Sexualizing the Social

Power and the Organization of Sexuality

Edited by

Lisa Adkins
Lecturer in Sociology
University of Kent at Canterbury

and

Vicki Merchant
Principal Lecturer in Sociology
University of Central Lancashire
Preston

D1493943

MACMILLAN

First published 1996 by
MACMILLAN PRESS LTD
Houndmills, Basingstoke, Hampshire RG21 6XS
and London
Companies and representatives
throughout the world

ISBN 0–333–64999–0 hardcover
ISBN 0–333–65000–X paperback

A catalogue record for this book is available
from the British Library.

10   9   8   7   6   5   4   3   2   1
05 04 03 02 01 00 99 98 97 96

Printed and bound in Great Britain by
Antony Rowe Ltd
Chippenham, Wiltshire

Contents

List of Plates   vii
Acknowledgements   viii
Notes on the Contributors   ix

Introduction   1
Lisa Adkins and Vicki Merchant

Part I   Power and Consent

1   Heterosexuality as a Problem for Feminist Theory   15
    Stevi Jackson

2   Sinking into his arms . . . Arms in his Sink:
    Heterosexuality and Feminism Revisited   35
    Jo VanEvery

3   The Social Construction of Consent Revisited   55
    Lynn Jamieson

Part II   Identities

4   Beyond Victim or Survivor: Sexual Violence, Identity and
    Feminist Theory and Practice   77
    Liz Kelly, Sheila Burton and Linda Regan

5   Genital Identities: An Idiosyncratic Foray into the
    Gendering of Sexualities   102
    Tamsin Wilton

6   Irish Masculinities and Sexualities in England   122
    Máirtín Mac an Ghaill

7 Beyond the Predatory Male: The Diversity of Young
Glaswegian Men's Discourses to Describe Heterosexual
Relationships 145
Daniel Wight

Part III Sexual Exchange

8 Organized Bodies: Gender, Sexuality and Embodiment in
Contemporary Organizations 173
Anne Witz, Susan Halford and Mike Savage

9 Feminist Debates on Prostitution 191
Mary McIntosh

10 The Cultural, the Sexual, and the Gendering of the
Labour Market 204
Lisa Adkins and Celia Lury

Index 224

List of Plates

1 Tom of Finland (1963).
2 Tom of Finland (1986).
3 Advertisements from *Gay Times* (June 1993).
4 Advertisements from *The Pink Paper* (1989).
5 Phone lines for women: *Women Only* (1992).
6 Phone lines for men: *Knave* (1992).
7 'Lesbians' from phone advertisements for men: *Knave* (1992).
8 From safer-sex leaflet produced by the New Zealand AIDS Foundation (n.d.).
9 Cover of leaflet produced by San Francisco AIDS Foundation and San Francisco Department of Public Health Jail Medical Services (n.d.).

Acknowledgements

This book consists of chapters originally delivered as papers at the 1994 British Sociological Association (BSA) Annual Conference on the theme of 'Sexualities in Social Context', held at the University of Central Lancashire, 28–31 March 1994. It is one of three volumes produced from the papers given at that conference. The companion volumes are: *Sexual Cultures: Communities, Values and Intimacy*, edited by Jeffrey Weeks and Janet Holland, and *Sex, Sensibility and the Gendered Body*, edited by Janet Holland and Lisa Adkins.

The conference itself was one of the largest ever held by the BSA, and these three volumes offer a distillation of the 258 papers given at the conference. The editors of all three volumes had great difficulty in making a representative selection of the papers, and we would like to thank the forbearance and patience of all the contributors while we reviewed each paper and came to our often painful decisions concerning them. The editors of this volume would particularly like to thank the contributors for the speed and efficiency with which they responded to editorial comments and revisions. More broadly, we would also wish to thank all the participants at the conference, both those who gave papers, and those who participated in the various streams. We think that all who participated in the conference gained enormously from the intellectual vitality and excitement that was apparent there. We hope that this volume and its companions reflect some of that excitement, and contribute to the growing recognition of the significance of sexuality in understanding the social dynamics of contemporary societies.

That the conference was such a success is due to the efforts of countless people. We would like to thank members of the British Sociological Association staff for their support throughout this venture. We are grateful for the support given by staff at the University of Central Lancashire both before and during the conference itself. The editors of this volume owe a great debt of gratitude to their colleagues at the University of Central Lancashire and to former colleagues at the University of the West of England. We owe personal debts to our immediate partners and friends; they know who they are.

We dedicate this, and the companion volumes, to the many young sociologists who attended the BSA Conference, many for the first time. Their enthusiasm for the subject, and for the theme of the conference, gave us great hope for the future of the discipline.

Notes on the Contributors

Lisa Adkins is Lecturer in Sociology at the University of Kent at Canterbury. Her research interests are focused on the sociology of gender, especially sexuality, the labour market and the family. Her publications include *Gendered Work: Sexuality, Family and the Labour Market* (1995) and *Sex in Question: French Materialist Feminism* (edited with Diana Leonard, 1996).

Susan Halford is Lecturer in Sociology at Southampton University after having spent six years as Research Fellow in Urban Studies at the University of Sussex. She has published widely on the implementation of equal opportunities initiatives in local authorities and is the co-author of *Gender, Careers and Organisations* (forthcoming, with Mike Savage and Anne Witz).

Stevi Jackson is co-ordinator of the M.Litt. in Women's Studies at the University of Strathclyde. She is co-editor of *Women's Studies: A Reader* (1993), has a book on Christine Delphy forthcoming in the Sage 'Women of Ideas' series and has co-edited, with Shaun Moores, *The Politics of Domestic Consumption: Critical Readings* (forthcoming). She has also published a number of articles on romance and sexuality.

Lynn Jamieson is Senior Lecturer in Sociology at the University of Edinburgh. Her research interests are: family–household relationships, with reference to historical and life-cycle change; sexuality; 'sexual' assault; youth and childhood; and oral history. Her publications include: *State, Private Life and Political Change* (edited with H. Corr, 1990); *Country Bairns* (1992); and *Sex Crimes on Trial: The Use of Sexual Evidence in Scottish Courts* (with B. Brown and M. Burman, 1993).

Liz Kelly, Sheila Burton and Linda Regan have been working together for over five years at the Child and Woman Abuse Studies Unit (CAWSU), University of North London. The Unit exists to develop feminist research and methodologies, theory and practice which develop connections between forms of sexualized violence. Their work involves a creative combination of large and small scale research projects, training, policy development and networking, which requires bridging the worlds of academia, policy and practice, and activism. They sometimes think that the most creative part of their work together has been generating all the running costs of CAWSU!

Celia Lury teaches women's studies and cultural studies in the Sociology Department, Lancaster University. She is interested in exploring what theories of culture can offer to feminism, especially in the conceptualization of power. Publications include *Off-Centre: Feminism and Cultural Studies* (edited with Sarah Franklin and Jackie Stacey, 1991), *Cultural Rights* (1993) and *Possessing the Self* (forthcoming).

Máirtín Mac an Ghaill works in the School of Education, University of Birmingham. He is author of *The Making of Men: Masculinities, Sexualities and Schooling* (1994).

Mary McIntosh teaches at the University of Essex. She is currently working on a book on prostitution and public policy and has previously written 'The Homosexual Role' (1968) and, with Michèle Barrett, *The Anti-Social Family* (1982). She was a founding editor of *Feminist Review* and has contributed to debates on Marxism and feminism.

Vicki Merchant is Principal Lecturer in Sociology, University of Central Lancashire. She is Chair of the National Harassment Network and has research interests in power in organizations, computer pornography, and harassment and bullying at work and in higher education.

Mike Savage is Professor of Sociology at Manchester University and has a visiting part-time appointment at the University of North Carolina at Chapel Hill, USA. Among his recent publications are *Property, Bureaucracy and Culture* (with James Barlow, Peter Dickens, and Tony Fielding, 1992) and *Urban Sociology, Capitalism and Modernity* (with Alan Warde, 1993).

Jo VanEvery received her PhD in Sociology from the University of Essex in 1994. A book based on her doctoral research, entitled *Heterosexual Women Changing the Family: Refusing To Be a 'Wife'!* was published in 1995. She is currently developing research on the way sociologists conceptualize housework and pursuing some questions about heterosexuality and feminism. She is also trying to apply all this theory to the practice of having a long-term relationship with a man.

Daniel Wight is a researcher at the MRC Medical Sociology Unit, Glasgow University. He originally studied social anthropology, has conducted research on working-class culture, the employment ethic and consumption, and published *Workers not Wasters: Masculine Respectability, Consumption and Unemployment in Scotland* (1993). Following a qualitative study of young men's sexuality he is now (with Sue Scott, Charles Abraham, Gillian Raab and Graham Hart) developing a project to evaluate rigorously school sex education. Other interests include HIV in Uganda.

Tamsin Wilton is Senior Lecturer in Health and Social Policy at the University of the West of England, where she also teaches Women's Studies and Lesbian Studies. She is author of *Antibody Politic: AIDS and Society* (1993), *Lesbian Studies: Setting an Agenda* (1995) and *Engendering AIDS: the Sexual Politics of an Epidemic* (forthcoming), and editor of *Immortal, Invisible: Lesbians and the Moving Image* (1995) and *AIDS: Setting a Feminist Agenda* (with Lesley Doyal and Jennie Naidoo, 1994). She is currently working on *Fingerlicking Good*, a book on the politics of lesbian sex, and researching a handbook on lesbian health. She is a member of the Bristol Women and Health Research Group.

Anne Witz is Senior Lecturer in Sociology at the University of Strathclyde, and Marie-Jahoda Visiting Professor of Women's Studies at the Ruhr-University Bochum in Germany. She is the author of *Professions and Patriarchy* (1992) and co-editor of *Gender and Bureaucracy* (with Mike Savage, 1992).

Introduction
Lisa Adkins and Vicki Merchant[1]

The theme of this book is 'sexualizing the social'. It is concerned with the ways in which various aspects of social life – including employment, family life, representations, politics, identities, and the workings of the law and other bureaucratic organizations – are built on, and themselves build, sexuality. All the chapters show how it is now impossible to consider social life without considering how social relations may be constituted through and by sexuality. They thus bear testiment to the ways in which the sociology of sexuality has moved from occupying a marginal space in the discipline, to its centre (Gagnon, 1994). Indeed, one of the characteristics of contemporary sociology is its focus on sexuality. Many of the core concerns of the discipline – such as the nature of modernity and transformations within late modern societies – are now being examined in terms of sexuality, intimacy and the constitution of sexual identities (see, for example, Beck and Beck-Gersheim, 1995; Giddens, 1992).

The origins of this transformation of sociology has many strands (see Weeks and Holland, 1996), but in terms of the papers gathered in this volume, one stands out as particularly influential: the sexual politics of the women's and lesbian and gay movements. These movements contributed to a wholesale questioning of sexuality within sociology, which included a direct politicization of the sexual. Rather than constituting a 'natural' and 'private' matter, sexual practices, desires, and patterns of intimacy were located as socially made and organized. Moreover, radical sexual politics stressed the hierarchical organization and regulated nature of sexuality. Feminists stressed the hierarchical nature of heterosexuality: how heterosexuality was patterned by power relations between men and women; how it was linked to men's violence against women; and how it contributed to the constitution of gender. Lesbian and gay politics[2] similarly stressed the regulative organization of sexuality: the policing of lesbian and gay desire and how their vilification were linked to homophobia and the regulative power of heterosexuality; and early British sociological work on lesbian and gay identities (McIntosh, 1968; Plummer, 1975; Weeks, 1977) stressed the social construction of all these categories.

A lot of water has gone under the bridge since then, and in many

1

ways the sociological agenda has changed. For example, old certainties regarding the explanatory power of the social constructionist framework have been called into question (including by writers on sexuality;
see, for example, Vance, 1989; and other chapters in Altman *et al.*,
1989; Stein, 1992; and Wilton in this volume); and, in addition, there
have been shifts of agenda regarding sexuality itself. Early feminist
concerns with the coercive and violent aspects of heterosexuality are
giving way to, and/or being joined by, new emphases on agency, resistance and pleasures. While it is the transgressive and disruptive
potential of lesbian and gay identities which is now often emphasized,
rather than issues around their regulation.

However, despite these shifts, the chapters in this volume demonstrate that many of the 'old' concerns – power relations and the social
organization and regulation of sexuality – are still central to this field.
The organization of heterosexuality, its institutionalization, and sexual
violence against women, are all debated here.[3] But these 'old' concerns are also enmeshed with the new: the embodied nature of heterosexuality, the formation of sexual identities and subjectivities, the
relationship of sexuality to the self and selfhood, and the production
of sexual meanings are also at issue.[4] Indeed, one of the strengths of
this collection is the way in which many chapters bring together 'old'
and 'new' in innovative ways and address both long-standing and recent controversies in sociology. For instance, many chapters consider
the ongoing problem of structure and agency in different ways, also
issues of gender performativity, social diversity and culturalization.[5]
The chapters thus clearly demonstrate that rather than being a distinct
field or specialism, the sociology of sexuality is increasingly an integral part of 'sociology' itself.

All of the above implies that the majority of chapters in this volume
are concerned with sexuality in relation to gender. Indeed, one of the
ongoing controversies in the sociology of sexuality and feminist sociology – namely the relationship (and changes in the relationship) between gender and sexuality – is directly addressed in many.[6] This
confirms, once again, the significance of radical sexual politics and
especially feminism for this field. In particular, the chapters clearly
reveal that the connections between the sexual and the social are often
exposed through the category of sex or gender.

Early feminist work in sociology stressed the constructedness of the
private/public distinction in relation to gender (see, for example, Stacey,
1981), and in so doing revealed the centrality of gender to a range of
social institutions, including the labour market, the state and other

organizations. It is precisely this deconstruction of the private/public dichotomy which sociologists of sexuality (including many feminists) have built on and developed to unearth the different ways in which the sexual structures the social. Early writings on sexuality stressed that it should not be seen just as sexual practice, separate from other forms of social relations; nor as a discrete or ephemeral phenomena. Rather, sexuality is embedded in, and is intrinsic to, a whole range of social relations. In 1980, Rich, for instance, argued that rather than being a sexual practice, (hetero)sexuality constituted a system of social relations which operated in a range of institutions, that is, 'sexuality' operated across a range of domains. At that time there was relatively little research which explored this idea: that sexuality may be implicated in the constitution (and be constituted by) a range of social phenomena/ practices. However, this volume bears testament to the ways in which contemporary research is, indeed, locating a whole range of linkages between the sexual and the social or, more precisely, the way in which the social is sexual; and also the increasingly sophisticated ways in which these linkages are being viewed. Thus, organizations, occupations, the law, nations, and representational practices are all exposed as being both significantly organized in terms of sexuality, and as organizing sexuality.[7] Moreover, such mutual construction involves not only sexuality and gender, but also sexuality and ethnicity, nationality, and class, as is also stressed throughout the chapters. The heavy reliance on gender as an analytic category exposing these connections thus reveals the ongoing debt of the sociology of sexuality to feminism.

The significance of feminist interventions for contemporary research and writing on sexuality is immediately apparent in Part I, which is concerned with issues of power and consent. First, Stevi Jackson tackles the social organization of heterosexuality from a materialist feminist perspective. She seeks a way of addressing 'how we become sexual' which relates both to discourses on sexuality and those on structural inequalities, especially on gender:

> We need to weave these strands together in such a way as to recognize the force of cultural and ideological constructions of sexuality and the constraints of social structure but without denying human agency and therefore the possibility of resistance and change.

Jackson wants to find a way of understanding heterosexuality which denies neither structural inequalities nor agency – since, as she shows, such denials have been problematic in existing approaches. As a way out of this impasse, Jackson suggests a need to consider four aspects of heterosexuality: its institutionalization, the practices it entails, how it is experienced, and the political and social identities associated with it. Such an analysis allows her to uncover the intervening processes between, for example, practice and processes of institutionalization; and, therefore, to expose the over-determined position of those who assume that patterns of power between men and women in heterosexual practice can 'simply be read off from the structural level'. But whilst Jackson's analysis provides us with a multi-layered account, she also insists that all these aspects of heterosexuality need to be understood in terms of gender: of the hierarchical relations between men and women. These, she argues, involve a lot more than sexuality. Her argument implies, therefore, that the social should not be overly sexualized; and, in particular, that heterosexuality represents far more than sexual practice and experience, and that gender should not be conflated with sexuality.

Jo VanEvery also warns of the dangers of oversexualizing the social, again in relation to gender. Like Jackson, she notes that while lesbian and gay identities have been recognized as constituting far more than sexual identities, much recent discussion of heterosexuality has been limited to its sexual aspects. This focus on the sexual, she suggests, is problematic because it divorces sexual acts from social contexts. Economic, social and political factors then get located as external to the sexual. Such a separation, she suggests, acts to re-privatize heterosexuality. Moreover, it has lead to a 'dichotomized debate about repression and choice'. VanEvery seeks to demonstrate the socio-economic character of heterosexuality through her study of the gender division of labour in anti-sexist living arrangements. She emphasizes that despite a greater than average chance of constructing a non-oppressive heterosexuality, women living in such relationships have a difficult task to make them equal, because, rather than constituting a discrete area of living arrangements and relationships, heterosexuality is implicated in their social organization: '[H]eterosexuality . . . implicates many women in long term domestic arrangements with men in which their paid and unpaid labour is appropriated.' Thus VanEvery's chapter points to the ways in which (hetero)sexuality is intimately connected to the gender division of labour.

In the following chapter, attention shifts from the gender division of labour to the law, where Jamieson is concerned with legal discourses on rape. In particular, she examines the emergence and use of 'mistaken belief in consent' as a defence in rape trials, and the significance of this defence for the constitution of men and women's interactions outside the formally legal sphere. She is therefore concerned with the power of the law, and in particular with the power of the law in constituting sexuality. Through a detailed examination of courtroom constructions of consent, and especially the continued reliance on a simplistic notion of rape/not rape in legal discourse, Jamieson shows how the 'mistaken belief in consent' defence rests on blatant inequalities in the treatment of men and women. '[I]f a woman believes what is occurring is rape and the man does not, then in the law it is, indeed, not rape.' Whilst she shows that the use of this defence is not common, she indicates that it is, nevertheless, of considerable significance because it constitutes a 'legal denial of rape' and 'bolsters macho male masculinity at the expense of all women and some men far beyond the courtroom'. Drawing on this and on a wide range of other recent research on sexuality, Jamieson ends up questioning some of the optimism found in recent sociological writings on intimacy and relationships between men and women, especially as regards the rise of 'confluent love' in late modernity.

Issues of power and consent are also discussed in the chapters in Part II, which focuses on the constitution of identities. Kelly, Burton and Regan, for example, are concerned with current struggles over the meaning of victimization. They link the rise of 'power feminism' and its juxtaposition to its predecessor 'victim feminism', with medicalization and therapization, and also with shifts in feminism, especially the development of what they term commercialized feminism. What is at issue for them is the way in which important areas of feminist work on sexual violence are being negated as a consequence of these processes. One of their concerns is the recent popular and intellectual questioning of findings on the prevalence of sexual violence towards women and young people. They show this questioning often rests itself on the operation of a simple binary logic – similar to that operating in legal knowledges – which denies the complexity of experience. For example, there is often a simple opposition between a victim and a survivor identity at play in both popular and intellectual discourses. Through a detailed analysis of this dichotomy, which is shown to operate across a range of settings, including research and counselling, Kelly *et al.* are able to demonstrate how a range of problems are created, and how neither 'victim' nor 'survivor' is a useful identity over the long term in relation to sexual violence. This chapter thus reveals how on-going feminist activism and research in the area of sexual violence is producing increasingly sophisticated analyses: how the link between a range of long-term and some more recent processes helps us understand the construction of the meaning of sexual victimization.

Wilton continues the theme of the constitution of identities, but her discussion returns to sexuality and gender – or as she terms it sex/ erotic and sex/gender identities – and the relationship between the two. She argues that the pervasive conflation of the sex/erotic and sex/ gender through discursive and textual practices constitutes the hetero- sexual imperative and heteropolarity; and, moreover, that this elision is crucially inscribed onto the body. Thus 'genital identities' – or a kind of 'heterosexual bodily fuctionalism' – are key to the construc- tion of heterosexuality. In her analysis, Wilton examines two specific representational practices: HIV/AIDS health promotional material and telephone sex-line advertisements. In these apparently diverse texts, Wilton exposes an 'unquestioning obedience to heteropolarity': sexualities are always gendered and gender is always sexualized. Her argument, therefore, adds weight to those of Jackson and VanEvery – that sexu- ality must be analysed in terms of heterosexuality, and that gender is regulated through sexuality. But Wilton adds an additional dimension, that of the body. She locates radical feminist and queer theorists as particularly important in recognizing the significance of the body, both in the construction of heteropolarity and in attempts to decouple gender and sexuality, through their stress on disobedient bodies. In so doing she creates an unusual fusion of these often differentiated positions.

The constitution of sex/gender identities is also the subject of Mac an Ghaill's chapter, which looks at the interplay between sexuality, ethnicity and masculinity in relation to young Irish gay men living in England. He is particularly concerned to examine the range of sexual identities these men inhabit and the formation of these identities. Like other sociologists who analyse the inter-play of power relations, Mac an Ghaill is keen to avoid an additive model of oppressions and seeks instead to understand the diverse identities of these young men in terms of 'the multi-layered connectedness between different social categories'. He therefore examines the ways in which social relations and the accompanying discourses around gender, sexuality, class, 'race', Irish ethnicity and nationalism combine and interact in contingent circum- stances to constitute specific, and variable, sex/gender identities. Mac an Ghaill shows how social relations and discourses around sexuality are embedded in a range of phenomena, including specific national- isms and ethnicities – discourses which simultaneously 'speak' gender and sexuality.

In the following chapter, Wight is also concerned with the diversity of sexual identities; especially the diversity of masculine sexuality found among a particular group of white, working-class, (mostly) heterosexual, young men. Through an analysis of these men's accounts of their sexual relationships, Wight identifies four gendered discourses within which the young men position themselves: the uninterested, the predatory, the permissive and the have/hold or romantic discourses. Whilst he stresses the diversity of young men's accounts, he also shows how many of the discourses are linked to the regulation of women, especially by dichotomizing the latter into slags or drags. Like Jamieson, Wight is led to question the idea that 'confluent love' has been achieved within late modernity. He also questions simple characterizations of young men's gender identity as tied to sexual behaviour, for many of the young men in his sample did not prioritize sexual encounters, and in terms of gender other activities seemed more important. This chapter clearly exemplifies some of the recent shifts in sex research. In particular, its critical focus on men, heterosexuality and masculinity denotes an expansion of the research agendas in this field, such that not only women's and gay sexualities are questioned, but also male heterosexuality is now at issue. It therefore highlights ways in which critiques of heterosexuality are being taken up by a variety of constituencies, and the increasing impact of these critiques.

In Part III, three chapters examine the different kinds of ways in which routine exchange relationships, many of which have previously been completely disconnected from sexuality, and arenas in which exchange relationships take place, such as the labour market and organizations, may be organized in terms of sexuality. First, Witz, Halford and Savage consider the relationship between sexuality and gender in terms of organizations, and specifically how current approaches to organizations and bureaucracy tend either to foreground gender with little attention to sexuality (which they term the 'gender paradigm') or to focus on sexuality with little account of gender (the 'sexuality paradigm'). They suggest that a focus on the embodied nature of organizational life – and the ways in which this embodiment may be gendered – may offer a way out of this impasse, allowing a focus on both gender and sexuality and the articulation of the two. This chapter therefore has direct parallels with Wilton's, in that the body is located as key to understanding sexuality and gender, and to the relationship between the two. Drawing on new empirical material from three organizational settings – a hospital ward, a local authority and a branch of a bank – they show how sexualities are deployed in organizations with reference to gendered bodies and how a number of tacit organizational rules – spatial, verbal, and physical – govern the forms of (sexual and other) interaction between embodied organizational members. They reveal how both sexuality and gender, and the relationships between them which are played out in various organizational settings, turn around various forms of body politics. In the process, Witz *et al.* not only propose a new way (as they say) to 'flesh out' the inter-connections between gendered sexuality and gendered organizational hierarchies, but also reveal the ways in which the deployment of sexuality and forms of sexual interactions which take place in organizational contexts are integral to organizations themselves.

The theme of embodiment is also taken up by McIntosh in her critical evaluation of feminist analyses of prostitution. She discusses the links that have been made between the exchange of sex for money in the context of prostitution, and the exchange of sex for something else, such as economic support, in what are regarded as non-prostitute relationships, such as marriage. Specifically, she questions Pateman's (1988) analysis of prostitution as involving the selling of the self for women, and the latter's assertion that within modernity women cannot enter any bodily contracts without selling their selves. What is at issue for McIntosh is that the relationship between the body and the self is specific to prostitution (and to other bodily contracts involving women, such as marriage and surrogacy), and that women's selves are involved in prostitution in a different way from the way in which the self is involved in other occupations. In questioning this, she considers the ways in which personal service occupations, such as waitressing or bar work, may be analogous to prostitution, and argues that whilst these jobs often require bodily work, they also and (increasingly) involve personality and emotional work – which may be just as important in terms of the constitution of gendered selves as the selling of the body. Thus McIntosh not only questions the pervasive assumption that prostitution is disconnected from other types of work, but also whether it is just the body and its uses, especially in terms of the heterosex act, which are integral to the gendered self. Hence, she argues that the notion of the self used by Pateman is far too narrow, as it ignores the ways in which the self is much more various in terms of sexuality. She suggests that possibly some men, may, for example, be weakened by sex with women, and some women empowered by sex with men.

Similar issues concerning self-hood and embodiment are raised by Adkins and Lury in the final chapter. Drawing on empirical material on similar service occupations in tourism, they show how men and women are employed on quite different terms even when they are nominally employed to do the same jobs. Women are routinely required to produce and maintain a sexualized identity or sexual 'self', and to carry out various forms of sexual labour as part of the job, while men are not. This analysis leads them to consider the gendered constitution of the self in the workplace. They argue that gendered relations of production – where women workers are both required to present a sexual 'self' and where this self is subject to appropriation – means that:

> such identity practices cannot be detached from the person, contracted out and freely exchanged: on the contrary, these identity practices are rendered intrinsic to women workers through relations of appropriation. That is to say, the gendered relations of production . . . ensure that women's labour (including the production of workplace identities) is always embodied as part of their selves. Thus women cannot 'own', and therefore contract out, their workplace identities because their 'selves' are produced through the relations of production and are the subject of appropriation.

Men, on the other hand, they suggest, because they are not required to maintain a particular self, are better placed to detach their labour (including the performance of a work identity) and to claim their 'selves' as a labour market resource.

Adkins and Lury's analysis, like McIntosh's, thus shows how bodily and sexual work are routinely involved in personal service occupations, and how labour is embodied rather than being an abstract category. But their analysis of the constitution of gendered selves is more in line with Pateman's, since they suggest that, for women, the self and the body are not detachable in gendered relations of production and appropriation in service workplaces.

Despite their disagreements these three chapters do, however, demonstrate the centrality of sexuality in organizations and in various forms of (gendered) exchange. They show how considering social relationships and key social institutions through sexuality not only transforms our understanding of the organization of the social, but also transforms sociological concepts: our understandings of 'organizations', 'the labour market', 'exchange' and 'selfhood' are all questioned and recast. Indeed, all the chapters in this book demonstrate how contemporary research and writing on sexuality is 'sexualizing' – and therefore transforming understandings of – the social. Some also show how in the process the 'social' itself is becoming increasingly de-centred and contested. Mac an Ghaill, for example, stresses the contingency of the category in relation to the constitution of sex/gender identities, while other chapters attempt to rebuild the social as an analytic term. Adkins and Lury, for example, are critical of earlier taken-for-granted understandings, and emphasize the need to historicize the social as a specific field in order to understand its significance in terms of sexuality and the relationship of sexuality to gender. The chapters, as a collection, therefore highlight the ways in which the sociology of sexuality is contributing to a new reflexivity within the discipline, and to an interrogation of its central concepts.

NOTES

1. With thanks to Diana Leonard for her editorial suggestions.
2. Although, of course, there were, and continue to be, divisions between lesbians and gay men: see, e.g., Stanley (1982), Hanmer (1990) and Jeffreys (1990).
3. On the organization of heterosexuality see the chapters by Jackson, VanEvery and Wilton; on its institutionalization, see Adkins and Lury, and Jamieson; and on sexual violence against women see Jamieson, and Kelly *et al.*
4. On the embodied nature of heterosexuality see Adkins and Lury, McIntosh, Wilton, and Witz *et al.*; on the formation of sexual identities and subjectivities see Kelly *et al.*, Mac an Ghaill, VanEvery, Wight, and Wilton; on the relationship of sexuality to the self and selfhood see Adkins and Lury, and McIntosh; and on the production of sexual meanings see Kelly *et al.*
5. On structure and agency see Adkins and Lury, Jackson, and Witz *et al.*; on gender performativity see McIntosh, and Wilton; on social diversity see Mac an Ghaill, and Wight; and on culturalization see Adkins and Lury.
6. On this relationship see Adkins and Lury, Jackson, McIntosh, VanEvery, Wight, Wilton, and Witz *et al.*
7. On organizations see Witz *et al.*; on occupations see Adkins and Lury, and McIntosh; on the law see Jamieson; on nations see Mac an Ghaill; and on representational practices see Wilton.

REFERENCES

Altman, D. *et al.* (eds) (1989), *Which Homosexuality? Essays from the International Scientific Conference on Lesbian and Gay Studies* (London: Gay Men's Press).
Beck, U. and Beck-Gernsheim, E. (1995), *The Normal Chaos of Love* (Cambridge: Polity Press).

Gagnon, J. (1994), 'News from the Margin: The Progress of Sex in Sociology', Opening Plenary Address to the *British Sociological Association Annual Conference, Sexualities in Social Context*, 28–31 March, Preston.

Giddens, A. (1992), *The Transformation of Intimacy: Sexuality, Love and Eroticism in Modern Societies* (Cambridge: Polity Press).

Hanmer, J. (1990), 'Men, Power and the Exploitation of Women', in J. Hearn and D. Morgan (eds), *Men, Masculinities and Social Theory* (London: Unwin Hyman).

Jeffreys, S. (1990), *Anticlimax* (London: The Women's Press).

McIntosh, M. (1968), 'The Homosexual Role', *Social Problems*, **16**:(2), pp. 182–92.

Pateman, C. (1988), *The Sexual Contract* (Cambridge: Polity Press).

Plummer, K. (1975), *Sexual Stigma: An Interactionist Account* (London: Routledge & Kegan Paul).

Rich, A. (1980), 'Compulsory Heterosexuality and Lesbian Existence', *Signs*, **5**:(4), pp. 631–60.

Stacey, M. (1981), 'The Division of Labour Revisited, or Overcoming the Two Adams', in P. Abrams, R. Deem, J. Finch, and P. Rock (eds), *Practice and Progress in British Sociology, 1950–1980* (London: Allen & Unwin).

Stanley, L. (1982), '"Male Needs": The Problems of Working with Gay Men', in S. Friedman and E. Sarah (eds), *The Problem of Men: Two Feminist Conferences* (London: The Women's Press).

Stein, E. (ed.) (1992), *Forms of Desire: Sexual Orientation and the Social Constructionist Controversy* (London: Routledge).

Vance, C. (1989), 'Social Construction Theory: Problems in the History of Sexuality', in D. Altman *et al.* (eds), *Which Homosexuality? Essays from the International Scientific Conference on Lesbian and Gay Studies* (London: Gay Men's Press).

Weeks, J. (1977), *Coming Out: Homosexual Politics in Britain from the 19th Century to the Present* (London: Quartet).

Weeks, J. and Holland, J. (1996), 'Introduction', in J. Weeks and J. Holland (eds), *Sexual Cultures: Communities, Values and Intimacy* (Basingstoke: Macmillan).

Part I
Power and Consent

1 Heterosexuality as a Problem for Feminist Theory

Stevi Jackson

Despite the emphasis on the social construction of sexuality in both feminist and wider social theory, we have yet to find satisfactory ways of conceptualizing sexuality as fully social. In part this derives from a lack of consensus as to what is meant by social construction and how it should be analysed. Feminists are also deeply divided on the politics of sexuality: on what it is about sexuality as currently constituted that needs to be challenged and on strategies for change. In this paper I will explore some of these problems and debates in order to seek a way forward for feminist analysis. I am not proposing some new definitive perspective on sexuality, nor will I attempt to answer all the questions I raise. I will, however, suggest some preconditions for theorizing about sexuality which I think are fundamental to an approach which is both feminist and sociological.

Sexuality has been contested terrain within feminism since the nineteenth century and resurfaced as a central issue in the earliest days of second wave feminism. At that time we did have a common point of departure: that the current ordering of (hetero)sexual relations was detrimental to women and implicated in our subordination. In making sexuality a political issue we also conceptualized it as changeable and therefore challenged the prevailing assumption that sexual desires and practices were fixed by nature. Viewing sexuality as socially constructed therefore followed from politicizing it. We have since followed diverging paths, guided not only by our political convictions about such issues as pornography and sexual diversity, but also by the theoretical directions we have taken. Three main strands of analysis have developed over the last two decades, none of which is necessarily limited to any one theoretical or political position but which have, in practice, become associated with particular variants of feminism. What is distinctive about each of these tendencies is the object of their analysis, precisely what they see as being socially constructed. Each foregrounds

15

a specific aspect of sexuality – the centrality of male domination, the variability and plasticity of sexuality and the construction of our individual desires. It is my contention that each of these facets of the social construction of sexuality must be addressed and that we should find ways of exploring their interlinkages. What has tended to happen, however, is that particular groups of theorists concentrate on one aspect of sexuality to the exclusion of others and, because each is pursuing its own theoretical and political agenda, little genuine interchange of ideas takes place. Moreover, the ways in which these issues have been theorized has produced some irreconcilable differences between those who have analysed sexuality in relation to patriarchal structures, those who have emphasized its historical construction as an object of discourse and those primarily concerned with its constitution at the level of individual subjectivity.

In mapping out these divisions I am not trying to find some neutral 'middle ground': I write from a particular theoretical and political position as a materialist radical feminist and from a specific personal location as a White heterosexual academic feminist. I will begin by outlining the main issues addressed by the three strands of analysis I have identified, drawing out some of the essential insights that we need to build on, as well as pinpointing some problems and lacunae. In so doing I will begin to signpost some elements of a more adequate theorization of sexuality before dealing more specifically with the institution and practice of heterosexuality.

FEMINIST THINKING ON SEXUALITY

The first tendency I have identified, which identifies sexuality as a site of male power, had its roots in feminist political activism, in efforts to challenge men's sexual appropriation and abuse of women. This has given rise to analyses of sexual violence and pornography and, more generally, of the ways in which sexuality had been defined and constructed from a masculine perspective. The social construction of sexuality is here seen as patriarchal, as serving the interests of men, as coercing women into compulsory heterosexuality (Rich, 1980). It is therefore linked to a structural analysis of patriarchy (for example, MacKinnon, 1982). Moreover, the erotic itself is understood as culturally constituted, so that currently prevailing definitions of eroticism are themselves the product of gendered patterns of domination and submission intrinsic to patriarchal societies and written into their cultural representations (Kappeler, 1986; Cameron and Frazer, 1987). This form of analysis has been pursued primarily, but not exclusively, by radical feminists.

Curiously, radical feminist perspectives of this kind are often misread as essentialist, as implying that men are naturally sexually violent and predatory, and that women are innately loving and egalitarian (see, for example, Weedon, 1987). I say curiously because it is indeed odd that a perspective dedicated to challenging and changing both male and female sexuality and to radically transforming our ideas about what is erotic should be seen as biologically determinist.[1] The emphasis on coercive aspects of sexuality and on the interconnections between sexuality and women's oppression has led to the charge that radical feminists cannot deal with sexual pleasure and are simply anti-sex. This is a caricature which both ignores the diversity of opinion among radical feminists and equates opposition to specific sexual practices with an anti-erotic stance. There are, none the less, aspects of sexuality which are under-theorized from this perspective. Radical feminists have not devoted much attention to the ways in which sexuality is constructed at the level of our individual subjectivities. While constantly asserting that specific sexual desires and preferences are learnt, they have had little to say about how this happens. Sometimes this leads to overly voluntaristic accounts of the potential for change in our personal sexual lives, as in the slogan 'any woman can' become a lesbian. Radical feminism's focus on power raises further issues of agency and subjectivity, specifically of tracing the connections between the structural bases of patriarchal power and the ways in which it is exercised and resisted at the level of personal sexual relations (Ramazanoglu and Holland, 1993).

The idea that human sexuality is historically and culturally variable is fundamental to all forms of social constructionism. Not only does it hold out the possibility of transforming sexual relations, but it is also an effective means of challenging biologistic notions of the fixity of human sexuality. This has provided the impetus for historical work on sexuality from a range of perspectives. Radical feminist contributions have included work on the pathologizing of lesbian relations (Jeffreys, 1985) and the constructions of sexuality within sexology (M. Jackson, 1987, 1994). As others have pointed out, the idea that radical feminists regard sexual relations as fixed and unchanging is another false stereotype (Walby, 1990; Richardson, 1993). The agenda for much academic work in this area has, however, been set by Foucauldian perspectives. The appeal of Foucault to feminists lies in his radical anti-essentialism and his view of power as constitutive of sexuality, rather than merely repressive (Foucault, 1981). It is worth remembering that some of Foucault's ideas, hailed as radically innovative, were current in less fashionable areas of social theory well before the publication of first volume of *The History of Sexuality*. For example, Gagnon and Simon (1974) had already critiqued the concept of repression and questioned the privileged place accorded to sexuality within modern culture. There were also analogous ideas circulating among feminists concerning how the 'truth' of sex was produced, particularly with regard to the sexualization of women.

Feminists have found fault with Foucault's acute gender-blindness and the difficulty of linking his conception of socially diffuse power to structural analyses of inequality (see, for example, Ramazanoglu, 1993). Those working within a Foucauldian framework have made gender more central, exploring the construction of female sexuality as an object of regulatory discourses and practices. Often, however, such historical analyses are too obsessed with disjunctions – in particular with the Victorian 'discursive explosion' – at the expense of continuities, thus playing down the resilience and flexibility of patriarchal domination under changing historical conditions.[2] Too much attention tends to be focused on 'women' as an unstable category (Riley, 1988) at the expense of the persistance of gender hierarchy.

Sexuality is also subject to synchronic variability. We need to consider the intersections of gender and sexuality with class, 'race' and other social divisions, to think about the ways in which dominant discourses around sexuality have been framed from a predominately White and middle-class, as well as male and heterosexual perspective, about how we each live our sexuality from different locations within social structures. Although some attention has been given to these issues, particularly to the racism embedded in Western sexual discourses and practices, Foucauldian inspired perspectives tend to focus on sexual diversity *per se*, on 'sexualities'. With this pluralization of sexuality, the lack of attention to structural bases of power can become acutely problematic especially when coupled with the denial of importance of gender, as in Rubin's (1989) work. There is then no way of establishing regularities underpinning diverse 'sexualities', of relating them to dominant modes of heterosexual practice or of locating them within power hierarchies. Instead attention is directed to the 'outlaw' status of various 'sexual minorities' each judged, from a libertarian perspective, as equally worthy of protection from oppression and opprobrium. That there is a world of difference between a street prostitute and a millionaire pornographer, and between a man who has sex with a child and that child, is not attended to.

Libertarian arguments draw on Foucault only selectively, emphasizing that aspect of his work which sees 'bodies and pleasures' as the point of resistance to power while losing sight of the constitutive effects of power in creating desire (see Foucault, 1981, pp. 156–7). The danger here lies in treating bodies and pleasures as unproblematic. As Nancy Fraser has commented, it is difficult to see 'what resistance to the deployment of sexuality . . . in the name of bodies and pleasures would be like', given that 'the disciplinary deployment of sexuality has, according to Foucault, produced its own panoply of bodily pleasures' and that 'disciplinary power has thoroughly marked the only bodies that we potential protesters have' (Fraser, 1989, p. 63). Hence diverse forms of sexuality are taken as given, already there to be outlawed, bringing us back to the repressive hypothesis which Foucault so effectively critiqued. The false equation of the transgressive with the progressive is in fact framed from within the very discourses it seeks to subvert. As I have argued in the past (from a pre-Foucauldian position), both libertarian and authoritarian perspectives on sexuality tend to afford it an overly privileged position; sexual licence is seen either as the route to personal fulfilment and social liberation or as leading to individual degradation and social disintegration (S. Jackson, 1982a).

While I find Foucauldian analyses interesting in the way that they sensitize us to the multiplicity of often contradictory ways in which sexuality has been constructed and regulated, their inability to deal with the regularity and pervasiveness of patriarchal power, with the ways in which what counts as sexual has been constructed in terms of gender hierarchy is problematic. The idea that our sense of what is sexual, including our desires and practices, is discursively constituted is potentially productive. But, whereas Foucault (1980) sees the concept of discourse as antithetical to ideology, I would argue that we need to retain a concept of discourses as ideological – in that they can serve to obscure or legitimate relations of domination and subordination. Discursive constructions of sexuality have produced very particular 'truths' which have defined hierarchically ordered heterosexual relations as natural and inevitable.

This still leaves us with the problem of the relationship between our individual desires and the discourses circulating within society. Some feminists have applied Foucault to the problem of subjectivity by analysing how we locate or position ourselves within discourses (Hollway, 1984a; Weedon, 1987), or have suggested that Foucault's later work on technologies of self might be productive (McNay, 1992). This has not, however, led to any consistent theorization of the processes by which we become gendered, sexual subjects. Indeed, when it comes to this question, Foucault is frequently abandoned in favour of psychoanalysis. Much of poststructuralist and postmodernist thinking is premised on the assumption that it is possible to draw simultaneously on both Foucault and Lacan, despite Foucault's contention that psychoanalysis is just another discursive formation producing its own disciplinary regime of truth.[3]

Psychoanalysis has established a virtual monopoly on theorizing the construction of sexuality at the level of subjectivity, despite the numerous cogent critiques of it. Many feminists and sociologists agree that psychoanalysis is ahistorical, that it rests on essentialist premises. While the Lacanian version suggests that sexed, desiring subjects are constituted through their entry into language and culture, this refers not to an historically specific language and culture, but to the very process of becoming a 'speaking subject'. Moreover, psychoanalysis depends upon interpreting infantile emotions through a filter of adult assumptions and then makes incredible conceptual leaps from presumed infantile frustrations and gratifications to adult sexual desires and practices. Importantly, psychoanalysis makes no distinction between gender and sexuality: the two are conflated and ultimately reduced to the gender of our 'object choice'. 'One either identifies with a sex or desires it, but only these two relations are possible' (Butler, 1990b, p. 333).

The influence of psychoanalysis is, in part, attributable to the lack of viable alternatives. It is not that there are no other theories, but that they are either inadequate or underdeveloped. Most of us have long since abandoned conventional models of socialization and, indeed, the concept of socialization itself, as far too simplistic and mechanistic to reveal much about subjectivity at all. Gagnon and Simon's (1974) work on sexual scripts, although flawed, might have proved productive if used critically, but few of us bothered to try.[4] Foucauldian perspectives on discourses and technologies of self could be applied to the problem, but this too has not been attempted in any consistent way. These two perspectives still seem to offer the best way forward, in that they allow for active agency in the construction of individual sexualities, but remarkably little progress has been made in this area over the last twenty years. While we are engaging in ever more sophisticated modes of theorizing about gender, sexuality and subjectivity, we still have no satisfactory way of approaching the very basic question: How did I get this way?[5] For those who are sceptical of psychoanalysis, the lack of a convincing theory of subjectivity is a major gap in feminist and sociological theory.

In theorizing sexuality we need a means of understanding how we become gendered and how we become sexual without conflating gender and sexuality, without assuming that particular forms of desire are automatically consequent upon acquiring feminine or masculine gender. We need, too, to think about how we acquire our sexual desires in all their complexity and how these might relate to our identity as heterosexual or lesbian without positing 'heterosexual desire' and 'lesbian desire' as monolithic entities. Such an analysis should also include emotions, especially love, within its scope. While psychoanalysis has always assumed that desire is heavily invested with emotion, elsewhere sexuality has often been theorized as if it were emotionless. Empirical work, on the other hand, has often drawn attention to the emotional meanings of sexuality, particularly the relationship between love and sexual desire expressed by many young women (Lees, 1986; Thomson and Scott, 1991). Bringing emotions into the picture does not mean assuming that all sexual desire is equally emotionally charged. Nor should we forget that emotions themselves are socially constructed as gendered (S. Jackson, 1993).

What I have suggested so far is that in addition to finding ways of theorizing how we become sexual, we need some understanding of how this is related to discourses on sexuality circulating within our culture and how these in turn are related to structural inequalities, particularly gender inequality. We need to weave these strands together in such a way as to recognize the force of cultural and ideological constructions of sexuality and the constraints of social structure, but without denying human agency and therefore the possibility of resistance and change. This enterprise, in my view, requires that we do not over-privilege sexuality. Part of the problem we have in thinking about sex derives from the weight we make it carry, the way we think of it as qualitatively different from other aspects of social life. This is one of the few points on which I am in agreement with Rubin (1989). Running through much feminist thought, as well as some interactionist and Foucauldian work (Gagnon and Simon, 1974; Heath, 1982), is the idea that we should question the way in which sexuality is singled out as a special area of existence, as fundamental to individual and social well being, as defining who and what we are. While I would insist on the necessity of relating sexuality to gender, I am firmly convinced that the latter is more important than the former. Here I would argue a position derived from Delphy's (1984, 1993) materialist feminism that gender, the existence of 'men' and 'women' as social categories, is a product of hierarchy. Rather than gender being premised on anatomical sex or on sex in the sense of the sexual (*pace* Rubin, 1975), hierarchy precedes division (Delphy, 1993). Sexuality, in particular institutionalized heterosexuality, is woven into this hierarchy, but I would resist any attempt to root explanations of women's subordination in sexuality: it is not possible to locate the source of patriarchal domination in a single area of social life (Delphy, 1984).

WHY HETEROSEXUALITY?

Although little attention has been given to theorizing heterosexuality as a form of sexuality, feminists have always seen heterosexuality as problematic. Those writing on sexual violence, where male sexual power is starkly evident, have stressed the continuities between apparently 'deviant' acts and the 'normal' expression of (socially constructed) masculinity (S. Jackson, 1978; Kelly, 1988; Scully, 1990) Work on diverse aspects of heterosexuality – from the analysis of sex manuals to research on young women's sexual relationships – has sensitized us to the complexity and ubiquity of power relations within sexuality. One reason why it is important not to lose sight of these feminist perspectives on heterosexuality is the important role they have played in anchoring critiques of a range of sexual practices both heterosexual and non-heterosexual, particularly from anti-libertarian positions within the 'sex wars' debates.

A serious social constructionist position has to accept that there is no total escape from the heterosexual framing of desire within a social order where heterosexuality is so privileged. We all learn to be sexual within a society in which 'real sex' is defined as a quintessentially heterosexual act, vaginal intercourse, and in which sexual activity is thought of in terms of an active subject and passive object. As many feminists have pointed out, this has also had an impact on lesbian and gay sexuality (Cameron and Frazer, 1987; Jeffreys, 1990) While feminists, both lesbian and heterosexual, are challenging the construction of sexuality in terms of active masculinity and passive femininity, our creativity in developing alternative forms of eroticism is necessarily limited by the social conditions which have shaped our desires. Thus it seems to me that a critique of heterosexuality needs to underpin all theorizing about sexuality.

It is precisely such a critique which is missing from much libertarian theory. In defending sexual 'pluralism' it is often forgotten that feminist theories of sexuality began by questioning the relations of dominance and submission inscribed in conventional heterosexual practice, suggesting that such relations were neither natural nor inevitable but resulted from the hierarchical ordering of gender. Many of the 'sexualities' currently being defended or promoted reproduce these hierarchies whether in the form of sado-masochism or 'cross-generational relations' (Rubin, 1989). There is no questioning of where such desires come from: 'the analysis begins from existing desires and thereby takes them to be "natural", immutable and ultimately valid' (Cameron and Frazer, 1987, p. 173). Hence such arguments are, at root, essentialist, as some erstwhile defenders of libertarianism are beginning to admit (see Seidman, 1992).

Moreover, in celebrating diversity these theorists frequently regard heterosexuality as unproblematic, as the singular norm against which diversity must be defended. Quite simply, heterosexual sex is boring – unless it is redefined by virtue of the ambiguity of its participants or practices as 'queer'. Lying inside Rubin's (1989) 'charmed circle' of acceptable sexual activity, heterosexual sex escapes scrutiny and is represented as surprisingly monolithic. A similar thing happens in some postmodernist arguments which seem, at first sight, to be questioning and deconstructing all gender and sexual categories – a point Mary Evans has recently made about Judith Butler's work (Butler, 1990a, 1993; Evans, 1994). While Butler aims to destabilize the 'regulatory fiction' of gender and the heterosexual ordering of desire it gives rise to, heterosexuality itself is denied the possibility of being anything other than an unexamined norm.

Heterosexuality can also appear monolithic from a quite opposing perspective: that of its radical lesbian feminist critics. Here heterosexuality is certainly problematized, but in the process is frequently denied any complexity: it *is* simply eroticized power (as in Jeffreys, 1990). Reducing it to this single dimension works against a fuller theorization of it. The relative silence heterosexual feminists have, until recently, maintained around their own sexuality has not helped. The critique of compulsory heterosexuality (Rich, 1980) and the vision of lesbianism as a positive, politically informed, alternative has meant that lesbians have generated a good deal more theory on heterosexuality than have heterosexual women themselves. It is not that the latter have had nothing to say about sexuality – many are in fact doing research in this area – but we have been less willing to engage with debates on heterosexuality as such. Unless we begin to do so, we may unwittingly contribute to perpetuating the heterosexual norm and the 'otherness' of homosexuality in relation to it (Robinson, 1993). Moreover, leaving the discussion of heterosexuality to lesbians and avoiding dialogue with them inevitably skews the form of theory produced.

RETHINKING HETEROSEXUALITY

Feminist discussions of heterosexuality frequently distinguish between heterosexuality as institution and as practice or experience, a clarification which is essential if we are to deal with its complexities (Richardson, 1993; Robinson, 1993).[6] In terms of meeting the needs I have identified above in thinking about sexuality at the level of social structure and culturally constituted discourses as well as at the level of individual agency and subjectivity, more distinctions may be necessary. I would suggest that we need to consider four aspects of heterosexuality – its institutionalization within society and culture, the practices it entails, the experience of it, and the social and political identities associated with it. These are, of course analytical distinctions which, as heterosexuality is lived, intersect and interrelate. I have also argued that we should not over-privilege sexuality in relation to other aspects of social life. While here I am concentrating on the specifically sexual aspects of heterosexuality, I should make it clear that as institution, practice, experience and identity, heterosexuality is not merely sexual. Moreover, while heterosexuality's central institution is marriage, the assumption of normative heterosexuality operates throughout society and even its specifically sexual practice is by no means confined to the private sphere (see, for example, Hearn *et al.*, 1989).

As it is institutionalized within society and culture, heterosexuality is founded upon gender hierarchy, upon men's appropriation of women's bodies and labour: the implicit terms of the marriage contract (Delphy and Leonard, 1992). The benefits men gain through their dominant position in the gender order are by no means reducible to the sexual and reproductive use of women's bodies. Men may say that 'women are only good for one thing', but as Delphy (1992) points out, this is no reason why we should accept this at face value. In marriage, for example, the home comforts produced by a wife's domestic labour are probably far more important to a man's well-being and his ability to maintain his position as a man than the sexual servicing he receives.

None the less, a man does acquire sexual rights in a woman by virtue of marriage and a woman who is not visibly under the protection of a man can be regarded as fair sexual game by others. Fear of sexual violence and harassment is also one means by which women are policed and police themselves through a range of disciplinary practices – from restricting their own access to public space, to where they choose to sit on a bus or train, how they sit and whom they avoid eye contact with (Bartky, 1990). Here the macro-level of power intersects with its micro-practices. The institutionalization of heterosexuality also works ideologically, through the discourses and forms of representation which define sex in phallocentric terms, which position men as sexual subjects and women as sexual objects.

At the level of heterosexual practice, the structural and cultural ordering of gender hierarchy can be reinforced or contested. Complicity in and resistance to heterosexual practice is not just about what does or does not happen between the sheets, but about who cleans the bathroom or who performs emotional labour on whom. In the specifically sexual sense it is here that phallocentricity, the privileging of male pleasure and eroticized power relations involve our material bodies, where male sexual privilege is acted out or where we try to negotiate activities and forms of pleasure which challenge it.

Experience and practice are perhaps too closely linked to be easily disentangled, but the distinction is intended to signal experience as what is felt both sensually and emotionally and what is thought. Specifically sexual experience encompasses our desires, our pleasure and displeasure. Sexual experience, although felt in its impact on our physical bodies, is not simply accessible to us in raw form as bodily sensation: it is actively worked over and made sense of. How we make sense of it depends on the discourses, narratives and scripts available to us, and it is through these interpretative processes that we link our experience and practice. The way we narratively construct our experience will depend on our location within our society and culture – whether, for instance, we have access to feminist discourses that might challenge dominant, patriarchal ones and thus enhance our ability, in practice, to resist.

The question of sexual identity, in particular lesbianism as a political identity, has been much debated by feminists. Heterosexuality, however, is still infrequently thought of in these terms and the vast majority of heterosexual women probably do not define themselves as such. None the less, many of the identities available to women derive from their location within heterosexual relations – as wife, girlfriend, daughter or mother. Attachment to these identities affects the ways in which women experience the institution and practices of heterosexuality. For example, women's ambivalent feelings about housework, their unwillingness to be critical of the appropriation of their labour, even when they are aware of the inequity of their situation, springs from their feelings about those they work for and from their desire to be good wives and mothers (Westwood, 1984). In sexual terms, too, women's identities are likely to be shaped by heterosexual imperatives – the need to attract and please a man. The desire to be sexually attractive appears to be profoundly important to women's sense of self-worth and closely bound up with the gendered disciplinary practices through which docile, feminine bodies are produced (Bartky, 1990). Hence heterosexuality, while uninterrogated, is pivotal to conventional feminine identities.

To name oneself as heterosexual is to make visible an identity which is generally taken for granted as a normal fact of life. This can be a means of problematizing heterosexuality and challenging its privileged status; but for women, being heterosexual is by no means a situation of unproblematic privilege. Heterosexual feminists may benefit from appearing 'normal' and unthreatening, but heterosexuality as an institution entails a hierarchical relation between (social) men and (social) women. It is women's subordination within institutionalized heterosexuality which is the starting point for feminist analysis. It is resistance to this subordination which is the foundation of feminist politics. It is hardly surprising, then, that heterosexual feminists prefer to be defined in terms of their feminism – their resistance – rather than their heterosexuality, their relation to men (Swindells, 1993). Resisting the label heterosexual, though, has its problems. It can imply a refusal to question and challenge both the institution and one's own practice; it can serve to invalidate lesbianism as a form of resistance to patriarchy and to deny the specific forms of oppression that lesbians face. For these reasons Kitzinger and Wilkinson are sceptical about those who 'call for the dissolution of the dichotomous categories "lesbian" and "heterosexual"' (1993, p. 7).

Questioning this binary opposition, however, need not be a way of avoiding the politics of lesbianism or getting heterosexual feminists off the hook, but can represent an honest attempt to problematize heterosexuality (see Gergen, 1993; Young, 1993). Nor is it only heterosexual feminists who are engaged in this deconstructive enterprise, but also lesbian queer theorists such as Diana Fuss (1991) and Judith Butler (1990a, 1991, 1993). When such arguments are framed from a postmodernist stance, this does make it difficult to account for the systematic structural bases of any form of oppression (see S. Jackson, 1992). None the less, treating the categories 'lesbian' and 'heterosexual' as problematic is by no means antithetical to radical feminism: indeed, I would argue that it is essential. This is not merely a matter of competing identities, but is fundamental to an appreciation of the social construction of gender and sexual categories.

The categories heterosexual, homosexual and lesbian are rooted in gender – they presuppose gender divisions and could not exist without our being able to define ourselves and others by gender. If we take Delphy's (1984, 1993) argument that 'men' and 'women' are not biologically given entities but social groups defined by the hierarchical and exploitative relationship between them, then the division between hetero- and homosexualities is, by extension, also a product of this class relation. Where materialist feminism differs from postmodernism is that these categories and divisions are not seen simply as discursive constructs, but as rooted in material inequalities. Within this perspective it is possible to see gender and sexual categories as both social constructs and material realities. 'Women' are a social rather than natural category defined by their relation to men. Contrary to Wittig's (1992) assertion that lesbians are not women, lesbianism is defined by gender and in relation to heterosexuality. It is certainly not a category outside patriarchal relations.

Recent analyses of heterosexuality, whether attacking it (Kitzinger and Wilkinson, 1993; Kitzinger, 1994) or defending it (Hollway, 1993; Segal, 1994), have tended to focus on sexual experience and practice, particularly on desire and pleasure. These debates have been centrally concerned with power – its structural underpinnings and its micro-practices, the implications of its erotic dimensions and the degree to which women can subvert or challenge it within heterosexual relations.

WHAT DO HETEROSEXUAL FEMINISTS DO IN BED? (AND DOES IT MATTER?)

To desire the 'other sex' or indeed to desire 'the same sex' presupposes the prior existence of 'men' and 'women' as socially – and erotically – meaningful categories. Desire as currently socially constituted is inevitably gendered. What is specific to heterosexual desire is that it is premised on gender *difference*, on the sexual 'otherness' of the desired object. From a materialist feminist perspective this difference is not an anatomical one but a social one: it is the hierarchy of gender which 'transforms an anatomical difference (which is itself devoid of social implications) into a relevant distinction for social practice' (Delphy, 1984, p. 144). Since it is gender hierarchy which renders these anatomical differences socially and erotically significant, it is hardly surprising that heterosexual eroticism is infused with power. However, this eroticization of power is not reducible to the mere juxtaposition of certain body parts. There is nothing intrinsic to male and female anatomy which positions women as passive or privileges certain sexual practices above others. There is no absolute reason why the conjunction of a penis and a vagina has to be thought of as penetration, or as a process in which only one of those organs is active. The coercive equation of sex = coitus = something men do to women is not an inevitable consequence of an anatomical female relating sexually to an anatomical male, but the product of the social relations under which those bodies meet. Those social relations can be challenged. Even the most trenchant critics of heterosexuality and penetrative sex such as Jeffreys (1990) and Dworkin (1987) recognize that it is not male and female anatomy nor even, in Dworkin's case, the act of intercourse itself which constitutes the problem, but rather the way in which heterosexuality is institutionalized and practised under patriarchy.

Conventional (patriarchal) wisdom tells us that sexual attraction and excitement depend upon the power difference between men and women. While some lesbians and feminists strive to 'eroticise sameness and equality' (Jeffreys, 1990, p. 315), others argue that desire and pleasure depend upon power and therefore 'don't want to do away with power in sex' (Hollibaugh, 1989, p. 408). It is difficult to support the contention that power – a *social* relation – is intrinsic to desire without slipping back into essentialism. Even if what we understand by desire presupposes some degree of difference, does this inevitably entail hierarchy? All of us are 'different' from each other: no two human beings are 'the same' and a lover is always someone 'other'. It is therefore possible to envision the ideal of egalitarian sexual relations in which there is still the potential erotic charge of otherness. The point is that there are some differences which are of little social significance – such as the colour of our hair – and others which are constructed as socially significant by virtue of hierarchy – such as the configuration of our genitals. To imagine that the abolition of gender difference would do away with all difference is absurd (see Delphy, 1993). So too is the assumption that doing away with gender, or other power differentials, would necessarily eradicate desire – although it would no doubt transform it.

Where does this leave those of us who relate sexually to those defined as different within the hierarchy of gender? Is power an inescapable feature of heterosexual eroticism? To argue that the power hierarchy of gender is structural does not mean that it is exercised uniformly and evenly at the level of interpersonal sexual relations, nor that our practice and experience is wholly determined by patriarchal structures and ideologies. There is some room for manoeuvre within these constraints. To deny this is to deny heterosexual women any agency, to see us as doomed to submit to men's desires whether as unwilling victims or misguided dupes. Heterosexual feminists, here as elsewhere in their lives, have struggled against men's dominance. We have asserted our right to define our own pleasure, questioned phallocentric models of sexuality, tried to deprioritize penetration or reconceptualize it in ways which did not position us as passive objects (Campbell, 1980; S. Jackson, 1982b; Robinson, 1993). More recently some have admitted – cautiously or defiantly – that even penetrative sex with men can be enjoyable and that its pleasure is not merely eroticized submission (Hollway, 1993; Robinson, 1993; Rowland, 1993; Segal, 1994).

Critics of heterosexuality are unimpressed by such claims. Kitzinger and Wilkinson, for example, are scathing about heterosexual feminists' attempts to develop egalitarian sexual practices and to change the meaning of penetration. Such strategies, they say, 'obscure the problem of the *institutionalization* of penile penetration under heteropatriarchy' (1993, p. 21). They see the institution as totally determining practice so that each and every instance of penetration is an enactment of men's power. While it is the case that penetration within patriarchy is loaded with symbolic meanings which encode male power and is often, in fact, coercive, it cannot be assumed that it invariably carries this singular meaning. To argue that it does is to treat the physical act as meaningful in itself, as magically embodying male power without any intervening processes. It is here assumed that the micro-processes of power can simply be read off from the structural level. It certainly cannot be assumed that if women like heterosexual sex we must all be wallowing in a masochistic eroticization of our subordination – the consistent message of the radical lesbian position (Jeffreys, 1990; Kitzinger and Wilkinson, 1993; Kitzinger, 1994).[7] This is also a very static view of sexuality, which denies the experience of those heterosexual feminists whose desires and practices have changed over time (see, for example, Bartky, 1993).

We need to retain a critical perspective on heterosexual pleasure, but one which is more subtle and less condemnatory. However, we should not underestimate the pervasiveness of male power either. This is a problem in Wendy Hollway's (1984b) analysis which demonstrates that women can produce discourses which contest 'the power of the penis', but ignores the material power accruing to men as social group. Even if, as Lynne Segal suggests, 'sex places "manhood" in jeopardy', threatening the 'masculine ideal of autonomous selfhood' (1994, p. 255), the hierarchical ordering of gender and sexuality is not as easy to subvert as she implies. Power operates at a variety of levels. Although we can contest it at the level of individual practice (and enhance our sexual pleasure in the process), this may have little effect elsewhere.

There are, as Caroline Ramazanoglu reminds us, very real material constraints on seeking heterosexual pleasure. As she says, we need 'to distinguish between the undoubted possibilities of heterosexual pleasure, and the extremely powerful social forces which constrain these possibilities from being more widely realised' (1994, p. 321). For many women pleasure remains elusive, as has been demonstrated by the Women Risk and AIDS project (WRAP). Not only sexual coercion, but also an inability to find a language in which to discuss and assert their own pleasures serve as obstacles to the practice of safer sex among young women (Holland *et al.*, 1990, 1991; Thomson and Scott, 1991). They discipline their own bodies and pleasures to suit men in ways their partners are unlikely even to be aware of. In so doing they concede to men's definitions of what is pleasurable and acceptable, continuing to define sex as 'penetration for men's pleasure in which women find fulfilment primarily in the relationship, in giving pleasure' (Holland *et al.*, 1994, p. 31).[8] This attribute of femininity is hardly confined to sexuality: the ethic of service to men is fundamental to other aspects of gender relations, to men's appropriation of women's labour as well as their bodies.

It is difficult to imagine a truly egalitarian form of heterosexuality while gender hierarchy and, hence, gender division persists; and if that division were eradicated heterosexuality would no longer exist in any meaningful sense. In the last analysis, what we do in bed, or who we do it with will not undermine the hierarchy of gender. Sexual practice is just one gendered social practice among many, and needs to be placed in context as such. To give too much weight to sexual desire, practice and identity is to ignore the many other ways in which male domination is colluded with and resisted and the many other means by which women's subordination is perpetuated.

NOTES

1. The reasons for this misrepresentation are beyond the scope of this paper. For an excellent analysis of the 'trashing' of radical feminism see Cameron (1993).
2. See, for example, Smart's (1992) analysis of the construction of women as unruly subjects (as if out of nowhere) in the Victorian era. A more convincing analysis is provided by Poovey (1989), who calls our attention to the co-existence of new definitions of femininity with older ones. She is also alert to the material social relations underlying contested constructions of femininity.
3. For example, Wendy Hollway (1984a) has produced the most systematic application of Foucault to issues of sexual desires and practices; yet elsewhere, in discussing how such desires come into being, she resorts to psychoanalysis (1989, 1993).
4. Gagnon and Simon's interactionism has two major, interrelated problems (aside from certain sexist assumptions which are not the product of the perspective itself). First, there is no way of analysing the social origins of particular sexual scripts or their deployment throughout society and, second, like Foucauldian analysis, it is unable to deal with the structural bases of power and inequality. See my early (1978) attempt to apply this perspective to the problem of rape and Walby's (1990) critique of it.
5. This weakness in social construction theory gives biological determinism a new foothold. The popularity of the idea of the 'gay gene' and similar biological theories is in part due to the lack of a convincing alternative explanation of how we acquire specific desires.
6. Such distinctions are also necessary in order to avoid interpreting a critique of heterosexuality as an attack on heterosexual women.
7. The inevitability of women's sexual masochism (whether for all time or just under patriarchy) is also asserted from other perspectives, whether in psychoanalytic accounts like Naomi's Segal's (1992) claim that new men just aren't sexy or libertarian celebrations of S/M.
8. Segal (1994) is dismissive of this evidence, claiming that WRAP interpreted it to fit their own preconceptions. Had she read their publications more carefully she would have discovered that they looked for a discourse of pleasure among the young women they interviewed, but failed to find it.

REFERENCES

Bartky, S. (1990), *Femininity and Domination* (New York: Routledge).
Bartky, S. (1993), 'Hypatia Unbound: A Confession', in S. Wilkinson and C. Kitzinger (eds), *Heterosexuality* (London: Sage).
Butler, J. (1990a), *Gender Trouble: Feminism and the Subversion of Identity* (New York: Routledge).
Butler, J. (1990b), 'Gender Trouble, Feminist Theory and Psychoanalytic Discourse', in L. Nicholson (ed.), *Feminism/Postmodernism* (New York: Routledge).

Butler, J. (1991), 'Imitation and Gender Insubordination', in D. Fuss (ed.), *Inside/Out* (New York: Routledge).

Butler, J. (1993), *Bodies that Matter* (New York: Routledge).

Cameron, D. (1993), 'Telling It Like It Wasn't: How Radical Feminism Became history', *Trouble and Strife*, **27**: pp. 11–15.

Cameron, D. and Frazer, E. (1987), *The Lust to Kill* (Oxford: Polity Press).

Campbell, B. (1980), 'Feminist Sexual Politics', *Feminist Review*, **5**: pp. 1–18.

Delphy, C. (1984), *Close to Home: A Materialist Analysis of Women's Oppression* (London: Hutchinson).

Delphy, C. (1992), 'Mothers' Union?', *Trouble and Strife*, **24**: pp. 12–19.

Delphy, C. (1993), 'Rethinking Sex and Gender', *Women's Studies International Forum*, **16**(1): pp. 1–9.

Delphy, C. and Leonard, D. (1992), *Familiar Exploitation: A New Analysis of Marriage in Contemporary Western Societies* (Oxford: Polity Press).

Dworkin, A. (1987), *Intercourse* (London: Secker & Warburg).

Evans, M. (1994), 'Desire Incarnate: Review of Judith Butler's *Bodies that Matter*', *The Times Higher Education Supplement*, 18 February.

Foucault, M. (1980), 'Truth and Power', in C. Gordon (ed.), *Michel Foucault: Power/Knowledge* (Brighton: Harvester).

Foucault, M. (1981), *The History of Sexuality*, volume 1 (Harmondsworth: Penguin).

Fraser, N. (1989), *Unruly Practices: Power, Discourse and Gender in Contemporary Social Theory* (Oxford: Polity Press).

Fuss, D. (1991) (ed.), *Inside/Out: Lesbian Theories, Gay Theories* (New York: Routledge).

Gagnon, J. and Simon, W. (1974), *Sexual Conduct* (London: Hutchinson).

Gergen, M. (1993), 'Unbundling our Binaries – Genders, Sexualities, Desires', in S. Wilkinson and C. Kitzinger (eds), *Heterosexuality* (London: Sage).

Hearn, J., Sheppard, D. L., Tancred-Sheriff, P., and Burrell, G. (1989) (eds), *The Sexuality of Organization* (London: Sage).

Heath, S. (1982), *The Sexual Fix* (London: Hutchinson).

Holland, J., Ramazanoglu, C., Scott, S., Sharpe, S. and Thomson, R. (1990), *"'Don't Die of Ignorance' – I Nearly Died of Embarrassment": Condoms in Context* (London: Tufnell Press).

Holland, J., Ramazanoglu, C., Scott, S., Sharpe, S. and Thomson, R. (1991), *Pressure, Resistance, Empowerment: Young Women and the Negotiation of Safer Sex* (London: Tufnell Press).

Holland, J., Ramazanoglu, C., Sharpe, S. and Thomson, R. (1994), 'Power and Desire: The Embodiment of Female Sexuality', *Feminist Review*, **46**.

Hollibaugh, A. (1989), 'Desire for the Future: Radical Hope in Passion and Pleasure', in C. Vance (ed.), *Pleasure and Danger: Exploring Female Sexuality* (London: Pandora).

Hollway, W. (1984a), 'Gender Difference and the Production of Subjectivity', in J. Henriques, W. Hollway, C. Urwin, C. Venn and V. Walkerdine (eds), *Changing the Subject* (London: Methuen).

Hollway, W. (1984b), 'Women's Power in Heterosexual Sex', *Women's Studies International Forum*, **7**(1): pp. 63–8.

Hollway, W. (1989), *Subjectivity and Method in Psychology* (London: Sage).

Hollway, W. (1993), 'Theorizing Heterosexuality: A Response', *Feminism and Psychology*, 3(3): pp. 412–17.

Jackson, M. (1987), '"Facts of Life" or the Eroticization of Women's Oppression? Sexology and the Social Construction of Heterosexuality', in P. Caplan (ed.), *The Cultural Construction of Sexuality* (London: Tavistock).

Jackson, M. (1994), *The Real Facts of Life: Feminism and the Politics of Sexuality* (London: Taylor & Francis).

Jackson, S. (1978), 'The Social Context of Rape', *Women's Studies International Quarterly*, 1(1): pp. 27–38.

Jackson, S. (1982a), *Childhood and Sexuality* (Oxford: Basil Blackwell).

Jackson, S. (1982b), 'Masculinity, Femininity and Sexuality', in S. Friedman and E. Sarah (eds), *On the Problem of Men* (London: The Women's Press).

Jackson, S. (1992), 'The Amazing Deconstructing Woman: The Perils of Postmodern Feminism', *Trouble and Strife*, 25: pp. 25–31.

Jackson, S. (1993), 'Even Sociologists Fall in Love', *Sociology*, 27(2): pp. 201–20.

Jeffreys, S. (1985), *The Spinster and her Enemies* (London: Pandora).

Jeffreys, S. (1990), *Anticlimax: A Feminist Critique of the Sexual Revolution* (London: The Women's Press).

Kappeler, S. (1986), *The Pornography of Representation* (Oxford: Polity Press).

Kelly, L. (1988), *Surviving Sexual Violence* (Oxford: Polity Press).

Kitzinger, C. (1994), 'Problematizing Pleasure: Radical Feminist Deconstructions of Sexuality and Power', in H. L. Radtke and H. J. Stam (eds), *Power/ Gender: Social Relations in Theory and Practice* (London: Sage).

Kitzinger, C. and Wilkinson, S. (1993), 'Theorizing Heterosexuality', in S. Wilkinson and C. Kitzinger (eds), *Heterosexuality: A 'Feminism and Psychology' Reader* (London: Sage).

Lees, S. (1986), *Losing Out* (London: Hutchinson).

MacKinnon, C. (1982), 'Feminism, Marxism, Method and the State: An Agenda for Theory', *Signs*, 7(3): pp. 515–44.

McNay, L. (1992), *Feminism and Foucault* (Oxford: Polity Press).

Poovey, M. (1989), *Uneven Developments* (London: Virago).

Ramazanoglu, C. (ed.) (1993), *Up against Foucault* (London: Routledge).

Ramazanoglu, C. (1994), 'Theorizing Heterosexuality: A Reply to Wendy Hollway', *Feminism and Psychology*, 4(2): pp. 320–1.

Ramazanoglu, C. and Holland, J. (1993), 'Women's Sexuality and Men's Appropriation of Desire', in C. Ramazanoglu (ed.), *Up against Foucault* (London: Routledge).

Rich, A. (1980), 'Compulsory Heterosexuality and Lesbian Existence', *Signs*, 5(4): pp. 631–60.

Richardson, D. (1993), 'Sexuality and Male Dominance', in D. Richardson and V. Robertson (eds), *Introducing Women's Studies* (London: Macmillan).

Riley, D. (1988), *Am I That Name? Feminism and the Category of Women in History* (London: Macmillan).

Robinson, V. (1993), 'Heterosexuality: Beginnings and Connections', in S. Wilkinson and C. Kitzinger (eds), *Heterosexuality* (London: Sage).

Rowland, R. (1993), 'Radical Feminist Heterosexuality: The Personal and the Political', in S. Wilkinson and C. Kitzinger (eds), *Heterosexuality* (London: Sage).

Rubin, G. (1975), 'The Traffic in Women', in R. Reiter (ed.), *Toward an Anthropology of Women* (New York: Monthly Review Press).

Rubin, G. (1989), 'Thinking Sex: Notes for a Radical Theory of the Politics of Sexuality', in C. Vance (ed.), *Pleasure and Danger* (London: Pandora).

Scully, D. (1990), *Understanding Sexual Violence* (London: Unwin Hyman).

Segal, L. (1994), *Straight Sex: The Politics of Pleasure* (London: Virago).

Segal, N. (1992), 'Why Can't a Good Man Be Sexy? Why Can't a Sexy Man Be Good?', in D. Porter (ed.), *Between Men and Feminism* (London: Routledge).

Seidman, S. (1992), *Embattled Eros: Sexual Politics and Ethics in Contemporary America* (New York: Routledge).

Smart, C. (1992), 'Disruptive Bodies and Unruly Sex: the Regulation of Reproduction and Sexuality in the Nineteenth Century', in C. Smart (ed.), *Regulating Womanhood* (London: Routledge).

Swindells, J. (1993), 'A Straight Outing', *Trouble and Strife*, **26**: pp. 40–4.

Thomson, R. and Scott, S. (1991), *Learning about Sex: Young Women and the Social Construction of Sexual Identity* (London: Tufnell Press).

Walby, S. (1990), *Theorizing Patriarchy* (Oxford: Blackwell).

Weedon, C. (1987), *Feminist Practice and Poststructuralist Theory* (Oxford: Blackwell).

Westwood, S. (1984), *All Day, Every Day* (London: Pluto Press).

Wittig, M. (1992), *The Straight Mind and Other Essays* (Hemel Hempstead: Harvester Wheatsheaf).

Young, A. (1993), 'The Authority of the Name', in S. Wilkinson and S. Kitzinger (eds), *Heterosexuality* (London: Sage).

2 Sinking into his Arms ... Arms in his Sink: Heterosexuality and Feminism Revisited

Jo VanEvery

This chapter is concerned with debates about heterosexuality and feminism. In particular, it focuses on the argument – made in writing and in verbal discussions, and to varying degrees – that heterosexuality is central to the practice of male dominance and to women's oppression (and is thus contradictory to feminist practice) and that lesbianism constitutes a feminist political practice (although not all lesbians are feminists). Some proponents of this argument were (and are) talking about specific sexual practices; others, about a more general way of life which may or may not include sex. In the past year or so, new academic attention has been brought to this topic with the publication of Sue Wilkinson and Celia Kitzinger's special issue of *Feminism and Psychology* in 1992 (and the subsequent *Reader*, 1993) on the topic of heterosexuality.

I come to this debate via an interest in feminism and the family, in particular how women have tried to arrange their domestic lives in ways which take account of feminist critiques of the family as an oppressive institution. I examined these issues by conducting a small study of self-defined anti-sexist living arrangements.[1] This research was conducted in an environment where several other researchers were involved in what might be called lesbian and gay studies. Their influence on my thinking led me to consider the sexuality of the participants in my study and the importance of sexuality to the analysis. I was concerned not to reproduce in my work the heterosexism implicit in so much academic writing.

During the course of the research I was also developing a friendship with a woman who was moving increasingly in the direction of lesbian separatism. Debates and discussions with her, about research, theory and our personal lives, also influenced my thinking in this area. Largely

35

as a result of these discussions and the reading that they provoked, I am aware that separatism is not a political stance specific to a particular historical moment in feminist movement, but is still lived and debated by some lesbians today. However, as a feminist who works in academia, I recognize that lesbian separatist theory and practice is often dismissed, marginalized or ignored. I believe that there are important insights to be gained by taking this body of theory seriously.

SEXUALITIES AS *SOCIAL* PRACTICES

I have noted two influences on my thinking about heterosexuality: lesbian and gay studies, and lesbian separatism. While the latter is influential to the structure of my argument as a whole, the former profoundly influences the way I conceptualize heterosexuality. The work of gay male historians such as Michel Foucault and Jeffrey Weeks has highlighted the way that the meaning of homosexuality has changed. No longer considered solely as 'acts', homosexuality is now considered as 'identity', 'lifestyle' and 'community'. One aspect of this historical change has been the rejection of the (medical) term 'homosexuality' in favour of 'gay' or 'lesbian' and the proliferation of lesbian and gay identities. These insights can be applied in the study of heterosexuality. Julia Penelope has noted that the term 'heterosexuality' was coined after 'lesbian', 'homosexual', 'invert' and 'Sapphist' (1993, p. 261). The reactions of many of the contributors to the Wilkinson and Kitzinger volume (1993) indicate that it has not developed as a conscious 'identity' or 'lifestyle'. For example, Sandra Lipsitz Bem says, 'although I have lived monogamously with a man I love for over 26 years, I am not now and never have been a "heterosexual"' (1993, p. 50).[2]

If sexualities are understood not solely as sexual acts but also as (potential) identities, lifestyles and communities, heterosexuality and lesbianism can be understood as *sexual* practices and as *social* practices. Lesbianism as a social practice is evident in the writings on 'political lesbianism' in the early 1980s. For example:

Our definition of a political lesbian is a woman-identified woman who does not fuck men. It does not mean compulsory sexual activity with women. (Leeds Revolutionary Feminist Group, 1981, p. 5)

and

Woman-identified Lesbianism is . . . more than sexual preference; it is a political choice. It is political because relations between men and women are essentially political; they involve power and dominance. Since the Lesbian actively rejects that relationship and chooses women, she defies the established political system. (Charlotte Bunch, quoted in *Bar On*, 1992, p. 49)

Thus political lesbians are not necessarily sexual lesbians (a major point of contention in the debate). This is also evident in Adrienne Rich's article of the same period in which she introduces the terms 'lesbian existence' and 'lesbian continuum':

> I have chosen to use the terms *lesbian existence* and *lesbian continuum* because the word *lesbianism* has a clinical and limiting ring. *Lesbian existence* suggests both the fact of the historical presence of lesbians and our continuing creation of the meaning of that existence. I mean the term *lesbian continuum* to include a range – through each woman's life and throughout history – of woman-identified experience; not simply the fact that a woman has had or consciously desired genital sexual experience with another woman. (Rich, 1980, p. 648; emphasis as in original)

Yet despite this recognition of lesbianism as more than sexual practice within the political lesbianism debates, much of the discussion of heterosexuality is limited to its sexual aspects – fucking men.

There are (at least) two problems which arise from concentrating on the sexual aspects of heterosexuality. The first is the focus on desire and individual women's ability to change it. As Rich notes, 'the assumption that "most women are innately heterosexual" stands as a theoretical and political stumbling block for many women' (1980, p. 648). This has led to a dichotomized debate about repression and choice. Indeed, the radical insight of Rich's article was precisely her characterization of heterosexuality as 'compulsory'. She provides numerous examples which demonstrate that women are physically, economically, emotionally and psychologically *coerced* into heterosexuality. Recent heterosexual contributors to the renewed debate about heterosexuality have turned this around to argue that it is possible in 1990s Britain for a woman to choose 'non-oppressive' heterosexual sex. For example, Wendy Hollway, in her response to the special issue of *Feminism & Psychology*, argues that 'The absence of discourses which make sense of the pleasures, desires and satisfactions, for women, of heterosexual relationships is damaging both to feminist theory and feminist politics' (1993, p. 412). But she never addresses the issue of coercion. Moreover, the examples Hollway uses of the pleasures, desires and satisfaction of heterosexuality for women – penetration, and the embrace of 'strong arms' – reduce 'heterosexual relationships' to heterosexual sex. In addition, the influence of her context is ignored in the discussion of the meaning of these acts:

> I love the experience of being wrapped in my partner's 'strong arms' and 'adored'.... Later I will be out there in the world doing my own thing, on my own (though – I hope – in the knowledge that my partner is there for me). However, for those moments I am safe, protected and loved. (1993, p. 414)

This brings us to the second problem with the focus on the *sexual* aspects of sexualities – it divorces sexual acts from the social contexts in which they happen (e.g. relationships, family) thus separating discussions of sexual practices from those about these contexts. As Hollway's argument illustrates, feminist defenders of heterosexuality rarely consider research on families. How many women go out there to do their own thing, on their own? In addition, the debates about sexuality have had little explicit impact on analyses of the 'family', the division of labour, etc.:[3] heterosexuality is usually not problematized in analyses of these topics; and lesbian and gay living arrangements are treated in that literature (if at all) as part of a new diversity of family forms.[4]

Carol Pateman (1988), in an analysis of political theories based on social contract, points out that the social contract is based on a sexual contract and the division between these two appears as a division between the public and the private spheres of society. Economics and politics are considered part of the public sphere; personal relationships based on care and altruism, the private. She points out that this is a political fiction necessary for the maintenance of male dominance. The two problems highlighted above perpetuate this division. In the first situation, economic and social factors are discussed as external factors coercing women into heterosexuality or constraining their escape from abusive heterosexual relationships. Economics and politics remain external to the relationships themselves. 'Good' sex is freely chosen sex, a concept only making sense (according to Pateman) in the public sphere of social contract. In the second, even where political and economic aspects of family and marriage are discussed, this is rarely related to an analysis of heterosexuality. Sexuality seems to become a new private sphere.[5]

Feminists have been instrumental in highlighting the economic aspects of the private sphere. It is now widely accepted that a lot of necessary work gets done (usually by women) in the home. And recent research has highlighted inequalities in access to financial and other resources. Most of this research has focused on married couples with children, yet none of it discusses heterosexuality. There is almost no research on the division of labour or the allocation of resources in lesbian or gay couple households, and thus sexuality never arises when the findings of several studies are compared. Perhaps because of this, this research is also never discussed in debates about heterosexuality.

A recent conference paper by Becky Rosa, a radical lesbian feminist, on lesbian anti-monogamy indicates some of the issues which may be important to an understanding of the links between heterosexuality as a sexual identity and as a social identity. Through an examination of the importance of couples and monogamy in the separatist lesbian community, she demonstrates the strength of cultural connections between sexual practices and domestic arrangements through monogamy.

When we meet a woman who we are 'attracted to', why does this indicate to us the start of a sexual relationship, rather than a friendship? What if we already have a sexual relationship (remember we are only allowed to have one)? Within a monogamous framework, if we 'fall in love' with a woman and we already have a Girlfriend our choices are to finish with our current Girlfriend and start a new relationship, to have 'an affair' or to openly continue two relationships with little or no support, and few models of how other Lesbians may have made them work. Our energy is taken up trying to sort these out rather than with the wider Lesbian community, and often ultimately cause the break up of relationships. However, we can have an unlimited number of friends, it would serve us better if we didn't separate off feelings of lust/attraction from those of feeling we might like to get to know a woman better and be her friend. (Rosa, 1993, p. 4)

Transferring her insights to an understanding of heterosexuality, we can see that even if we reject radical or revolutionary feminist analyses of heterosexual sexual acts (e.g. that of Jeffreys, 1990), heterosexuality is still problematic *because it usually involves long-term monogamous relationships in which the partners share living space.*

Opposite sex bonding *per se* is not the complete package. Even if we are in a heterosexual relationship there are many other social conventions we are then expected to follow that are built upon it: marriage, house-owning, children, tax incentives, dinner parties, social success and being 'normal', being able to join in everyday conversations. We (heterosexual or not) are expected to buy into a whole way of life that goes far beyond being involved in, or being prepared to be involved in, sexual relations with men. (Rosa, 1993, p. 1)

I believe it is important to bring these areas of concern together. When feminists assert that women should be able to choose heterosexuality, they overlook the fact that women usually do not choose just any heterosexual relationship. They choose long-term monogamous cohabiting relationships. At the very least this is often their ideal. Numerous studies have shown that women are disadvantaged in long-term, monogamous, co-resident relationships with men through the unequal division of domestic labour, and the unequal access to large amounts of discretionary income.[6] Some of the articles in the volume edited by Kitzinger and Wilkinson indicate an awareness of this link without making it central to their analyses (e.g. Croghan, 1993; Rowland, 1993). It is this aspect of heterosexuality which I believe needs to be given more attention.

There is also a broader claim being made by some radical lesbian feminists, that heterosexuality is intrinsic to the construction of gender difference (e.g. Wittig, 1992). In making this claim, they are not only talking about erotic desire. For example, Marilyn Frye argues that women's oppression is in their being defined as 'for men' not just sexually but in myriad ways.

In cultures most shaped by male domination, wives' (female slaves', or servants') compulsory sexual accessibility and service is of a piece with their economic and domestic service and subordination to the man or men to whom they are attached and in some cases to those men's whole fraternity, family or clan. (Frye, 1992, p. 129)

In another essay she talks about the construction of men and men's activities as the most/only important things around. 'The maintenance of phallocratic reality requires that the attention of women be focused on men and men's projects ... and that attention not be focused on women.' (Frye, 1983, p. 172) Thus the 'problem' of heterosexual feminism is not one of desire but one of how to enter such relations while challenging the arrogant male perception that it is 'how things are'.

Her discussion of female heterosexuality (Frye, 1992) encompasses the social/economic aspects that I address in this chapter. But in a recent critique of Frye's notion of 'virginity', Kitzinger and Wilkinson (1994) distort much of what Frye is actually saying about the pervasiveness and complexity of women's subordination, by focusing on the sexual as the most important determining factor in defining women as subordinate.

Heterosexual sex acts are but one part of the institution of heterosexuality. Feminists need to consider not only whether fucking is bad for women or whether women are coerced into heterosexuality, but they also need to consider the economic and social character of heterosexual relationships. All of these issues are linked to identity. Do the acts and relationships work out the same way if a woman identifies as heterosexual as if she identifies in some other way (e.g. bisexual)?

ANTI-SEXIST LIVING ARRANGEMENTS AND HETEROSEXUALITY

My interest in this topic arose out of a study of anti-sexist living arrangements[7] (VanEvery, 1994). Although many feminist texts speak of the unsatisfactory nature (or even failure) of 'alternative families' in the 1970s (e.g. Yuval-Davis, 1993, p. 53; Nava, 1983, p. 76), there has been little analysis of them. I interviewed members of 26 self-defined anti-sexist living arrangements in order to begin to understand the possibilities and problems of such 'personal' attempts at political change.

Because it was important that participants were *explicitly* anti-sexist in their motivation, they were recruited through advertising. The 26 living arrangements interviewed were drawn from a list of 62 including seven who responded to an advertisement in *Everywoman*; two who responded to a notice in the Working Mothers association newsletter; 48 who responded to an advertisement in the *Guardian*; one who I met at a conference entitled 'Men, Masculinity and Socialism'; and four who were referred by other respondents, whether in an interview or in the initial response.[8] All lived in Britain.

I chose the living arrangements to be studied using two criteria – the type of living arrangement and geographical location. I wanted to have some variety in the living arrangements chosen, yet retain some basis for preliminary generalizations about particular arrangements. A preliminary categorization based on number of adults and the presence of children was used to this end. This classification was later modified into six groups which were of approximately equal size: (1) single mothers by choice; (2) voluntarily childless heterosexual couples; (3) heterosexual couples with children in role reversals; (4) heterosexual couples with children with shared roles; (5) multiple adult arrangements; and (6) others. The latter category included a lesbian couple with children, a voluntarily childless heterosexual couple who did not cohabit, and a voluntarily childless single woman. In order to maximize the geographical diversity without excessive cost, interviewees were chosen in clusters around Britain. Six of the living arrangements were in London; three in the South East; two in the South West; three in the West Midlands; three in the East Midlands; three in East Anglia; one on the South Coast; three in the North West; and two in southeast Scotland.

All of the participants were White. Most would also be considered middle-class although some reported having a working-class background. Incomes varied between Income Support and over £200 000 per annum. Most were well educated, many having university degrees (some, postgraduate degrees) or other post-secondary qualifications. While these characteristics could be argued to limit the applicability of any conclusions, I believe that there are advantages in the particular composition of the sample. Most of the participants could be described as having a better than average chance of being able to exert control over their personal lives. Any constraints on their ability to change would reflect, not factors such as poverty or racism but, rather, the resistance of particular constructions of gender and family to change.

Members of living arrangements were interviewed together, usually in their own homes. Who was present for the interview was largely decided by the members of the living arrangement, although I had made a decision not to interview children under 16. Organizational considerations meant that in larger living arrangements a member was often missing. Both partners of the couples were present except in two cases. In one, the man did not wish to be interviewed; in the other, the woman did not realize that I had wanted to interview both of them. The interviews were loosely organized around a list of 11 topics and usually lasted about 90 minutes.[9]

In my study I found that the defining characteristic of an anti-sexist living arrangement was the rejection of and resistance to being a 'wife' (defined by the appropriation of her paid and unpaid labour, financial dependence, sexual availability, subordinate position and the accompanying psychological characteristics). While it was not impossible for those living with men to reject being a wife, it was easier in many ways for those women in living arrangements without men. In addition, it was in these latter living arrangements that the greatest degree of rejection was found. This was true whether or not the women in these living arrangements identified themselves as lesbian.

Living Arrangements including Men

For those living arrangements in my study which included men, the difficulties were greater. In comparison to the findings of other studies, the men in my study were exceptional in the amount of housework that they did. This is most obvious for the role-reversals. In these living arrangements, the division of housework was described as one in which men were responsible for everything. Specific tasks were only mentioned where women did them, usually for a particular reason. These were few and usually infrequent. The rationale behind this was the equalization of 'time spent with the children'. Thus, men did housework so that women could spend time with the children in the evenings and at weekends.

Graeme Russell (1987) reviews the limited literature on role-reversals, including his own study. The implicit definition of a role-reversal used by Russell is men taking on child-care and women being main earners. He concludes that

> reversing employment and child-care jobs, does not necessarily lead to fathers assuming the overall responsibility for children in the way that traditional mothers do. Many mothers retained greater responsibility for children, and 'took over' when they arrived home from work. (pp. 163–4)

He also notes that women experienced difficulties similar to women in dual-earner couples related to *their dual roles*.

In sharp contrast, the men in role-reversals in my study took on the bulk of the housework. While this finding indicates that it *may be* possible to radically alter the division of domestic labour in living arrangements including men, I did not interpret it in this way. Given the rarity of the situation which I found (indicated by studies such as Russell's), I concluded that women's ability to reject being a wife in such a living arrangement was severely limited by the willingness of the man involved to take on the housework and child-care. This

understanding of men's commitment as a constraint can be extended
to all of the living arrangements with men in them (all of which had
heterosexual couples, although in larger arrangements not all adults
were related to each other as couples).

I identified three ways in which housework was divided. The first,
used in all arrangements, was to increase the amount of work for which
members of the living arrangement were individually responsible, including the cleaning of individual space (e.g. bedrooms) and laundry.
This was, in effect, to define certain tasks as 'not housework'.[10] Communal tasks were then divided either by swapping, in which tasks were
divided up and each was treated as the individual responsibility of one
member, or sharing, in which tasks were shared out evenly amongst
all members over time, either by doing them together or by alternating
regularly. Both methods raised different problems but there was evidence of struggle to achieve equality.[11] Some participants even mentioned less tangible aspects of the division of housework like thinking
about when things needed to be done.

However, regardless of the amount of work they do, men can be
understood to be in control of the division of housework (their traditional role) because their *agreement* is crucial to the form of the
living arrangement. This was particularly evident in one living arrangement centred on a heterosexual couple. The woman, Val,[12] said that
she thought Jason (her husband) should have ironed shirts and that she
was willing to do his ironing but he would not let her. Compared to a
case discussed by Arlie Hochschild (1989, p. 202) in which men used
a strategy of 'needs reduction' in order to get their wives to do things,
this arrangement looks good: Jason does not want his wife to do his
ironing for him even though he is unwilling to do it himself. However, *it is Jason who decides* what housework will be done and who
will do it, an aspect of the traditional division of labour identified as
crucial to the oppression of women by Delphy and Leonard (1992).

The unequal division of domestic labour is not the only issue. My
study had a higher than usual incidence of independent management
systems for the allocation of financial resources.[13] In this system neither
partner has access to all the money. Women's contributions to joint
expenditure remain visible and they retain control over the portion of
their income which exceeds this contribution. Two-thirds of my sample
used this system of money management, spread across all categories
of living arrangements with or without children. All of the women
using this system explicitly mentioned the importance of independence
at some point during the interview.[14]

Where it was not used, it was usually because the minimum condition of two independent incomes was not met. In only one case was a man the sole earner and this couple described their financial situation as unsatisfactory. This factor did not explain all cases, though. It was striking that, although not all the married couples used a joint management system (where all money is pooled and both partners have access to the pool), all of the heterosexual couples using this system were married. Where the minimum conditions for independent management were met, there were some cases in which an ideology of marriage as (equal) partnership led to the adoption of a joint management system. Other research has provided some evidence of a link between 'love' and joint bank accounts (Duncombe and Marsden, 1993, p. 227). Roseanna Hertz (1986) has found that, when she discussed her research with heterosexual academic friends of hers, they had an extremely negative reaction to the adoption of the independent system of financial management, as it contradicted expectations that couple-relationships were sharing and trusting. Some studies have shown that joint management can lead to a devaluation of women's income (e.g. Hertz, 1986).

Sarah Berk (1985) has suggested that in order to explain the division of housework in heterosexual couple households we must take into account the fact that

At least metaphorically, the division of household labor facilitates *two* production processes: the production of goods and services and what we might call the production of gender. (Berk, 1985, p. 201; emphasis as in original)

She conceptualizes gender as a power relationship in which men are dominant and women subordinate (a conceptualization which I share). I would argue that her insights can be extended to the explanation of the allocation of financial (and other) resources within living arrangements. Thus both the organization of housework (what needs to be done and who does it) and the management of money construct men as dominators (people who earn more money, control spending and do not have to do housework) and women as subordinates (people who are financially dependent and do housework), as 'man and wife'.

It is this construction that those in my study were trying to reject. However, the equality of a living arrangement including men is never certain: men can change their minds or decide there are limits to their commitment to anti-sexist living. These changes need not be overt.

For example, Lynne and Dave instituted a role-reversal over ten years ago, largely to enable Lynne to pursue higher education and a career. At that time, they had five young children at home and, given that grants are only available for full-time education, it made sense for Dave to stay home full-time although he did some freelance building work. Now all but one of the children has left home, and Lynne is in a job with some scope for flexibility. Housework is divided by swapping, rather than sharing, tasks. Dave is responsible for activities related to eating, including shopping and cooking. Lynne is responsible for cleaning, which is mostly ensuring that it gets done. They have a paid cleaner two days a week. Lynne earns considerably more than Dave. They use a joint management system of financial allocation.

However, Lynne has begun to doubt Dave's willingness to take on more paid work if she decided to cut back her paid work. Despite the lack of (or extremely reduced) appropriation of Lynne's *unpaid* work, the appropriation of her *paid* work (as discussed by Delphy and Leonard, 1992) is becoming apparent. It could be argued that their division of paid work is constructing Dave as a man (as dominator) in the sense of a person who can get someone else to earn the money necessary for his maintenance so he can pursue more fulfilling (unpaid) activities like pottery. Their system of financial allocation masks this process.

Changes in commitment are not inevitable. Many of the participants spoke of their living arrangements in terms of struggle or evolution – as a project never finished. What I would like to highlight here is that they were dependent on *men's* commitment and thus vulnerable to *men's* decisions about the extent of that commitment. If men change their minds or say 'thus far and no further', women have few choices *if they are to remain in heterosexual relationships.* As I have already pointed out, the men who participated in my study are exceptional – if one of these women were in a position to leave her particular man, she would be unlikely to find another who will be any better. In fact, she would be extremely likely to find one who would be worse. Arlie Hochschild (1989) found in her study of two-earner couples that men use this fact to limit the amount of work they actually do by routinely comparing themselves to other men (and rarely to women). *This strategy can only work if living alone or with other women is ruled out as an option for their partners.* What is striking about Hochschild's study is that the women were so strongly committed to preserving their marriages despite extreme dissatisfaction with the division of domestic labour and (in some cases) unusually high earnings. Although she points out, as do many researchers in this area, that women are aware of the statistics on women's standard of living post-divorce, she does not point out that *particular* women in her study have resources unlikely to put them in such dire straits. We need to recognize that *some* women are in an economic position to make such choices. The way we talk about (value and devalue) living arrangements without men contributes to their perception of the choices actually available to them.

Living Arrangements without Men

Although most of the women in my study were heterosexual, not all were in living arrangements that included men. For example, Kate, a single mother by choice, identifies as heterosexual. Her sexual practice is mostly celibate. She has no desire for a long-term couple relationship. The fathers of her children have/had no control over the raising of them. Her primary relationships are with women (including her mother, sister, friends, a network of other single mothers). She has been involved in political activism around lesbian issues such as Section 28. To put her in the same category as married or cohabiting heterosexual women is to bury the different meanings heterosexuality has in different women's lives.

For women living on their own or only with their children, the division of housework could be interpreted as taking individual responsibility. While this is not inevitable, particularly for single mothers, those in my study had little or no contact with the fathers of their children.[15] For those in non-cohabiting heterosexual relationships, the lack of communal space meant that individual responsibility was maximized. Communal activities (such as shared meals) were the responsibility of the person whose space the activity took place in (which usually alternated).

Women living only with other women needed to negotiate a division of housework. Sarah Berk (1985) assumes that the production of gender would not happen in this situation. I do not have enough evidence to support or refute this as a general statement but for those in my study this was certainly the aim. For example, Miriam, a single mother who co-owns her house with a woman friend and has two women lodgers, told me that

[having men living in the house] made it a less equal household as far as both of us were concerned. And you're bringing all kinds of power struggles in that I can really do without in the home. I'm quite prepared to battle them out in other places but I want a home to be a nice, safe, comfortable, easy sort of place. I'd really rather keep that out on a permanent basis. (Miriam, multiple adult living arrangement)

The one lesbian couple were constantly negotiating the balance between spending time with the children (one partner was working full-time, the other part-time) and not 'servicing' one partner or the children. They tended to share tasks. The one woman-only household (two co-owners, one child, two lodgers) tended to share overall responsibility between the co-owners who also did irregular tasks. Routine cleaning tasks were swapped with each person responsible for one area of the house. Tasks related to eating were an individual responsibility (although Miriam took responsibility for her daughter).

Since most of the women-only living arrangements were single mothers or single women, the independent system of financial management prevailed. Only Kate had received any maintenance from the father of one of her children and she had no other contact with him during this period. Kathryn and Amy, the lesbian couple, used a joint management system which they related to the 'joint project' of having and raising the children. They also noted that they might think differently about this system of financial allocation if it were not for the 'basis of equality' provided by both of them being women.

Although most of the feminist literature on the advantages of living without men focuses on lesbians, the position of single heterosexual women is addressed by Becky Rosa:

Single women, similarly to Lesbians, dispel the myth that women should be dependent on a man, and are thus penalized for it. However, unlike single or coupled Lesbians, heterosexual single women are not necessarily creating structures for women to bond with other women to provide real alternatives to heterosexual monogamy. (Rosa, 1993, p. 8)

This is evident in one of the living arrangements which did not revolve around a couple. Miriam and Sally bought a house together six years before I interviewed them. Both identify as heterosexual and Miriam has a daughter (Becki, aged 8). The house is large enough to have two lodgers in addition to the co-owners and Becki. After a few bad experiences with short-term male lodgers, they decided to enforce a decision that only women could live in the house although boyfriends were welcome to visit. Miriam prefers the autonomy of part-time, temporary contracts in further education to the pressures of a full-time, permanent post, but at the time of the interview her ability to survive on the lower income this generates was in jeopardy.

Sally had moved out about a year earlier to live with her boyfriend. Miriam's sister had bought Sally's share but she had also moved out for the same reason (although she continued to pay the mortgage for an agreed period). In order to afford to keep the house on her own, Miriam needed to increase her paid work and take an extra lodger even though she would have preferred the shared responsibility of a co-owner. Miriam's ability to form 'a real alternative to heterosexual monogamy' was limited by the other women's lack of commitment to creating new structures despite their commitment to feminism.

It appears from this evidence that *some* heterosexual single women are trying to create new structures. However, Miriam's difficulties are but one example of the scarcity of that sort of commitment. In contrast, Kathryn and Amy, the one lesbian couple in the study, had formed or joined a lesbian mothers group in every area they lived. This gave them support in a society hostile to lesbian mothers. Similarly, Ann, a single mother by choice, stated that she had 'gradually become lesbian over the last 10 years' and that she was 'committed to working things out with women' despite the fact that she was not in a couple relationship nor looking for one.

CONCLUSION

Heterosexuality, in the sense of an erotic orientation, clearly implicates many women in long-term domestic arrangements with men, in which women's paid and unpaid labour is appropriated. Even for those who are resisting this appropriation, men are in control of the character of the relationship to the extent that women rely on their commitment to anti-sexism. Women's commitment to a heterosexual identity (particularly one which values cohabiting relationships) further disadvantages them as it opens up strategies for the avoidance of equality by men – they only need to be better than other men.

I would go further and argue that heterosexuality does more than implicate women in oppressive relationships. These relationships are the hegemonic construction of heterosexuality. Despite recent panic about declining marriage rates and increasing numbers of out-of-wedlock births, the vast majority of the population do marry, and the majority of such births are registered to both parents (usually giving the same address).[16] In addition, as David Clark and Douglas Haldane have pointed out, despite higher than ever rates of divorce, about two-thirds of marriages will be 'for life'. (1990, p. 24). It is not enough to say that women can choose heterosexuality without considering what that choice means for different women. The women who participated in my study have a better than average chance of being able to construct a non-oppressive heterosexuality. Yet, my evidence shows that it is difficult for women to make cohabiting heterosexual relationships equal. Not only is it rare for men to be committed to equality, but even when they are, the process is a struggle. Some women have decided to choose other forms of heterosexuality and, while there are still constraints, are better able to avoid being constructed as wives.

Lesbian separatists do not intend their theory to be used to think through new ways for women to be with men. However, the focus of their theory on the limits to change imposed by particular social and sexual relationships provides a fruitful avenue for thinking about heterosexuality. For heterosexual feminists, focusing on defending their heterosexuality as a *sexual* identity leads to a situation in which the form of most heterosexual relationships, and the information about the social and economic relationships within them is ignored. In addition, the liberatory possibilities of living arrangements such as Kate's or Miriam's, and the *work* that goes into sustaining them, has not been sufficiently explored.

In many ways, I have avoided direct engagement in the debate about heterosexuality which frames this chapter (which usually addresses the question of whether heterosexuality is a valid practice/identity for feminists/women) in order to address the underlying issue of defining what it is we are talking about in this debate. It is my belief that recent revival of the political lesbianism debate as an academic debate about heterosexuality is limited by its focus on the sexual. This debate would be enriched by making more central some of the insights of lesbian and gay theorizing about sexualities which start from the distinction between sexualities and sexual acts. Analyses of heterosexual relationships – usually called marriage and the family – need to be integrated into the analysis of heterosexuality.

NOTES

1. This research was conducted for a PhD in sociology at the University of Essex, awarded in 1994. The thesis was entitled 'Anti-sexist Living Arrangements: A Feminist Research Project'. A revised version, entitled *Heterosexual Women Changing the Family: Refusing to be a 'Wife'!* was published in 1995.
2. I would argue, however, that this resistance to naming is an indicator of the hegemony of a particular construction of heterosexuality as natural, a recognition that it does not need to be named.
3. While some radical feminist texts in these fields may be understood as analyses of heterosexuality (e.g. Christine Delphy and Diana Leonard's *Familiar Exploitation* (1992)), this reading is rarely made explicit and one wonders to what extent their work is indeed being read in such a way.
4. The latter is not necessarily positive: Jeffrey Weeks (1991) criticizes such inclusive definitions of family for not being useful sociological categorizations; Bar On (1992) sees them as part of a depoliticizing naturalization of lesbianism.
5. This was highlighted in a conversation with a fellow academic who said he resented the way I, and other feminists, wanted to *bring politics in* to sex in a way which assumed that there could and should be a sphere of life free of politics. I found this a rather strange notion, not only because I thought I was only highlighting what was already there, but also because I find it hard to imagine anything being apolitical.
6. Morris (1990) provides a review of the UK and US research in these areas.
7. I use the terms 'living arrangement' and 'residential group' to overcome some of the problems with the use of 'family' and 'household'. Among these problems are a confusion between 'family' as a kin-group and the residential kin group (the nuclear family household), the difficulties incorporating a diversity of family forms into definitions without losing conceptual clarity, and the assumptions about relationships within families and households (particularly communality and sexual relationships). (See VanEvery, 1994, pp. 10–13.)
8. The advertisement that appeared on the *Guardian* Women's Page was worded as follows:

> Calling all alternative lifestyles . . . PhD student Joanne VanEvery is researching Anti-Sexist Alternatives to the Patriarchal Family and wants to interview people from all types of anti-sexist arrangements, including heterosexual parents who share the work, parents single by choice, voluntarily childless couples and collective households with or without kids. Write to her at the Department of Sociology . . .

The other advertisements had similar wording.
9. The topics were: (1) general information; (2) attitudes and ideas about child-care and mothering; (3) work; (4) child-care; (5) school; (6) relationships both within the household unit and with others who live elsewhere; (7) state support; (8) money; (9) division of labour in the home; (10)

politics; and (11) feelings about space (public and private). They may have been covered in any order. I usually started by describing briefly the purpose of my research and asking them to describe their living arrangement to me.

10. Following Delphy and Leonard (1992) I define housework not solely by the tasks done but by the social relations in which they are done.
11. While there are these general patterns, the division of housework in each living arrangement was unique. Thus space does not allow me to provide details in this paper. (see VanEvery, 1995).
12. All names are pseudonyms.
13. Morris (1990) notes that it is totally absent in several studies.
14. Weston (1992) has found that the sharing of income was relatively uncommon in her study of lesbian and gay 'families' who also stressed autonomy and choice in family formation.
15. I have stated elsewhere (VanEvery, 1995) that they are thus dependent on the commitment of men to not taking on the powerful role available to them. Delphy and Leonard raise the issue of the continued appropriation of women's unpaid labour after divorce (1992, p. 127, footnote 6).
16. Using 1992 statistics published in *Population Trends* 77 (Autumn 1994) I have calculated that 77.2 per cent of women aged 16 and over have 'ever married' (ie. have got married even if they are no longer married). For women aged 24 and over the figure is 87.6 per cent. When the figures are broken down by birth cohort, it becomes obvious that age at first marriage is increasing (OPCS, 1993, Table 3.12). Thus, there may be a significant proportion of the 24–35 age group who will marry but have not yet done so. Furthermore, the 1991 General Household Survey reports that 23 per cent of unmarried people aged 16–49 in their sample were cohabiting. For an analysis of the trends in the registration of births see Cooper (1991).

REFERENCES

Bar On, B.-A. (1992), 'The Feminist Sexuality Debates and the Transformation of the Political', *Hypatia*, 7: 4, pp. 45–58.
Bem, S. L. (1993), 'On the Inadequacy of Our Sexual Categories: A Personal Perspective', in Wilkinson S. and Kitzinger, C. (eds), op. cit., pp. 50–1.
Berk, S. F. (1985), *The Gender Factory: The Apportionment of Work in American Households* (London: Plenum Press).
Copper, J. (1991), 'Births outside Marriage: Recent Trends and Associated Demographic and Social Changes', *Population Trends*, **63**: pp. 8–18.
Clark, D. and Haldane, D. (1990), *Wedlocked?* (Cambridge: Polity Press).
Croghan, R. (1993), 'Sleeping with the Enemy: Mothers in Heterosexual Relationships', in Wilkinson, S. and Kitzinger, C. (eds), op. cit., pp. 243–5.
Delphy, C. and Leonard, D. (1992), *Familiar Exploitation: A New Analysis of Marriage in Contemporary Western Societies* (Cambridge: Polity Press).
Duncombe, J. and Marsden, D. (1993), 'Love and Intimacy: The Gender Division of Emotion and "Emotion Work"', *Sociology*, **27**: 2, pp. 221–41.

Frye, M. (1983), *The Politics of Reality: Essays in Feminist Theory* (Trumansburg, NY: The Crossing Press).

Frye, M. (1992), *Wilful Virgin: Essays in Feminism* (Freedom, CA: The Crossing Press).

Hertz, R. (1986), *More Equal than Others: Women and Men in Dual-Career Marriages* (Berkeley, CA: University of California Press).

Hochschild, A. (1989), *The Second Shift: Working Parents and the Revolution at Home* (London: Piatkus).

Hollway, W. (1993), 'Theorizing Heterosexuality: A Response', *Feminism & Psychology*, **3**: 3, pp. 412–17.

Jeffreys, S. (1990), *Anti-Climax: A Feminist Perspective on the Sexual Revolution* (London: The Women's Press).

Kitzinger, C. and Wilkinson, S. (1994), 'Virgins and Queers: Rehabilitating Heterosexuality?', *Gender and Society*, **8**: 3, pp. 444–63.

Leeds Revolutionary Feminist Group (1981), 'Political Lesbianism: The Case Against Heterosexuality', in Onlywomen Press (eds), *Love Your Enemy? The Debate between Heterosexual Feminism and Political Lesbianism* (London: Onlywomen Press).

Morris, L. (1990), *The Workings of the Household: A US–UK Comparison* (Cambridge: Polity Press).

Nava, M. (1983), 'From Utopian to Scientific Feminism? Early Feminist Critiques of the Family?', in L. Segal (ed.), *What is to be done about the Family?* (Harmondsworth: Penguin), pp. 65–105.

Onlywomen Press (eds) (1981), *Love Your Enemy? The Debate between Heterosexual Feminism and Political Lesbianism* (London: Onlywomen).

OPCS (1993), *Marriage and Divorce Statistics, 1991* (London: HMSO).

OPCS (1994), 'Table 7: Population: age, sex and marital status', *Population Trends*, **77**: p. 45.

Pateman, C. (1988), *The Sexual Contract* (Cambridge: Polity Press).

Penelope, J. (1993), 'Heterosexual Identity: Out of the Closets', in Wilkinson, S. and Kitzinger, C. (eds), op. cit., pp. 261–5.

Rich, A. (1980), 'Compulsory Heterosexuality and Lesbian Existence', *Signs*, **5**: 4, pp. 631–60.

Rosa, B. (1993), 'Anti-Monogamy: A Radical Challenge to Compulsory Heterosexuality?', unpublished, WSN(UK) Conference, Nene College, Northampton, UK. (A revised version is in G. Griffin, M. Hester, S. Rai and S. Roseneil (eds) (1994), *Stirring It: Challenges for Feminism* (London: Taylor & Francis).)

Rowland, R. (1993), 'Radical Feminist Heterosexuality: The Personal and the Political', in Wilkinson, S. and Kitzinger, C. (eds), op. cit., pp. 75–9.

Russell, G. (1987), 'Problems in Role-reversed families', in C. Lewis and M. O'Brien (eds), *Reassessing Fatherhood* (London: Sage).

VanEvery, J. (1994), 'Anti-sexist Living Arrangements: A Feminist Research Project', unpublished PhD dissertation, University of Essex.

VanEvery, J. (1995), *Refusing to be a Wife! Heterosexual Women's Strategies for Liberation* (London: Taylor & Francis).

Weeks, J. (1991), 'Pretended Family Relationships', in D. Clark (ed.), *Marriage, Domestic Life and Social Change* (London: Routledge), pp. 214–34.

Weston, K. (1992), *Families We Choose: Gays, Lesbians, and Kinship* (New York: Columbia University Press).

Wilkinson, S. and Kitzinger, C. (eds) (1993), *Heterosexuality: A Feminism and Psychology Reader* (London: Sage).

Wittig, M. (1992), *The Straight Mind and Other Essays* (Brighton: Harvester Wheatsheaf).

Yuval-Davis, N. (1993), 'The (Dis)Comfort of Being "Hetero"', in Wilkinson, S. and Kitzinger, C. (eds), op. cit., pp. 52–3.

3 The Social Construction of Consent Revisited

Lynn Jamieson

INTRODUCTION

On 19 January 1994 in Scotland, the Court of Criminal Appeal quashed the rape conviction of Brian Jamieson[1] who had been found guilty of this and other independent crimes in May 1993. Jamieson was immediately released from custody (on bail awaiting the outcome of a continued appeal on a separate charge of attempted murder) to the consternation of the complainer (whose parents expressed their disgust to the press). A guilty verdict is a rare and hard-won occurrence (78 per cent of cases in Scotland going to trial involving a single charge of rape result in not guilty or not proven verdicts).[2] The ground for the Jamieson appeal was the fact that the judge had told the jury that if a man believed a woman consented *and* he had a *reasonable basis* for his belief then he could not be found guilty of rape. The three appeal judges, (Lord Hope, the Justice General, Lord Allanbridge and Lord Cowie) upheld the view that a man cannot be guilty of rape if he honestly, genuinely, believed that the women consented to sex *even if* the man had *no reasonable basis* for his belief. The trial judge's (Lord Osborne) comments were a misdirection. A miscarriage of justice had therefore occurred and the conviction had to be quashed with the very exceptional possibility of a retrial. No retrial was requested.

Feminist commentators on the law have noted ways in which it encapsulates double standards in sexual conduct. There is a substantial body of feminist writing which accuses the law of at best failing women and at worst being inherently phallocentric and patriarchal (Smart, 1989; MacKinnon, 1987). The treatment of consent by the law can certainly be read in this way. The legal denial of a woman's experience of rape because a man unreasonably believed she consented is a recent and powerful reaffiirmation of the phallocentricity[3] of the law. Legal discourse around rape is a key way in which 'the law' claims to know the truth about how men and women interact and do sexual acts. While there is debate about precisely how constitutive (as opposed to reflective) the law is of men and women's everyday social worlds, no commentator denies the power of law. Smart (1989), for example, suggests that the truth claims of legal discourse support phallocentric culture – predatory heterosexual masculinity predicated on women's social and sexual subordination – by suppressing alternative visions of gender and sexuality. It is important to re-examine the defence of 'mistaken belief in consent' as an example of resilient and significant phallocentricity. The significance of the 'unreasonable but mistaken belief in consent' defence depends on whether it is regarded as potentially constitutive of men and women's interaction or a legal anachronism ineffectually emerging after its time.

The causal effect of legal discourse around rape is a matter of debate that cannot be resolved empirically. Nevertheless, there are relevant research-based literatures. Most obviously there is the literature documenting how the law actually deals with women complaining of rape and men accused of rape. But also the pronouncements of the law on sexual relationships between men and women made in the process can usefully be compared with sociological writing on sex and intimacy. For example, the case for regarding the law as an irrelevant anachronism would receive a boost if sociological research on sexual interactions between men and women documented growing equality and declining phallocentricism. And, indeed, there are such hopeful sociological accounts. One of the most optimistic accounts of social change in the intimate lives of men and women is Giddens' (1992) description of the apparent ascendancy of confluent love 'opening oneself out to the other' and the search for 'the pure relationship'. Sex in the context of such a relationship is mutually negotiated, on an equal footing, seeking the full satisfaction of both partners. Giddens certainly does not suggest that all is well in relationships between men and women. He discusses male violence, (adopting the suggestion made by feminists over twenty years ago that male violence increases in reaction to women's growing power). He itemizes various forms of obsessive and destructive ways of seeking and doing sex and intimacy. His text makes it clear that the transformation of intimacy he describes is resisted, with men a long way behind women. Nevertheless, the book exudes a sense of optimism concerning the future of sexual pleasure and intimacy. While Giddens discusses the law as a system of legitimation and an expression of modes of domination elsewhere, this text puts forward the possibility that legal discourse is already becoming and will ultimately be wholly out of tune with the transformation of intimacy. Hence it lends support to downgrading the power of law, and to regarding the law as an anachronism. Unfortunately, Giddens' optimism concerning the transformation of intimacy is not weighed carefully in any empirical balance. Indeed his account is so weakly empirically based that it should be treated as a vision of an incipient alternative world rather than documentation of an established process of transformation. Empirically grounded feminist contributions to discussions of sex and intimacy provide a starkly contrasting picture. These feminist studies confirm the grim view of exploitative and pleasureless sex which, as is illustrated below, is legitimated as normal by the law. Indeed, there is no support in any empirical work for the view that the law is an anachronism. Rather empirical work on sex and intimacy between men and women indicates that the law is at least in tune with, if not actually constitutive of, how men and women often 'do sex' in our society.

LEGAL PRONOUNCEMENTS REGARDING RAPE AND 'NORMAL SEX'

The law, in fact, offers no positive definitions of consensual sex but specifies its boundaries. For example, who can and cannot give consent to certain sexual acts is legally specified. So a man cannot legally have sexual intercourse with a girl under the age of sixteen as she is below the age of consent (although there is a special defence of mistaken belief in age). Similarly, a woman who is certified mentally defective is legally incapable of consent. In principal, then, the interactional process between the participants in such an act of sexual intercourse is irrelevant to the fact of the crime. In practice, observation of such court cases indicates that the process is often as much under scrutiny as in a rape trial, by way of trying to mitigate the man's offence (Brown *et al.*, 1993, pp. 120–3; Burman, forthcoming). The crime of rape is, by definition, the antithesis of consensual sex, but at the same time the law keeps considerable distance in legal principal and court practice from a view of consensual sex as mutually negotiated on each and every occasion of a sexual encounter. The most obvious examples with respect to the legal principals are the difficulty the law has had in recognizing rape in marriage in England and the inability to recognize rape of an unconscious woman in Scotland.

In court practice, the most common defence is that sex took place with the consent of the complainer/complainant and, hence, there is considerable manoeuvring to establish consent and its absence by defence and prosecution. Again, this process is documented in considerable detail both north and south of the border (Adler, 1987; Brown *et al.*, 1993; Chambers and Millar, 1986; Edwards, 1986; Lees, 1989). The shadow of 'normal sex' cast by these contests, when the defence and prosecution portray events and their aftermath as 'not rape' and 'rape', is typically far removed from mutually negotiated, mutually satisfactory sex between equals. Rather, 'normal sex' encompasses women acquiescing to sexual use by men. Mutual negotiation is not a test of normality.

In taking evidence from a complainer/complainant, the prosecution focus on how the woman made her lack of consent clear. The implied interactional pattern is not of confluent love but one in which men are actively seeking sex and women say yes or no. This sets up a situation in which the absence of any of the standard pieces of evidence which the prosecution use to support their case of 'sex refused' is turned into positive evidence of consent by the defence. Hence, the defence will typically suggest to the jury that the absence of medical evidence of injuries suffered by the complainer/complainant indicates consent; the absence of any ear-witness evidence of screams indicates consent; the absence of medical evidence of marks of resistance on the accused indicates consent.[4] The questioning makes clear that the burden of negotiating consent is not mutually shared, but rather that women are responsible for giving or denying sexual access. The accused, if he chooses to go into the witness box, is not generally asked about how he tried to establish consent in detail. There are no equivalent 'why did you not do this and that' questions put to the accused to match questions to the complainer like 'why did you not scream', 'why did you not kick him between the legs', 'why did you not poke him in the eyes'. The accused is not generally asked such questions as 'did you ask her if she wanted to have sex with you?', 'did you ask her if what you were doing to her was OK/what she wanted/felt all right?' The stereotype of women as relatively passive acceptors or refusers of sex also fits with the pernicious notion that women need to be persuaded to have sex and hence some resistance is part of the normal sequence of events; hence the currency of resistance is further inflated.

In cases where the accused and the complainer/complainant had a previous sexual relationship, it is taken absolutely for granted that the fact of sex in the past has a bearing on whether or not the woman consented in the present. The assumption is that sex in the past legitimates a man's presumption of consent in the present unless the woman makes it abundantly clear that it is otherwise. In such cases there is an even greater burden on the woman who has to make it clear that she does not want sex. It is as if because a woman has sex with a man on one occasion he can reasonably assume consent on a subsequent occasion. In this sense the law remains close to a view of women as men's sexual property. In relationships in which women have suffered violence from the accused in the past, the defence are liable to suggest this is part of normal sex in that relationship (Adler, 1987, pp. 91–2). Lack of negotiation and pleasure for women can also be cast as a normal part of the sexual relationship. For example, the man acquitted of raping his wife in the first marital rape case brought to court in Scotland testified that she was 'like a zombie as usual' during the events he was describing as normal sex.

While women may be characterized as men's sexual property and relatively passive sexually, the defence also routinely construe women as seeking sex – either being out looking for sex on that particular occasion or as being generally sexually promiscuous or voracious. The issue of negotiating sexual encounters can again be side-stepped by such typifications. In many cases the emphasis is on the kind of woman that the complainer is. As Adler puts it 'it takes very little to discredit the victim's sexual reputation' (Adler, 1987, p. 88). Observation of Scottish courts similarly found the routine use of innuendo, sexual history and sexual character evidence to construct an image of 'that kind of women' who would have had sex with anybody anytime or at least was indiscriminately seeking sex on the day in question (Brown *et al.*, 1993, pp. 73–5, 92–102, 153–61). Defence practitioners admitted that they would do their best to create 'a smoke screen of immorality around the girl' (Brown *et al.*, 1993, pp. 107–11).

These strategies fit together within the framework of conventional double standards in conduct for men and women in which 'good women' are asexual or the sexual property of one particular man, and 'bad women' are promiscuous seekers of sex. The types of questioning these strategies generate do not engage with a view of sex as a mutually negotiated encounter between equals. The issue of negotiating consent is touched on in the many cases where the interaction between an accused and complainer/complainant, who were not previous sexual partners, is scrutinized for signs of intimacy leading up to the incident in question. It is a common defence tack to suggest that willingness on the part of the woman to enter into a *degree* of intimacy with the accused implies willingness to have penetrative genital sex (Adler, 1987, pp. 111–12; Brown *et al.*, pp. 89–91). Choosing to be alone together is taken as evidence of consensual intimacy – walking alone with somebody, going to their house, inviting them into your house, getting into their car. Since flirting, cuddling or kissing can be preliminary steps towards consensual sexual intercourse, complainers who had been intimate with the accused to this degree invariably face hostile questioning concerning their willingness to go so far but no further towards sexual intercourse. The questioning generally fits with the 'leading the man on' characterization of the sexual encounter which again lays responsibility unequally on the woman. The defence are particularly eager to show woman's active participation in intimacy 'did you not choose to sit next to him?' 'did you not put your arm round him?' A similar emphasis is put on the enjoyment of the alleged intimacy 'you were laughing and joking', 'you were flattered', 'you were happy to have a kiss and cuddle'.[5] Both prosecution and defence questioning generally focuses more on behaviour than feeling and thinking but the defence are more likely to investigate enjoyment than the prosecution. The image of the sexual encounter that is suggested by the defence is generally one of a behavioural chain in which 'one thing leads to another'. Smart (1989) has argued that legal method relies on the use of binary oppositional categories – consent/non-consent, active/passive – to resist more complex understandings of rape. Hence she suggests that jurors are discouraged from viewing women as consenting-to-go-so-far-but-no-further and incited to conclude that if she went this far she must have consented to go all the way because she either consented or she did not – there is no halfway house. Certainly legal practitioners are skilled manipulators and remakers of categories and, arguably, the use of binary opposites is just one tactic among many. In either case, the concept of a behavioural chain clearly confuses the distinction between consent and non-consent and is used by the defence in their quest to undermine claims of guilt and to deny proof 'beyond reasonable doubt'.

THE MISTAKEN-BELIEF-IN-CONSENT DEFENCE

Putting forward a view of sexual encounters as a behavioural chain in which 'one thing leads to another' implicitly raises for the jury questions about what the accused might have believed at the time. By suggesting that if a woman is prepared to enter into some degree of intimacy then she is actually prepared to go on from there to participate in penetrative genital sex, the defence imply that this is a good general logic which any man might reasonably follow when orienting himself in an encounter with a woman. Indeed, all arguments made by the defence to convince the jury that a woman was consenting can also be heard as arguments about why a man would believe she was consenting. The defence discussion of the absence of evidence of injuries, screams, etc., suggesting that resistance was 'weak' or 'lacking' could obviously be heard in this way. The persistent pernicious misconception that when women refuse intercourse they do not really mean it (Adler, 1987, p. 9; Brown *et al.*, 1993, pp. 115–16) could only assist in this hearing. Consensual sex in the past could be heard as a reason why the accused believed the woman consented rather than simply being heard as evidence that she did consent. Similarly, defamation of a woman's sexual character, her sexual history and any intimate or sexually interested behaviour with the accused could be heard in this way. In other words, if it is plausible for the defence to argue that if a woman behaves in a particular way then this implies consent, then it is plausible and reasonable for anyone, including the accused, who is the focus of jurors' attention, to use this logic.

Research into the use of evidence in Scottish sexual offence trials shows that an *explicit* defence of mistaken-belief-in-consent is very rare in the Scottish courts. Adler's (1987) work suggests a similar absence of this defence south of the border, despite all the concern it has generated. Did this appeal indicate a shift in practice? Was the fact that the appeal was successful an indication of a significant shift, given that the well-known appeals establishing a mistaken-belief-in-consent defence had not resulted in convictions being quashed.[6] Could the successful deployment of the mistaken-belief-in-consent defence become yet another route by which the ordeal of the trial would culminate in a guilty accused walking free?[7] The building blocks of the courtroom constructions of consent could readily be turned to building an explicit mistaken-belief-in-consent defence. Rather than arguing that a woman consented and trying to show this was so, for example by the lack of evidence of injuries, screams, etc., it could be argued that the accused believed she consented, for example because her resistance was 'weak' or 'lacking'. It is interesting that such explicit reference to the accused's beliefs are not typically made by the defence. Indeed, the fact that it is judges rather than the defence who sometimes introduce a mistaken-belief defence supports the suggestion that the case is put implicitly in the process of suggesting the woman consented. In a sample of 54 rape trials observed in Scotland, the mistaken-belief-in-consent defence was only referred to in two cases and then it was an issue put to the jury by the judge rather than explicitly developed by the defence. In the first case, in which the husband described his wife as 'like a zombie as usual', the judge made the following statement in his address to the jury: 'There is no reason why a husband should assume his wife is not consenting to intercourse unless she makes it abundantly clear to him that she is refusing consent. Rape must be committed with intent. The accused must know he is doing wrong. If an accused has an honest and genuine belief that a woman is consenting then no crime is committed' (Brown *et al.*, 1993, p. 92). The second case did not involve the uncontested fact of a previous sexual relationship between the complainer and the accused, but rather an alleged previous sexual encounter (alleged by the accused and denied by the complainer). Judge: 'Had she had intercourse with the accused the week before? This must put things in a different light. The accused maintains she was leading him on, having had sex the week before. Did the accused force himself upon the complainer or did she consent? You are here to consider if the accused could honestly hold that belief' (Brown *et al.*, 1993, p. 92).

The legality of a mistaken-belief-in-consent defence was originally established in England in 1976 by the appeal case of *Morgan* which went to the House of Lords.[8] It took another six years before an appeal was lodged in Scotland seeking a similar judgement referring to *Morgan* (Brown *et al.*, 1993, pp. 4–6). This appeal against the convictions of *Meek and Others*, argued along the lines of the *Morgan* case as follows: the law north and south of the border is substantially the same; in each jurisdiction the crime of rape requires the criminal intention of forcing intercourse upon a woman against her will; hence, if a man genuinely, honestly, believes a woman is consenting there is no criminal intent and no crime; if a man genuinely believes the women consented, there is no criminal intent whether or not his belief in consent is reasonable (*Meek and Others* v. *HMA*). The Scottish judges basically accepted these arguments, with some qualification discussed below. So by 1982 it was affirmed in both jurisdictions that it is only right and proper to acquit a man of rape if he believed what occurred was consensual sex, while the woman was experiencing sex against her will. In other words, if a woman believes what is occurring is rape and the man does not, then in the law it is, indeed, not rape. Having ruled that no crime has occurred, the law does not have to answer the question 'what is it then, if it is not rape?' or 'if it is not rape, is it consensual sex?' Logically, however, defenders of the mistaken-belief-in-consent defence should be sympathetic to a new crime standing in relation to rape in the way manslaughter stands to murder. The legal response to accusations of foul play, and blatant inequality in the treatment of men and women with respect to the principals underlying the mistaken-belief-in-consent defence is to point to the consistency with judgements concerning other types of crime to which intentionality is a central element and, indeed, to the centrality of criminal intention, *mens rea*, to the legal understanding of the essence of crime. However, academics of the law continue to contest the scope of the honest-belief defence and the basis for the notion that it holds good even when 'unreasonableness' is involved.

Tempkin (1983) notes that in English law the *Morgan* judgement that belief in consent was a protection against the accusation of rape, was qualified by concern with 'recklessness'.[9] She argues that after *Morgan*, belief in consent can be no defence if a man realizes that the woman may not consent but hopes that she does, carries on regardless, closes his mind to the risk or alternatively never considers the issue. Moreover, she believes that the circumstances in which men would be regarded as reckless in their belief in consent have been further extended by subsequent cases involving other crimes where recklessness is an issue. However, the fact remains that English law does not recognize as rape, situations in which 'The defendant, having realised that the woman might not be consenting, wrongly and quite unreasonably concludes that she is' (Tempkin, 1983, p. 6). Rather than seeing this as consistent with the general doctrine of the law, Tempkin argues that an honest but unreasonable mistake is not a defence in the case of other offences under English law. Moreover, even if it would be inappropriate and unjust to require that a mistake was reasonable with respect to some offences, this is not the case with rape. This is because it is possible for a man to ascertain whether a woman is consenting or not with minimal effort. She is there next to him. He only has to ask. Since to have sexual intercourse without her consent is to do her great harm, it is not unjust for the law to require that he inquire carefully into consent and, it may be added, process that information carefully as well. An unreasonable mistake in the context of rape is [quoting Professor Pickard in the University of Toronto Law Journal, 1980] "an easily avoided and self-serving mistake produced by the actor's indifference to the separate existence of another"' (Tempkin, 1983, pp. 15–16).

The qualifications made by the Scottish judgement in the *Meek* appeal case are important because they had implications for how the law might operate in practice in Scotland and the scope for addressing Tempkin's concerns. It was clearly stated that a jury would be expected to weigh the reasonableness of the grounds for belief in consent when deciding whether a man's alleged belief in consent was genuine or not.

'We have no difficulty in accepting that an essential element in the crime of rape is the absence of an honest belief that the woman is consenting. The criminal intent is, after all, to force intercourse upon a woman against her will and the answer to the certified question given by the majority of their Lordships in *Morgan* is one which readily accords with the law of Scotland. The absence of reasonable grounds for such an alleged belief, will, however, have a considerable bearing upon whether any jury will accept that such an "honest belief" was held' (*Meek and Others* v. *HMA*, reported in Scots Law Times, 1983, p. 281).

In other words, 'reasonable grounds', while not being a necessary requirement of an honest or genuine belief, nevertheless could be used by a jury to weigh up whether or not a genuine honest belief was present.

These qualifications offered some reassurance to those who feared that the *Morgan/Meek* judgements could be a rapist's charter. The outcome of the *Meek* case was essentially the same as in that of *Morgan*; the principal of an honest-but-mistaken-belief defence was accepted, but the appeal against the convictions of *Meek and Others* was rejected. In both appeals it was argued that injustice had been done because the judge had not drawn the juries attention to the fact that if a man believes a woman is consenting then he has not committed rape. Both these cases were group rapes. In *Morgan* the appellants argued that they believed the woman consented because they had been told that she did by the woman's husband. In *Meek* the appellants argued that they believed the woman consented because other men were already having what they believed to be consensual sex with her when they arrived on the scene. The appeal judges however ruled that in the course of the trial the defence had consistently contradicted the complainer/complainant's testimony of resistance and lack of consent. Hence the jury were presented with a straightforward choice between the woman's account and that of the accused men. As the Lord Chancellor put it in the case of *Morgan*: 'The choice before the jury was thus between two stories each wholly incompatible with the other . . . the one of a violent and unmistakable rape of a singularly unpleasant kind, and the other of active co-operation in a sexual orgy. . . . I am utterly unable to see any conceivable half-way house' (*DPP* v. *Morgan and Others*, quoted in *Meek and Others* v. *HMA*, Scots Law Times, 1983, p. 281) The Lord Justice-General (then Lord Emslie) quoted this passage in the case of *Meek* and went on to say concerning *Meek* and his co-appellants: 'the evidence of the appellants was not that they failed to detect resistance on the complainer's part, or that they honestly believed that in spite of certain signs of distress which they observed, the complainer was not really resisting and, indeed, wanted them to have intercourse with her. Their evidence was that she not only did not exhibit any signs of unwillingness but that she actively co-operated and encouraged them in a sexual orgy' (*Meek*, 1983, pp. 281–2). In such circumstances, no 'half-way house', it was ruled there was no need for the judge to alert the jury to the possible defence of mistaken belief in consent.

In terms of this reasoning, it seems that it was unnecessary for the judges to refer to the mistaken-belief-in-consent defence in their summing up to the jury in the two Scottish cases referred to above. In both of these cases, accused and complainer offered wholly disparate accounts. For example, in the marital rape case, the woman's account was of being physically abused, tied to the bed with climbing ropes and gagged, in contrast to the accused's account of normal sex with his wife 'like a zombie as usual'. In each of these cases known or alleged previous consensual sex (uncontested in the marital rape case and in the other case alleged as having occurred once at the complainer's house with the complainer denying any previous sex or visit to her house) is taken as a basis for mistaken-belief-in-consent despite contrasting accounts of the contested events.

Interviews with practitioners gave some insight into why a mistaken-belief-in-consent defence was not used more often by the defence in the Scottish courts. The defence regarded the mistaken-belief-in-consent argument as more complicated than a straightforward contradiction of the complainer's testimony and an assertion of consent. An explicit mistaken-belief argument might involve closer questioning of the accused, who currently is not required to enter the witness box. Frankly, the defence did not need mistaken-belief-in-consent as they had a very high success rate in simply arguing consent. One offered an ideal typical summing-up speech in a case where there had been a history of intimacy between the complainer and the accused leading up to the incident in question.'Well this is what happened: x, y, and z in the pub, kissing and cuddling in the bus, back to her house, couple of large vodkas and a wee bit more kissing and cuddling happened there. And we don't know what happened after that. The accused said she consented. The girl said she didn't. Well you've got to look at the whole background, what happened that night, and you've got to decide, she had no bruises on her, no scratches or anything like that, her clothes weren't torn, did she consent, did she get out of these skin tight jeans single-handed, being pulled off her with no bruises or anything like that? Even if you don't accept it was total literal consent, if you're left with a reasonable doubt, then that's the end of the story' (Brown *et al.*, 1993, p. 116).

One defence added that in any case they could rely on the judge to raise the mistaken-belief-in-consent argument. It was their opinion that mistaken-belief-in-consent arguments would only come into play when medical evidence indicating non-consent is going against the accused: 'I think the most common defence, as you know, is consent, but [when it is raised] the belief-in-consent one is virtually always put to the jury by the judge, and it's a lot more difficult. Because the straight-forward consent one normally comes in where the girl doesn't have any injury at all. The belief-in-consent one is normally a situation where there's been a bit of a struggle and the man says he thought she was doing a token protest, as very often happens' (Brown *et al.*, 1993, p. 115).

My knowledge of the case involving Brian Jamieson, is restricted to summary given in the appeal judgement. It relates that a 17-year-old woman met Brian Jamieson for the first time at the village dance the evening of the incident. He asked her if she wanted to go for a walk with him. They walked to the primary school which Jamieson had at-tended as a boy. The rape took place in a bike shelter in the primary school playground. The woman testified that she tried to push the ac-cused away, told him that she did not want 'that', struggled, screamed and bit him. The appellant in his evidence agreed the young woman had offered resistance. 'But he said that he thought at the time that she wanted to have sexual intercourse with him. His defence was that she consented to intercourse and that in any event he believed that he had her consent.' Here then is the reference to 'the half way house' to which the Lord Chancellor referred, the possibility that he believed she consented while in fact she did not. Two defences are simultaneously being deployed (a practice not uncommon in itself), on the one hand a straightforward 'she consented' and on the other, a mistaken-belief-in-consent defence. Presumably because of the reference to the possi-bility of mistaken belief in consent, the trial judge Lord Osborne alerted the jury to this defence in his summing up. However, it was Lord Osborne's remarks which became the basis of the appeal. The offend-ing remarks were as follows 'Reasonable belief, and that is to say a belief based on reasonable grounds, on the part of the male to the effect that the woman was a consenting party is a defence even though the belief, was, in fact, mistaken' (*Jamieson* v. *HMA*). This clashes with the notion that a genuine honest belief in consent, albeit unreasonable, is grounds for acquittal. It places reasonable grounds as a necessary part of an honest belief, rather than as something the jury might consider when deciding what was and what was not honestly believed. But Lord Osborne's 'mistaken' formulation is, of course, precisely the position for which Tempkin has argued. The trial judge defended himself citing cases in his support prior to *Meek* and saying that the direction given in *Meek* was not supported by any previous Scottish authority on mistake. However, the Solicitor-General, the second-ranking law officer who acts for the Crown in Scotland, informed the appeal judges that he was not seeking to challenge the observations in *Meek* as unsound in law and that the Crown accepted a misdirection in Jamieson's case. The references to 'reasonable belief' and 'reasonable grounds' were then accepted as 'misdirection' leading to Brian Jamieson's release from jail. The fact that the jury was misdirected requires either the conviction be quashed entirely or very exceptionally a retrial and, as I have said, no request for a retrial was made. Obviously, it is a matter of speculation whether Brian Jamieson would have still been convicted if the jury had been given a 'correct' statement of the law regarding mistaken-belief-in-consent. However, the fact that he was convicted in the first case was already against the balance of probabilities.

CONCLUSION

There is no reason to conclude that introducing the defence of mistaken-belief-in-consent (whether reasonable or not) is becoming more common on the basis of one appeal case. Detailed documentation of rape trials suggests that explicit use of a defence of mistaken-belief is unlikely to become routine; the defence practitioners themselves confirm this, saying that they see such a defence as a fall-back position rather than a first choice. However, juries are routinely exposed to claims concerning the basis for believing that a woman consented. It can be argued that an explicit defence of mistaken-belief-in-consent is redundant; standard successful defence tactics suggesting that the woman complaining of rape did in fact have consensual sex with the accused are simultaneously providing the story of why the accused knew the woman consented. Indeed it is only when the evidence against consent is very strong, for example when the woman suffered serious injuries, that the defence consider explicitly acknowledging that the accused's belief may have been mistaken.

The relative absence of explicit use of mistaken-belief-in-consent defences in actual trials in no way diminishes the significance of this defence as a legal possibility. The nonchalant reaffirmation of the legal denial of rape if a man mistakenly and unreasonably believes a woman is consenting is of considerable significance. If it is accepted that the law is a powerful discourse which stifles alternative accounts, then it is reasonable to assume that this piece of phallocentrism bolsters macho male masculinity at the expense of all women and some men far beyond the courtrooms. It is not possible directly to trace and demonstrate the effects beyond the courtroom however. But it can be shown that this defence is more in step with how men and women are 'doing sex' much of the time in our culture than with Giddens' vision of confluent love. Exploitative sex in which men sexually use women with little regard for their feelings or pleasure is not, unfortunately, an anachronistic phenomenon resulting from the activities of a minority of unreformed men. Consider briefly three bodies of British empirical evidence – the literature on domestic violence, work on teenage young people's sexual and intimate relationships, and the new studies of adult heterosexual couples' sexuality and intimacy. The literature on domestic violence suggests that its incidence has been seriously underestimated; the status of consent in sexual encounters in which women live in constant fear of violence from their partners is clearly highly problematic (Dobash and Dobash, 1980, 1992; Hanmer and Saunders, 1983; Kelly, 1988; Smith, 1989). However, it might still be argued that violent relationships are the extreme end of the continuum, but many young people's accounts of their first sexual experiences offer cold comfort. Many of the victims and attackers involved in sexual offence cases are young. Documenters of young people's heterosexual encounters note the persistence of a double standard in sexual conduct whereby young women's reputations can be ruined by accusations of promiscuity in a way that young men's cannot, and where young men set the agenda of sexual activity and pleasure in a way that young women cannot (Willis, 1977; Wilson, 1978; Griffin, 1985; Lees, 1986, 1993; Wallace, 1987; Halson, 1991; Thomson and Scott, 1991; Stafford, 1992). The inability of young women to make demands in their heterosexual relationships has been noted as a factor working against condom use despite the efforts of health educators (Holland *et al.*, 1990). Finally, there is a small body of empirical work which has reaffirmed British adult men's relative emotional illiteracy in heterosexual relationships and flight from intimacy (Hollway, 1984; Mansfield and Collard, 1988; Duncombe and Marsden, 1993). Add to this the large bodies of literature on the peristence of inequality at many other levels between married couples.

What then is the basis of Giddens' optimism. At a general level the features of 'high modernity' foster self-reflective, 'reflexive', contemplation of self, life-style, intimacy and sexuality. It is as if leading a life without self-awareness is increasingly untenable. Men then are increasingly forced to confront their often unacknowledged emotional life and their dependence on women for its satisfaction. Details of how the key structures of gender and power will bend in the process are left largely to the imagination.[10] Will childhood patterning of emotional and relational life be transformed by equal parenting? Much of the literature on fathering in Britain, Australia and the USA suggests that shifts are rather modest (Backett, 1982; Russel, 1983; Kimmel, 1987; Lewis and O'Brian, 1987; Barker, 1994). Are conventional divisions of labour between men and women, and systems of distribution of resources making a fundamental shift? Again much of the literature suggests very modest changes (Edgell, 1980; Rubin, 1983; Gerson, 1985; Hertz, 1986; Brannen and Wilson, 1987; Rosen, 1987; Gershuny and Robinson, 1988; Mansfield and Collard, 1988; Pahl, 1989; Hochschild, 1990; Brannen and Moss, 1991; Gilbert, 1993; Goodnow and Bowes, 1994). It is, paradoxically, in sexual life itself that Giddens finds it easiest to indicate change, but only through a selective and partial reading of the research literature. He relies heavily on a North American feminist text for evidence: Ehrenreich *et al.* (1986) *Remaking of Love: the Feminization of Sex.* The authors argue that 'the sexual revolution' is an unclaimed victory for women; women have challenged the very definition and meaning of sex. The old definition which they claim women have successfully challenge can instantly be recognized as the 'normal sex' of courtroom questions and in much of British literature documenting sexual lives.

Sex, or 'normal sex', as defined by the medical experts and accepted by mainstream middle-class culture, was a two-act drama of foreplay and intercourse which culminated in male orgasm and at least a display of female appreciation. We reject this version of sex as narrow, male-centred, unsatisfying.[11] In its single-mindedness and phallocentrism, this form of sex does imitate rape; it cannot help but remind us of the dangers and ambiguities of heterosexuality. . . . for *women* to insist on pleasure was to assert power and hence to give an altogether new meaning to sex – as an affirmation of female will and an assertion of female power. The old meaning, which in one form or another was always submission to male power, could be inverted.   (Ehrenreich *et al.*, 1986, pp. 193, 195)

The unreasonable but mistaken-belief-in-consent defence is the antithesis of 'an affirmation of female will' and should be expunged from the law. Some feminist commentators suggest that it is pointless to tinker with the law as this will only reinforce its stifling phallocentric claims to truth (Smart, 1989). Surely blatantly regressive invidious law should always be challenged. And, if we are indeed in a period of 'high modernity', then no expert view is universally regarded as sacrosanct; rather people are increasingly sophisticated in their recognition of competing claims to truth. Forcing acknowledgement of bad law may help shake the power of the law. At the same time, the resilience of the law is awesome. The law already incorporates the use of uncertainty and is self-consciously reflexive, for example, in the way defence practitioners routinely create uncertainties in their pursuit of their client's acquittal. All the more reason to challenge the law on many fronts. Tempkin's arguments stand against the defence of mistaken-belief-in-consent by appealing for consistency and integrity in the law. By comparing how the law deals with rape and how the law deals with other crimes she concludes that a man's 'unreasonable' mistake regarding a woman's consent cannot justly be a defence against rape. Her arguments suggest that the persistent legal advocates of a mistaken-belief-defence must at least acknowledge the need for a new crime standing in relation to rape in the way that manslaughter relates to murder. I do not accept that to make such arguments within the legal discourse merely serve to strengthen the law. Let those who speak within legal discourse make these arguments while those of us who are outsiders resist phallocentricism by whatever other means are available.

NOTES

1. No relative of mine.
2. See Brown *et al.* (1993). This is higher than the figure of around 50 per cent which can be derived from the work of Adler (1987, p. 43) on English rape cases.
3. Smart (1989) describes 'phallocentric' as a concept which combines references to the problems of masculine sexual power and heterosexism.

'Loosely it implies a culture which is structured to meet the needs of the masculine imperative' (Smart, p. 27).

4. Disclosure and distress after the event are also investigated as evidence of lack of consent, and hence the absence of a witness who can testify to distress immediately after the event is presented by the defence as evidence of consent.

5. Smart has argued that in practice the woman must show, beyond all reasonable doubt, that she was unwilling to have intercourse and that she could not possibly have enjoyed it (1989, pp. 36–8).

6. In fact, the Jamieson appeal judgement refers to another rape conviction being quashed in 1985 on similar grounds (*HM Advocate* v. *Stevenson and Others*, 5 July, 1985 (unreported)).

7. I do not assume all accused are guilty but believe that cases of mistaken identity and false allegation are rare and, therefore, given the extremely high acquittal rate, can only conclude that many guilty men are acquitted.

8. This case caused a degree of public uproar which was an important part of the background to the reform of the English law, although in fact the consequent Sexual Offences (Amendment) Act 1976 did not alter the judgement made in the *Morgan* case (Adler, 1987).

9. Note that 'recklessness' does not have the same meaning in Scots law. See the Commentary on *Meek* in the Scottish Criminal Court Report.

10. While there are a number of ways of conceptualizing the key structures of gender and power, I find the framework offered by Connell (1987) particularly useful. He identifies three key levels at which gender hierarchies may be being produced in any setting. These are: (1) 'cathexis' or the structuring of emotional attachment and emotional life; (2) division of labour; (3) distributions of power and resources.

11. Evidence of women's rejection includes the high sales of vibrators and other sex aids, the high incidence of female adultery, and various surveys in which women speak out about their determination to find sexual satisfaction.

REFERENCES

DPP v. *Morgan and Others* (1975), Criminal Appeal Report 136 [1976] AC 182.

Meek and Others v. *HMA* (1982), Scottish Criminal Court Report 613–621 and (1983) Scots Law Times, 280.

Jamieson v. *HMA* (1994) Transcript of the appeal judgement obtained from the Deputy Principal Clerk of Justiciary, Edinburgh High Court, not yet reported at the time of writing except in *Green's Weekly*.

Adler, Z. (1987), *Rape on Trial* (London: Routledge & Kegan Paul).

Backett, K. (1982), *Mothers and Fathers* (London: Macmillan).

Barker, R. (1994), *Lone Fathers and Masculinity* (Aldershot: Averbury).

Brannen, J. and Moss, P. (1991), *Dual Earner Households after Maternity Leave* (London: Macmillan).

Brannen, J. and Wilson, G. (eds) (1987), *Give and Take in Families* (London: Allen & Unwin).

Brown, B., Burman, M. and Jamieson, L. (1993), *Sex Crimes on Trial: The Use of Sexual Evidence in Scottish Courts* (Edinburgh: Edinburgh University Press).

Burman, M. 'Appearances of Consent: The Paradox of Sexual Offences Involving Women and Young Girls', submitted to *British Journal of Criminology* (forthcoming).

Chambers, G. and Millar, A. (1986), *Prosecuting Sexual Assault* (Edinburgh: HMSO, Scottish Office Central Research Unit Study).

Connell, R. W. (1987), *Gender and Power* (London: Allen & Unwin).

Dobash, R. and Dobash, R. (1980), *Violence Against Wives* (Shepton Mallet: Open Books).

Dobash, R. and Dobash, R. (1992), *Women, Violence and Social Change* (London: Routledge).

Duncan, J. and Marsden, D. (1993), 'Love and Intimacy: The Gender Division of Emotion and "Emotional Work"', *Sociology*, **27**(2): pp. 221–41.

Edgell, S. (1980), *Middle-class Couples: A Study of Segregation, Domination and Inequality in Marriage* (London: George Allen & Unwin).

Edwards, S. (1986) 'Evidential Matters in Rape Prosecutions from "First Opportunity to Complain" to Corroboration', *New Law Journal*, 28 March, pp. 291–3.

Ehrenreich, B., Hess, E. and Jacobs, G. (1986), *Remaking Love: The Feminization of Sex* (London: Anchor Books, Doubleday).

Gershuny, J. and Robinson, J. (1988), 'Historical Changes in Household Divisions of Labour', *Demography*, **25**: pp. 537–54.

Gerson, K. (1985), *Hard Choices: How Women Decide about Work, Career and Motherhood* (Berkeley: University of California Press).

Giddens, A. (1992), *The Transformation of Intimacy: Sexuality, Love and Eroticism in Modern Societies* (Cambridge: Polity Press).

Gilbert, L. (1993), *Two Careers/One Family: The Promise of Gender Equality* (Sage: London).

Goodnow, J. and Bowes, J. (1994), *Men, Women and Housework* (Melbourne: Oxford University Press).

Griffin, C. (1985), *Typical Girls* (London: Routledge & Kegan Paul).

Hanmer, J. and Saunders, S. (1983), 'Blowing the Cover of the Protective Male: A Community Study of Violence to Women', in E. Garmarnakow *et al.* (eds), *The Public and the Private: Social Patterns and Gender Relations* (London: Heinemann Educational Books).

Halson, J. (1991), 'Young Women, Sexual Harassment and Heterosexuality: Violence, Power Relations and Mixed-sex Schooling', in P. Abbott and C. Wallace (eds), *Gender Power and Sexuality* (London: Macmillan).

Hertz, R. (1986), *More Equal than Others: Women and Men in Dual Career Marriages* (Berkeley: University of California Press).

Hochschild, A. (1990), *The Second Shift: Working Parents and the Revolution at Home* (London: Piatakus).

Holland, J., Ramazanoglu, C., Scott, S., Sharpe, S., and Thomson, R. (1990), 'Sex Gender and Power: Young Women's Sexuality in the Shadow of AIDS', *Sociology of Health and Illness*, **12**, pp. 336–50.

Hollway, W. (1983), 'Heterosexual Sex: Power and Desire for the Other', in S. Cartledge and J. Ryan (eds), *Sex and Love: New Thoughts on Old Contradictions* (London: The Women's Press).

Kelly, L. (1988), *Surviving Sexual Violence* (Cambridge, Polity Press).

Kimmel, Michael (1987) (ed.), *Changing Men: New Directions in Research on Men and Masculinity* (Beverly Hills: Sage).

Lees, S. (1986), *Losing out: Sexuality and Adolescent Girls* (Harmondsworth: Penguin).

Lees, S. (1989), 'Trial by Rape', *New Statesman and Society*, 24 November.

Lees, S. (1993), *Sugar and Spice: Sexuality and Adolescent Girls* (Harmondsworth: Penguin).

Lewis, C. and O'Brian, M. (eds) (1987), *Reassessing Fatherhood: New Observations on Fathers and the Modern Family* (London: Sage).

MacKinnon, C. (1987), *Feminism Unmodified: Discourses on Life and Law* (London: Harvard University Press).

Mansfield, P. and Collard, J. (1988), *The Beginning of the Rest of your Life* (Basingstoke: Macmillan).

Pahl, J. (1989), *Money and Marriage* (Basingstoke: Macmillan).

Rosen, E. I. (1987), *Bitter Choices: Blue Collar Women in and out of Work* (Chicago: The University of Chicago Press).

Rubin, L. B. (1983), *Intimate Strangers: Men and Women Together* (London: Harper & Row).

Russel, G. (1983), *The Changing Role of Fathers* (Milton Keynes: Open University Press).

Smart, C. (1989), *Feminism and the Power of Law* (London, Routledge).

Smith, L. (1989), *Domestic Violence: An Overview of the Literature*, Home Office Research Study no. 107 (London: HMSO).

Stafford, A. (1992), *Trying Work* (Edinburgh: Edinburgh University Press).

Tempkin, J. (1983), 'The Limits of Reckless Rape', *Criminal Law Review*, January, pp. 5–16.

Thomson, R. and Scott, S. (1991), *Learning about Sex: Young Women and the Construction of Sexual Identity* (London: Tufnell Press).

Wallace, C. (1987), *For Richer for Poorer: Growing up in and out of Work* (London: Tavistock).

Willis, P. (1977), *Learning to Labour* (London: Routledge & Kegan Paul).

Wilson, D. (1978), 'Sexual Codes and Conduct', in B. Smart and C. Smart (eds), *Women, Sexuality and Social Control* (London: Routledge & Kegan Paul).

Part II
Identities

4 Beyond Victim or Survivor: Sexual Violence, Identity and Feminist Theory and Practice

Liz Kelly, Sheila Burton and
Linda Regan

In this chapter we examine recent debates about the meaning of sexual victimization. These struggles have implications for feminist praxis; for theory, research and practice. We explore several locations from which challenges to previous feminist re-definitions emerge; specifically, recent popularist publications which use, in a pejorative tone, the term 'victim' or 'victimhood' feminism and academic contestation of prevalence research. In the second half of the paper we connect these themes with a discussion of what we call 'the victim/survivor dichotomy', which represents another element in debates about the extent and meaning of sexual victimization.

Our concerns centre on the consequences of these developments for how feminism is understood and, within this, how sexual violence is explained, researched and responded to. The core of our argument is that there is a complex struggle occurring over the meaning of victimization. This struggle has multiple sites and locations; it is the combination of what, on one level, are disparate unconnected events, but which on another level act as reinforcers of one another. This chapter draws out analytically links between these developments, but we are not suggesting that they are part of a conspiratorial 'backlash'[1] against feminism. In order to develop these themes we have explored changes within feminism, and suggest an *additional way of classifying feminism*.

A central principle of feminism, particularly well-illustrated in work on sexual violence, has been to address the politics of naming. Creating and giving meaning to language in order to document the reality of women's lives has been a constant theme within feminist praxis (Raymond, 1986; Kelly, 1988; Stanley, 1990). Deborah Cameron has analysed the power of language as definer of reality; both setting limits

77

and opening possibilities of what it is possible to think and say (Cameron, 1985). It is this awareness of the power of meaning which makes 'discourse' such a useful concept within much contemporary feminist theory. It contains a recognition of the material consequences of ideas, that they play a key part in constructing what counts as 'real'; alongside an explicit acknowledgement of the power inherent in what become 'dominant' discourses. It is through naming various forms of victimization, and extending the limited definitions encoded in the law, medicine and research that feminist work has challenged dominant discourses on sexual violence. The resistance to feminist re-definitions and perspectives we explore in this paper are also not just 'ideas'. They are powerful ideas with a range of potential and actual consequences, not least being the possibility of re-working and re-instating pre-feminist meanings and definitions. We draw attention to these consequences for sexual politics, and in the final section for individual subjective identities.

RE-DEFINING FEMINISM

The emergence and popularity of a woman academic who has been constructed as, and represented herself as being, both the saviour of, and at the same time the most potent challenge to, contemporary feminism (Camile Paglia),[2] demands serious critical reflection.

The traditional distinctions between liberal, socialist and radical feminism, provide little purchase on this recent history. Neither do identity-based categories of, for example, Black or lesbian feminism. However, each has continued relevance in the ongoing history of the movements for women's liberation. In musing on what distinctions would enable a 'sense-making' of changing times we propose a different way of looking at feminist activity. The categories outlined below refer to the locations and purposes of forms of activity which currently constitute feminism in Western countries. They are neither mutually exclusive of one another (individual women can work in more than one location, although some combinations are more difficult and potentially contradictory than others), nor do we intend them as alternatives to previous distinctions.

Academic Feminism

Academic feminism is primarily in the business of creating knowledge from the perspective of women. Whilst there are many variations between feminists in the academy, there is no doubt that during the last decade the concerns of most academic feminists shifted; their focus moved to debates within the academy, and theory has become increasingly disconnected from attempts to create change outside the institution. It is no longer the case that the books which excite, incite and enrage are shared across contexts, many – if not most – academic feminist texts are inaccessible to the majority of feminists. Adrienne Rich's (1978) dream of a common language seems harder rather than easier to envisage. In the rush to claim a place at the institution's 'high table' the work of currently popular male gurus is far more likely to appear on Women's Studies reading lists than the exciting, challenging and accessible work of feminists such as Cynthia Cockburn (1992) or Cynthia Enloe (1983, 1989). We have referred to this shift elsewhere as a 'romance with epistemology' (Kelly *et al.*, 1994), or in our everyday office version, a preoccupation with long words beginning with 'e'.

The actual and potential consequences of this for the feminist challenge to language and dominant discourses are considerable. Not least is the extent to which academic feminism has accommodated to academic discourse, a powerful exclusionary form of language use. Of particular importance in the context of this discussion is the move *away* from the task of creating 'useful knowledge' (knowledge produced to better understand women's oppression in order to change it) and a move *into* the realms of abstract theory (or as Katie Grant (1994) has termed it 'theorrea'). Academic feminism is, in the main, currently failing to provide the women's movement with either useful knowledge, or the tools with which to make sense of current events/circumstances.

Commercialized Feminism

Commercialized feminism is primarily located in the market. Marketable/profitable feminism is the direct outcome of the success of women's movements in shifting cultural values. Two obvious areas are the media and therapeutic services (although this separation is somewhat artificial given the publishing success of therapeutic texts). There are now a number of highly successful and visible women who are not afraid to use the 'f' word (feminism), and their activities are frequently both glamorous and financially rewarding. Books and films are now marketed as feminist 'blockbusters' in ways that were inconceivable even a few years ago. The growth in therapy, self-improvement and self-help is also evident, with many elements of it drawing explicitly or implicitly on feminism for insight, theory, method and purpose. Both combine in the recent publications of Gloria Steinham (1993) and Naomi Wolf (1993).

What is most marked about 'marketable' feminism is its individualism. Absent from much of it is any serious reflection on the complicated questions which many academic and activist feminists are struggling with – such as which women are included or excluded from analysis and/or campaigns/services, or the multiplying material constraints on women's lives. The problem which had no name in the 1950s, and which in the 1970s was clearly named as one of men's power and men's behaviour, has, by a complicated alchemy, been transformed into women's unwillingness to use their own power, and their need to increase their self-esteem. Books exhorting us to 'sort ourselves out', 'take and use our power'[3] are now best-sellers. One simple illustration of how deep the shift into a therapeutic mode of communicating has been, is the extent to which the words 'I feel' are used when in fact what the speaker means is 'I think' or 'I believe'; a few minutes of participant observation of a conversation will prove the point.

We explore the particular consequences which this change has produced in two later sections – the concepts of 'power' and 'victim' feminism, and therapeutic understandings of the consequences of victimization.

Activist Feminism

Contrary to representations in some academic and commercialized feminist texts, activist feminism is still in the business of organizing in order to challenge the current social order. It includes campaigning groups, networks of women in organizations, direct action networks, publishing collectives, and women's organizations such as refuges and rape crisis lines. Groups, networks and coalitions may focus on a single issue or be broader in focus; local, regional, national or international in reach, with a mixed or identity-based membership. Whilst the shape and form of feminist activism may have adapted, many of the activities which characterized feminist activity in the 1970s remain, and new elements have been added (Griffin, 1995). What has changed is that little of this activity is recorded anywhere these days, especially in Britain. There is more than a little irony in the fact that it easier to find out about activism in other countries than one's own.

Even if there has been a decline in public visible protest in many Western countries[4] it is alive and thriving elsewhere in the world. Having said this, however, some of the forms which challenges to feminist knowledge and practice have taken create tensions and dilemmas which are not easily translated into forms of action. They require critical reflection before it is clear what kind of action should be taken.

'Power' and 'Victimhood' Feminism

What concerns us are the complex interconnections between these elements of feminist activity, and especially the constructed stories about the past and present which do a disservice to both. Many so-called histories of the contemporary women's movement draw on published work, which for the most part fails to record the breadth and complexity of local activism (Radford, 1994). The lack of awareness of current activism evidenced by the written and spoken word of many 'media feminists' is sometimes breathtaking and more than a little insulting to the countless women who maintain and sustain it.

The recent juxtaposing of the new 'power' feminism, and its lamentable predecessor 'victim' or 'victimhood' feminism is a case in point, and its promoters straddle the academic/commercialized feminism boundary (Wolf, 1993; Paglia, 1994; Roiphe, 1994). This neatly constructed dichotomy relies upon important elements of feminist history being either ignored or misrepresented. These include, but are not limited to:

- The lengthy and continuing questioning of power, and particularly 'power over' within feminist theory and practice.
- The fact that the documenting of, and resistance to, men's victimization of women has been one of the most powerful insights and organizing focuses in both waves of the women's movement. This is an issue which has prompted exchange and networking internationally to the extent that at the 1994 UN Human Rights Congress in Vienna a large, organized and passionate coalition of women from every continent successfully lobbied to have 'gender violence' recognized as a fundamental issue of human rights.
- That it was feminist awareness of the negative meanings which attached to the word 'victim' which led to use of the term 'survivor'; a shift later adopted by many professionals.
- The conceptual work of Kathleen Barry (1979), which has been developed by others since on 'victimism'.

There is no unproblematic relationship for feminists to power, be it of a personal, professional or institutional kind (Kelly, 1992). Just as the concept itself is intensely contested, so is its use in relationships with others. Moreover, 'using the power one has' for oneself departs markedly from the original ambition of feminism to end the systematic oppression of all women.

To elide the documentation of women's victimization with a suggestion that feminists have created a notion of 'victimhood', or constructed women as inevitable victims, is to confuse empirical reality with constructions of identity. The purpose of feminist activism on sexual violence began with the necessity of making the private pain and shame of women public; a collective refusal to keep men's secrets. From this beginning has grown a multitude of activities, many of which are still directed at removing the legacy of centuries of permission. Feminists have not just documented this reality, they have created alternative institutions, been the instigators of innumerable campaigns for change, and many of the women involved in these 'change-making' activities – activities which require using one's 'power to' act – have themselves experienced various forms of abuse.

In supporting individual women and children, most feminist organizations have placed the responsibility for violence and abuse on men and social institutions. They have noted, on the one hand, the courage, strength and creativity that coping with violation demands and on the other, the numbers of women and children who are murdered by men, and those whose lives are temporarily or permanently devastated by violations of the body, mind and spirit. This constitutes a refusal to position women and children as either inevitable victims or as strong survivors for whom abuse has minimal consequences.

Kathleen Barry's (1979) work addressed the ways in which traditional responses to women who are victimized positions them as victims; whereby the fact of victimization becomes the defining feature of an individual's identity and life experience. She argues: 'Victimism is an objectification which establishes new standards for defining experience, those standards dismiss any question of will, and deny that the woman even whilst enduring sexual violence is a living, changing, growing interactive person. . . . It denies the reality of [women's] circumstances and the very real human efforts they make to cope with those circumstances. . . . Surviving is the other side of being a victim. It involves will, action, initiative. Any woman caught in sexual violence must make moment-by-moment decisions about her survival' (pp. 38–9). The proponents of 'power' feminism have accused those they berate of creating 'victim' feminism; constructing women as lacking will and agency. Not only have we – in their view – represented women as passive victims, but we have also encouraged them to act as such. This is precisely the opposite of the activist feminist project in relation to sexual violence as we understand it. What the 'power' feminists may be drawing on – although this is never explicit – is a process of medicalization which has transformed the meanings of victimization and its aftermath (Kelly, 1989). This has several strands, which connect to and reinforce one another: the predominance of psychological approaches to the impacts of sexual violence, and the creation of syndrome and disorder diagnoses;[5] conceptualizations of the impacts of sexual violence which emphasize damage, and neglect both meaning and coping strategies; and the development of varieties of 'treatment' responses, within the health, therapeutic and self-help sectors.

The growth of therapeutic, rather than political, responses to sexual violence is most marked in the US (Armstrong, 1994) but can be discerned in Britain too. Whilst some individual feminists have contributed to this aspect of marketable feminism, there is considerable debate within the activist movement, and amongst engaged academics, about its consequences. The growth of 'to-be-paid-for' therapy and self-help guides have by-passed the existing network of feminist organizations, which attempted to provide *free* support to all women. There are also cogent feminist critiques of these responses, both in terms of what is being offered to individuals and the de-politicization of sexual violence (see, for example, Dobash and Dobash, 1992; Armstrong, 1994; Kitzinger and Perkins, 1994).

We have used this example to illustrate the complex interconnections between the locations and forms of feminism we outlined earlier, although we are aware that we have only sketched out some of the many connections and tensions. We hope, however, that we have indicated the kinds of analysis that it might be possible to undertake within this framework, and that previous ways of thinking about/representing feminism would not provide the tools which are needed for this task.

RE-DEFINING SEXUAL VIOLENCE

In this section we outline the processes of re-definition which feminism has engaged in, and some of the dilemmas and tensions within this. This is a necessary context for the discussion of challenges from inside and outside feminism to this work.

We have become accustomed to discussion of the 1970s and 1980s as the decades in which sexual violence was discovered: unearthed from layers of historical disbelief and denial. The unearthing took place at individual, institutional and social levels: adults of all ages remembered and/or began to speak; professionals and institutions acknowledged their failure to notice, hear or suspect; societies began to face the implications of this disturbing knowledge. But feminist historians (see, for example, Jeffreys, 1985; Clarke 1987; Gordon, 1988; Pleck, 1988) have documented the awareness of these issues in previous centuries. Linda Gordon, for example, argues:

> For most of the 110 years of this history, it was the women's rights movement that was most influential in confronting, publicizing and demanding action against family violence. Concern grew when feminism was strong and ebbed when feminism was weak. Women's movements have consistently been concerned with violence not only against women but also against children. But this does not mean that anti-family violence agencies, once established, represented feminist views about the problem. (Gordon, 1988, p. 4)

It was (and continues to be) feminists who insisted that forms of physical and sexual violence were named – words used and, if necessary, created, which made explicit both violation and agency (Kelly, 1988). This, in turn, encouraged a documentation of the extent of victimization. The sustained challenge to received knowledge over the last 25 years appears to have fundamentally shifted the grounds of credibility. But awareness existed previously, only to be re-buried and re-discovered.

The difference between the 1890s and the 1990s is that sexual violence has ceased to be unspeakable – and children and adults are graphically describing their experiences. What it is possible to tell, however, depends crucially upon what others are able and willing to hear. As women and children spoke the unspeakable, our vocabulary and emotions were continually stretched, as was our credulity. Both the extent and forms of abuse that children and adults revealed, alongside the findings of paediatricians in babies as young as a few months have combined in a catalogue of horror which has been difficult to contemplate let alone comprehend. But acknowledgement has resulted in legal and policy reform in many countries.

A central concern of contemporary feminist work on violence and abuse has been to create a language with which to make its many forms visible and 'speakable'. Whilst references to being 'silenced' have become something of a cliche, they none the less refer to a basic fact: if there is no language with which to name for oneself, and potentially communicate to others, events are literally 'unspeakable' and in significant ways also 'unknowable'.[6] Even where language exists, social denial in public and professional discourses encourages silence,[7] as do constructions of experiences as evidence of pathology or wilful carelessness. The ability of children and adults to speak about experiences of victimization is therefore dependent not just on access to meaningful language, but also on a context in which they have confidence that they will be heard and believed.[8] The last two decades have, undoubtedly, witnessed nothing short of a revolution in many Western countries – a movement from halting anonymous accounts to what can, at times, appear as an endless torrent of detailed public declarations.

Although what it has been possible to know and say has been totally transformed, there remain unresolved tensions within this changed discourse, which have direct correlations within research practice. Whilst a space has been opened up multiple barriers to speaking and naming experience remain: children still may not have access to words; abusers silencing tactics can be extremely effective; many children and adults continue to use minimizing as a coping strategy; minority cultural meanings may result in a range of negative consequences of telling; and 'common-sense' understandings of words and concepts may result in individuals excluding their experiences.

The power of dominant 'common-sense' limited definitions constitutes a recurring dilemma for feminists and researchers. One strategy used by both has been to attempt to extend the meanings of words such as 'rape' and 'incest'; to use them as 'collective nouns' covering a range of experiences. The rationale for this approach is that it constitutes an explicit challenge to definitions embodied in the law, and provides validation of violation through the powerful meanings which these words carry. It reflects the two-fold intention of naming for feminists: to make violation explicit and to draw attention to agency in the perpetration of such acts. The decision of Australian feminists to use the term child sexual *assault* is a further example of this strategy. Dominant 'common-sense' meanings remain, however, and constrain what individuals who have experienced some form of 'intimate intrusion' think it is legitimate to name. General understandings of the scope of concepts such as 'violence', 'assault' and 'abuse' vary, and are not shared between individuals and social groups.

A different strategy has been adopted by other feminists and re-searchers, which involves creating new concepts with which to name the variation of experiences, extending language itself, rather than the meaning of words. This strategy is often preferred by researchers for two reasons: it continues a long tradition of creating 'typologies' of events, but more usefully it allows attention to similarities and differ-ences. There is, however, no uncontested basis for deciding which dif-ferences are the most significant or meaningful. The relationship of the perpetrator to the victim, the frequency of abuse, the number of abusers involved, the context in which abuse takes place, the forms sexual violence takes have all been used singly or in combination to draw distinctions.

There are two interlinked dangers inherent in this strategy: first, that we create an unwieldy and ever-increasing typology in which dif-ferences are presumed and similarities lost; and, second, that connec-tions between forms of sexual violence are subordinated to detailed distinctions. The co-existence of abuse of women and abuse of chil-dren in the same household has long been recognized by refuge workers, but is absent in most research and policy on either domestic violence or child abuse (Mullender and Morley, 1994). The fact that in a pro-portion of sexual abuse cases what we are talking about is rape, and even repeated rape, is seldom named as such, with the euphemistic 'intercourse' or 'penetration' preferred.

We have noted elsewhere the impossibility of creating mutually ex-clusive categories (Kelly, 1988; Kelly *et al.*, 1991), not least because women and children experience a number of forms of abuse simul-taneously. We are also aware that typologies can rapidly become forms of regulation when they contain implicit or explicit hierarchies of serious-ness and harm.

The early 1990s marked a concerted groundswell of popular and intellectual questioning of recent prevalence findings, illustrated by two public debates in Britain in June 1991 and October 1993 about 'date rape', followed more recently by the publication of Katie Roiphe's book (1994). The use of the pejorative 'victimhood' feminism relates in part to these disputes about definition and prevalence. Extending what 'counts' as violating and abusive means that there will be more to count; in redefining violence we inevitably extend estimates of in-cidence and prevalence. The creation of 'False Memory Syndrome'[9] has added further fuel to debates about the credibility of individual accounts, and the extent of sexual abuse in childhood.

The most concerted challenge from within the academy to feminist re-definitions has come from Neil Gilbert in the US. Gilbert has been conducting something of a 'campaign', involving many media appearances and considerable publications, against not just the research findings on rape and sexual abuse in childhood, but also how they have been used in public policy. His argument is summarized in 'The phantom epidemic of sexual assault' published in 1991 in the journal *Public Interest*.

Neil Gilbert's challenge is premised on invoking the need for greater 'objectivity' in research. This appeal to a supposed neutrality is belied by his own language: referring to research findings as indicating a 'plague' (Gilbert, 1991, p. 54) or 'phantom epidemic' (p. 65) is not a value-free position. He presents a strident critique of aspects of contemporary research methodology, neglecting to provide readers with access to the rationales for such practices. What in the research literature is understood as increasing sophistication, based on what we now know about how sexual abuse/violence is understood and defined by individuals is not mentioned, but this knowledge is essential if findings are to be placed in context and assessed. Gilbert makes three substantive points to support his contention that prevalence findings are 'unbelievably high' (p. 55):

- 'whilst rigorous methods have been used the definitions are so broad that they become meaningless' (p. 63);
- 'the broad definitions used by researchers result in experiences being defined as 'rape' or 'sexual abuse' in many cases where the participants did not 'define themselves as victims' (p. 60);
- 'including a broad range of behaviour in definitions both denies individual meaning and trivialises serious assaults' (p. 61).

To support his argument he cites the fact that 41 per cent of women in Mary Koss's (1988) study of rape were virgins at time of the incident and that 42 per cent had sex again with the man. Consent is thus inferred from prior and subsequent events, rather than whether it was given for the time in question. This is precisely the strategy that defense lawyers use when conducting a consent defence in rape trials, and it is frequently successful in undermining women's credibility. Interestingly, Gilbert makes no reference to studies of marital rape, nor to the critical role that this new scholarship has played in challenging the prior legalistic definition of 'real' rape (Estrich, 1987), as that committed outside, at night by a stranger with a weapon. It is precisely this limited definition which prevents many women naming their experiences of forced sex as rape (Kelly, 1988).

What Gilbert is objecting to are feminist rejections of 'taken-for-granted' dominant definitions of violence/abuse. It has become clear over a number of research projects (see Koss and Harvey, 1991) that using the words 'rape' or 'sexual abuse' in questions produces lower prevalence findings than the words 'forced sex' or 'unwanted sexual experiences'. Most researchers now use the latter, and some may also ask if respondents would define any of the events they have reported as rape/sexual abuse. Additionally, in much of the US research Gilbert takes issue with, the incidents reported are compared to local statutes, and counted as rape if they would be prosecutable as such. Whilst it is a critical research question why so many women and men have more limited definitions of rape than the local statutes, there can surely be no principled objection to naming as rape or sexual abuse that which would be deemed so in law. Extending definitions beyond legal statutes presents a more complex issue, and we have already referred to the different strategies researchers have adopted in this respect.

That a large proportion of women do not name events obscures for Gilbert the fact that between a third and a half of young women report coercive experiences of heterosexual intercourse. The simplistic rape/not rape (see also Jamieson, this volume) position which Gilbert advocates denies the complexity of experience which he purports to want to take account of; a denial based primarily on the fact that he views the research findings as 'incredible'. Alongside disbelief concerning the extensiveness of sexual violence, Gilbert is also working with a model of what constitutes a 'victim' in terms of the meaning and impacts of experience, reflecting the meanings we present later in Table 4.1. His invoking of the concept of 'serious' assaults, presumption that women would name their experience consistently, and that they would not have further contact with abusive men all reflect his discomfort with not just feminist re-definitions of rape and sexual abuse, but also attempts to extend understanding of what it means to be victimized.

Gilbert concludes that contemporary prevalence research has produced 'advocacy numbers', and represents them as a feminist conspiracy to 'impose new norms' in which women will have 'complete control of physical intimacy between the sexes' (Gilbert, 1991, p. 61). This is an interesting interpretation, implying that researchers should ignore the social meaning/implications of their work and turning on its head the challenge feminists have made to violence in the name of intimacy. That Katie Roiphe (1994) has joined this challenge to feminist re-definitions of violation, which raise difficult questions about what should constitute consent in adult heterosexuality, is to be regretted.

It is little wonder that Roiphe has been courted by the world's press, since she has re-worked the ideology of coercive heterosexuality in men's favour. Men have always argued that what women defined as rape and/or intrusion was merely 'rough' or 'bad' sex. This raises the interesting possibility that commercialized/marketable feminism is that which represents minimal challenge to the *status quo*. Since what is at issue here is not simply the extent of women and children's experiences of violence, but the extent of men's perpetration of it.

Whilst Gilbert's position is that unless women (and presumably children) define themselves as 'victims', and he agrees with that definition, then victimization has not occurred, Roiphe and Paglia take an even more restrictive position. For them any subsequent redefinition of an event is a form of feminine 'sour grapes', an adoption of a position of powerlessness. To all intents and purposes what constitutes rape for them is 'stranger rape'; returning us to the position we began from over twenty years ago. Indeed, aspects of Camile Paglia's public position reminds one of the responses in the early 1970s of men like Norman Mailer (all quotes below taken from an in-depth interview in the *Irish Independent*, 12 January 1994).

If you have 10 tequilas, wear a Madonna frock and go back to some guy's room at 3 a.m., are you then surprised when he makes a pass at you!

We have to make women realise that they are responsible, that sexuality is something which belongs to them. It is up to them to use it correctly and to be wise about where they go and what they do.

If you have an unpalatable sexual encounter so what? Big Deal! You played Russian roulette and you lost.

The potential consequences of this position for two decades of feminist scholarship and activism are in one sense obvious, but unanticipated repercussions are also likely. We have outlined several attempts to undermine the process of feminist re-definition of sexual violence, from within and outside feminism. That some of these challenges have come from 'marketable' feminism means that the critique is more known, more powerful, and more read, than most of the research to which it refers.

BEYOND VICTIM AND SURVIVOR AS OPPOSITES AND/OR IDENTITIES

In this section we explore the problems associated with simplistic models of victimization, which inform the perspectives outlined in the previous section, but are by no means limited to those authors. In doing so we draw on our research on the abuse of women and children (see, for example, Kelly, 1988; Kelly *et al.*, 1991), especially data on resistance to and coping with assaults.[10] Both resistance and coping – the protective actions children, young people and adult women take on their own behalf – become marginal areas of knowledge and experience if we rely on simplistic models of victimization and its consequences.

The simplistic model which informs much research and practice can be summarized as a 'victim/survivor dichotomy'; a conceptual split which, albeit in different ways, underlies the thinking of Paglia, Roiphe and Gilbert. Table 4.1 illustrates this through a compilation of responses to an exercise we frequently use in training. Participants are asked to brainstorm the other words they associate with 'victim' or 'survivor'. What always emerges are series of oppositional words (although they are not volunteered directly as such); the table records the most frequently cited 'pairs'. In pointing this out during training we also note how most of the words associated with 'victim' are negative, whereas those under 'survivor' are much more positive. In one sense this is not surprizing, since the concept of 'survival', and it's associated noun 'survivor' was developed within the women's and self-help movements to shift the stigmatizing meanings which attached to 'victim'. Here we wish to explore the unintended consequences of this shift in language use which are neither helpful in understanding victimization or providing support for children and adults who have been victimized.

Before we develop these arguments though, note how many of the words which appear under the victim heading are the 'ways of seeing' women which the 'power' feminists object to. They, like most women, do not wish to see themselves or other women in this way and prefer, even promote, the meanings associated with survivor as sources of positive self-identity in women. This correspondence of valued and de-valued meanings creates an unhelpful framework for both understanding and responding to victimization.

Whilst in some written and spoken discussions of sexual violence 'victim' and 'survivor' are used interchangeably, they are more frequently represented as stages or phases. The notion of a journey from

Table 4.1   *The victim/survivor dichotomy*

Victim	Survivor
Passive	Active
Helpless	Resourceful
Weak	Strong
Vulnerable	Courageous
Shame	Pride
Small	Gutsy
Hurt	Angry
Powerless	Powerful
Confused	In control/coping
Controlled	Fighting back
Guilty	Not guilty

'victim' to 'survivor' is an extremely common metaphor which appears in self-help manuals, in research and informs much of the therapeutic work done with children and adults. Either explicit or implicit in the case of sexual abuse in childhood is a view of the child as a 'victim', who can be enabled to become an 'adult survivor'. These ideas are most evident in the commercialized feminism we outlined earlier, including: the rapidly increasing market of survival handbooks; the way in which published personal testimonies are now framed by commentaries from the woman's therapist; and the exponential growth in forms of therapeutic services offered to 'survivors' (see Armstrong (1991, 1994) in relation to child sexual abuse). The extent of abuse means that there is a large potential reservoir of 'consumers' for these materials and services.

There are a series of separate, but linked, problems with the victim/survivor dichotomy, some concern how experiences of abuse are represented, others are more strongly connected to the attribution/claiming of identity. Whilst the solidifying of these meanings into oppositional groupings has its origins within therapeutic perspectives, they have in turn become increasingly influential in some activist feminist support services.

Either 'Victim' or 'Survivor'?

The notion of phases or stages positions individuals as either 'victim' or 'survivor'. This misrepresents both material and emotional reality. All sexual violence involves an experience of victimization, and if individuals do not die as a consequence they have physically survived.

The conceptual separation over time produces an understanding which focuses on an either/or positioning of individuals, and prevents an alternative conceptualization where the two concepts refer to different aspects of experience: being victimized is what was done – a statement of historical fact; survival is what individuals who are victimized achieve in relation to, and often in spite of, that historical reality. It is also important to remember that not all who are victimized do survive: women and children are killed in the course of assaults, and some take their own lives when the pain and distress becomes unbearable.

In the setting up of the two as identities and opposites, a binary opposition of value results, where 'victim' carries all the negative meanings and 'survivor' the positive. Rather than challenge the stigmatizing meaning of 'victim' as initially intended, it is, in fact, reinforced, with the only route out being an identification with, or attribution of, the alternative of 'survivor'. One illustration of this is the frequent uses of the term 'victim behaviours' to describe actions or attitudes which researchers and/or clinicians define as problematic. Increasingly this orientation has moved into popular culture, to the extent that young people and adults now speak of their need to stop 'behaving like a victim'. In its crude forms this way of thinking reproduces, albeit in somewhat different form, a version of 'victim blame' (and the quotes from Camile Paglia earlier in this paper are particular examples of it in operation).

The Importance of Resistance and Coping

The chronological separation of victimization from survival feeds the neglect of resistance and coping strategies used during abuse, since passivity is presumed. These aspects of experience are often buried and minimized by children and adults, and they tend to be only remembered or mentioned if explicitly asked about. Once remembered, however, they offer a particularly fruitful starting point for exploring guilt and self-blame.[11] Most children, young people and adults who have been sexually abused/assaulted believe that they ought to have been able to stop the abuse.

This internalization of blame can, in part, be a way of exploring how they might prevent victimization in the future – hypothesizing what could have been different in order to make it different in the future (Kelly, 1988). This process of re-thinking also tends to result in the suppression of the unsuccessful tactics and strategies they did use, since their 'ineffectiveness' problematizes the desired construction of potential future safety. The reconstruction which takes place can have both positive and negative consequences – it may enable a sense of potential safety to develop, but at the cost of ignoring aspects of previous experience. Remembering that they were not passive, that they used strategies has similarly contradictory outcomes. It can shift the sense of blame for what happened, whilst at the same time making the creation of future safety more problematic.

Reinforcing or Challenging Disassociation

The opposition between 'victim' and 'survivor' leaves little room for exploring the complexity of coping/survival skills; for example, that necessary defenses are developed at the time of abuse, which are maintained over time, particularly if the child/young person/woman does not have access to others who believe and support them at the time. The maintenance and solidifying of defensive strategies can become a source of difficulty (Kelly, 1988). An obvious example here is the variety of disassociative responses which children and adults develop to limit the threat, fear and pain they are experiencing. As psychic defenses where abuse is occurring they are extremely effective, as the basis from which subsequent interactions with others take place they can become increasingly limiting and frustrating. For example, women and children may cope by living in the moment, or for/in the good times, forgetting/disassociating from the 'bad' (abusive) times. This can result in difficulties facing reality and/or coping with conflict, with a range of negative consequences in both practical everyday matters and relationships with others.

Dichotomizing 'victim'/'survivor', child/adult reinforces rather than challenges the splitting/disassociation which is so often a response to abuse. The powerful metaphor of 'the child inside', much used in therapy and counselling, whilst speaking to this aspect of experience, also serves to reinforce the separation. The fragmented and disconnected sense of self which some children, young people and women experience is not a source of creativity or positive tension, as much postmodernist theory suggests. Rather, for most, it is an obstacle to making desired changes in their lives.

Understanding that coping strategies connect directly to individual survival, enables us to understand that letting go of them, however unsuitable in current circumstances, is profoundly threatening. We believe that it is only through a tracing back to their origin as a survival strategy (in contrast to their labelling as a 'victim behaviour'), and a recognition of their appropriateness and necessity at the time, that it is possible for individuals to begin to let go of old coping strategies and develop new ones more appropriate to their changed situation.

Unhelpful Metaphors

The popular therapeutic notion of a 'journey' to survival, with accompanying notions of 'healing' are both naive and inappropriate. It is impossible to change what has happened in the past – although that may indeed be what many children and adults wish they could do, hence the potency of forgetting as a coping strategy. What is possible is to reach an understanding of those events and their consequences which explains feelings and responses; which makes sense of what happened, its many consequences and resonances in the past and present. It is finding some kind of resolution at the level of meaning which is fundamental to being able to achieve more sense of control over ones emotions and ones life. The medical metaphors of 'healing' and 're-covery' offer a false hope that experiences of abuse can be understood and responded to in a similar way to illness: where both symptoms and cause can be 'got rid of' if one can simply find the right 'treat-ment'. Thus interactional and social events which are fundamentally about inequality and the use of 'power over' are transformed into in-dividual encounters equivalent to the contracting of germs or viruses.

The implicit suggestion of a 'cure' has additional consequences. Anyone who has worked on their own experiences, and/or with indi-viduals who have experienced sexual violence knows that the two sets of understandings/feelings/responses/meanings in Table 4.1 co-exist; that strong, courageous children and adults can simultaneously feel hurt and damaged. We also know that the balance between these shifts, and that not all of the issues which experiences of abuse raise emerge at the same time. There is no absolute resolution, since changes in life experience and over the life cycle produce new areas of difficulty. Both research and practice must reflect this complexity, must acknowl-edge that both memory and meaning vary over time and in relation to other experiences. For example, the point at which someone who has been abused as a child becomes the parent/carer of a child is likely to be a powerful reminder of the vulnerability of children and result in a new set of concerns about protection of this child.

Failing to acknowledge that working through painful experiences is a process, that occurs throughout ones lifetime, can produce variants of resentment, preoccupation and despair. Resentment with 'helpers' that they have not provided the resolution can result in a desperate movement from one therapist to another, from group to group, and/or a voracious consumption of the literature – all in search of the 'answer', the 'cure'. There are a number of potential outcomes of this unsuccessful search: an angry difficult 'consumer' of services, cycling themselves round statutory and voluntary-sector organizations; a sense of personal failure, that one is a 'hopeless case' – still a 'victim'; a preoccupation with the experience of abuse such that it is the only aspect of experience a person focuses on, and becomes the explanatory framework for all feeling and behaviour.

Recognizing Harm

The 'healing' discourse and the positive connotations of 'survivor', which are most evident in the self-help manuals, but which also underpin much research and counselling, provide little room for recognition of just how damaging some experiences of sexual violence can be. Being systematically abused over a long period and having to find ways to survive this does not produce 'nice' or 'well-balanced' individuals. The extent of pain and suppressed rage which individuals carry varies, but we have to be able to acknowledge that for some children, young people and adults the levels and forms of damage are extensive.

At the same time, the 'damage' discourse which connects to the meanings associated with 'victim', suggests that without formal intervention, individuals who have been sexually victimized, especially in childhood, are 'emotional time-bombs waiting to go off'. This makes invisible (and also conceptually impossible) the incredible resourcefulness and creativity which many children and adults display in marshalling both their inner strengths and support from informal networks in successfully coping with experiences of abuse.

BEYOND EITHER/OR AND REMEMBERING FEMINIST PRAXIS

In recording what we regard as unintended consequences of the 'victim/survivor dichotomy' we are questioning whether either is useful over the long term as an identity. In this sense, and this sense only, we have some connection to elements of the arguments about 'victimhood'. But our point of departure is that victimization is extensive, rather than residual, and that these events have a range of consequences. For any individual struggling with the confusion, guilt, sense of being unworthy and undeserving, which experiences of abuse evoke, claiming an identity as a 'survivor' can be a positive move forward. For others, whose coping response has been to demonstrate to themselves and others how 'in control' and competent they are, acknowledging the pain and hurt which accompanies being a 'victim' may be an important step in integrating aspects of their experiences and emotions. But holding onto either as a key definer of the self over the long term means that selfhood is still fundamentally connected to the past. We are all far more that what was done to us and how we have coped with it, and survival must surely be the minimal, rather than the maximal goal. It is for this reason that throughout this paper we have not used either 'victim' or 'survivor' to refer to people, preferring children, young people, adults or women, and the words 'victimization' and 'survival' are employed to denote particular events and responses to them.

We begin from recognizing that when assaults occur, each child or adult has to make decisions at the time and later which are directed towards their survival. These decisions depend crucially on what they perceive as possible in their particular circumstances. This framework enables a more complex way of understanding and working with the impacts of abuse – a combination of physical, emotional and social effects and active coping responses, within which the actions/strategies children and adults take to prevent/avoid abuse and/or its most threatening meanings can be recognized and validated. Most of all we are arguing for a perspective which views and treats children, young people and adults as whole people for whom victimization is but one, albeit extremely important for many, aspect of their life experience.

We have come to this perspective through our work as feminist researchers and activists. Whilst we have taken women and children's experiences as our starting point, we have also used and developed our own (often drawing on work by other women) perspectives on them. We then 'use' this knowledge not only in our writing, but also in the support work and training we do within and outside our paid employment. The more we 'use' the knowledge, the more the perspective develops and in turn affects subsequent research.

This brings us (perhaps too neatly) back to our starting point: the increasing separation between feminist academics and activists, and the creation of a new location: commercialized feminism. It is the lack of connection between the first two which, in our view, adds power to the latter. In the absence of what Janice Raymond (1986) calls 'thoughtful theory' and 'considerate thinking' it becomes more possible for re-workings of dominant discourses, and even newly worked un-feminist ones to take root. She further notes:

> The need to think is inspired by the quest for meaning. Thus thinking should never be dissociated from the world of participation. (p. 215)

We would link this with Tania Modleski's (1991) observation that:

> We need to consider the extent to which male power is actually consolidated through cycles of crisis and resolution. (Modleski, 1991, p. 7)

The quest for meaning has been a recurring theme throughout this chapter; in terms of naming, definition, methodology, personal experience and personal identity. We have highlighted both attempts to challenge feminist meanings (redefining feminism and redefining sexual violence) and an attempt to continue developing it (beyond victim or survivor). What has been evident in the late 1980s and early 1990s are a number of significant attempts to contain the threat posed by feminist thought and action. But Modleski draws our attention to how these have been responded to within feminism: the relocation of feminist struggles against patriarchal power and relations to struggles within feminism. She asks the telling question why women have been more willing than any other oppressed group to yield the ground on which they (we) stand (Modleski, 1991, p. 15).

Being able to respond 'thoughtfully' to such challenges, and to continue creating feminist meaning in thought and action requires re-connecting the issues of concern between academic and activist feminists. A re-assertion of considerate feminist scholarship which attempts to provide useful knowledge, and a strong feminist praxis involving feedback regarding the uses to which that knowledge is put, and the new questions which emerge as a result. The outcome would be both stronger theory and stronger practice which benefitted women in the short term, and which provided us with clarity about targeting change in the longer term.

NOTES

1. We are uncomfortable with many of the current uses of the concept of 'backlash'. It is neither a 'new' notion, nor new phenomenon. Shulamith Firestone, in her much criticized but seldom read classic, *Dialectics of Sex: The Case for Feminist Revolution* (1972) uses it to describe the period between the first and second waves of Western feminism. She suggests that a range of strategies were used to diffuse fundamental challenges to patriarchal relations. She also makes the apposite point that no-one gives up power without a struggle; it is not possible for women to challenge, let alone 'take' power without there being reaction and resistance. 'Backlash' is frequently deployed in a simplistic and pessimistic formulation; implying an unfair and unkind response to women's hard-won victories, rather than being understood as a shorthand for an inevitable and persistent element in any struggle for liberation.

    The latter meaning presupposes that resistance to change should be anticipated and strategized around; that the emergence of 'counter-offensives' is evidence of a perceived threat to the *status quo*. In this meaning, what is indicated is less a defeat, but rather elements of success which need to be responded to; gains which need to be defended rather than prompting nostalgic recalling of some kind of 'golden' past. Paying attention to where, how and over what such reactions occur should be a rich resource in highlighting where the fault lines in patriarchal power lie. That many of these public struggles turn on sexuality, sexual violence and the ability of women to live independently of men is, in our view, enormously revealing, and demands our critical attention. Whilst some feminist thought does, indeed, do this, and we locate our own work within these attempts to analyse the current context, all too often 'backlash' is used as a substitute for analysis.

2. She has stated on more than one occasion that her ambition is to 'save feminism from feminists' (see, for example, *Irish Independent* 12 January 1994).

3. The questions of which women have access to material and social power, and whether they are using it as individuals or in order to improve the situation of all women are key feminist concerns.

4. This has become such a cliche that it drives out from memory the fact that, for example, the demonstration for abortion rights in 1993 in the US was the largest in living memory.

5. Examples here include Battered Women's Syndrome, Child Sexual Abuse Accommodation Syndrome, Post-Traumatic Stress Disorder and Multiple Personality Disorder. For a critique see Kelly *et al.* (1995).

6. The 'unspeakability' of experiences is literally true for some children and adults with disabilities who cannot use spoken language. Their ability to communicate about abuse is discussed by Kennedy (1992), and the implications of this for research methods by Kelly *et al.* (1994).

7. Currently, the form of sexual violence where this process is most evident is ritual abuse.

8. The most recent survey in Britain (Mihill, 1994), of students at universities in Oxford, reveals that many women are still not confident that

official agencies will respond sympathetically to reports of rape and sexual assault, although 93 per cent had told a friend.

9. We use the word 'creation' here deliberately, since the concept is the creation of organized groups of parents, who claim they have been falsely accused by adult daughters of sexual abuse. There is no such recognized 'syndrome' in clinical literature, although there is an ongoing debate about the status of 'recovered memory' (see Armstrong (1994), Kelly (1994) and the British Psychological Society document (1995) for more detailed discussions).

10. We all, in different contexts, have also done support work with adult women, and this combines with our research in the perspective we present here.

11. In support work it has become a commonplace that ensuring the basic message that 'you were not to blame' is communicated. In our experience, repeating this message is seldom effective where blame has been strongly internalized. Rather what needs exploration is *why* the person feels to blame, including how their abusers actions and words encouraged it and what avoidance/resistance they used at the time.

REFERENCES

Armstrong, L. (1991), 'Surviving the Incest Industry', *Trouble and Strife*, **21**: pp. 29–32.
Armstrong, L. (1994), *Rocking the Cradle of Sexual Politics: What Happened When Women Said Incest* (New York:, Addison-Wesley).
Barry, K. (1979), *Female Sexual Slavery* (Engelwood Cliffs, NJ: Prentice Hall).
British Psychological Society (BPS) (1995), *Investigation into Recovered Memory* (London: BPS).
Cameron, D. (1985), *Feminism and Linguistic Theory* (London: Macmillan).
Clarke, A. (1987), *Women's Silence, Men's Violence: Sexual Assault in England 1770–1845* (London: Pandora Press).
Cockburn, C. (1991), *In the Way of Women: Men's Resistance to Sex Equality in Organizations* (London: Macmillan).
Dobash, R. and Dobash, R. (1992), *Women, Violence and Social Change* (London: Routledge).
Enloe, C. (1983), *Does Khaki Become You? The Militarization of Women's Lives* (London: Pandora).
Enloe, C. (1989), *Bananas, Beaches and Patriarchy: Making Feminist Sense of International Politics* (London: Pandora).
Estrich, S. (1987), *Real Rape* (Cambridge, MA: Harvard University Press).
Faludi, S. (1991), *Backlash: The Undeclared War Against American Women* (London: Penguin).
Firestone, S. (1972), *The Dialectics of Sex: The Case for Feminist Revolution* (London: Paladin).
Gilbert, N. (1991), 'The Phantom Epidemic of Sexual Assault', *Public Opinion*, **103**: pp. 54–65.
Gordon, L. (1988), *Heroes of their Own Lives: The Politics and History of Family Violence, Boston 1880–1960* (London: Virago).

Grant, K. (1994), 'Queer Theorrea: And what it all might mean for Feminism', *Trouble and Strife*, 29/30: pp. 37–43.

Griffin, G. (ed.) (1995), *Feminist Activism in the 90s* (London: Taylor & Francis).

The Irish Independent (1994), 'Interview with Camile Paglia', 12 January.

Jeffreys, S. (1985), *The Spinster and her Enemies: Feminism and Sexuality 1880–1930* (London: Women's Press).

Kelly, L. (1988), *Surviving Sexual Violence* (Cambridge: Polity Press).

Kelly, L. (1989), 'From Politics to Pathology: The Medicalisation of Rape and Child Sexual Abuse', *Radical Community Medicine*, 36: pp. 14–18.

Kelly, L. (1992), 'The Contradictions of Power for Women', Keynote speech at the National Women and Housing Conference, Ormskirk.

Kelly, L. (1994), 'Stuck in the Middle', *Trouble and Strife*, 29/30: pp. 44–8.

Kelly, L., Regan, L. and Burton, S. (1991), 'An Exploratory Study of the Prevalence of Sexual Abuse in a Sample of 16–21 Year Olds', Final Report to the ESRC.

Kelly, L., Regan, L. and Burton, S. (1993), 'Beyond Victim to Survivor: the Implications of Knowledge about Children's Resistance and Avoidance Strategies', in H. Ferguson, R. Gilligan, and Torode (eds), *Beyond Childhood Adversity: Issues for Policy and Practice* (Dublin: Social Studies Press).

Kelly, L., Burton, S. and Regan, L. (1994), 'Researching Women's Lives or Studying Women's Oppression? Reflections on what Constitutes Feminist Research', in M. Maynard and J. Purvis (eds), *Researching Women's Lives from a Feminist Perspective* (London: Taylor & Francis).

Kelly, L., Burton, S. and Regan, L. (1995), 'The Dangers of using Syndromes and Disorders in Legal Cases', *Rights of Women Bulletin*, Spring.

Kennedy, M. (ed., with Kelly, L.) (1992), 'Special Issue: Disability and Abuse', *Child Abuse Review*, 1:2.

Kitzinger, C. and Perkins, R. (1994), *Changing Our Minds* (London: Onlywomen).

Koss, M. (1988), 'Hidden Rape: Sexual Aggression and Victimization in a National Sample of Students in Higher Education', in A. W. Burgess (ed.), *Rape and Sexual Assault*, vol. 2 (New York: Garland).

Koss, M. and Harvey, M. (1991), *The Rape Victim: Clinical and Community Interventions* (Newbury Park, CA: Sage).

Milhill, C. (1994), 'Student Sex Victims Fail to Inform Police', *Guardian*, 20 December, p. 7.

Modleski, T. (1991), *Feminism without Women: Culture and Criticism in a "Postfeminist" Age* (London: Routledge).

Mullender, A. and Morley, B. (1994), *Children Living with Domestic Violence: Putting Domestic Violence on the Child Care Agenda* (London: Whiting & Birch).

Paglia, C. (1993), *Sex, Art and American Culture* (London: Viking).

Pleck, E. (1987), *Domestic Tyranny: The Making of American Social Policy Against Family Violence from Colonial Times to the Present* (Oxford: Oxford University Press).

Raymond, J. (1986), *A Passion for Friends: Toward a Philosophy of Female Affection* (London: Women's Press).

Radford, J. (1994), 'The History of Women's Liberation Movements in Britain: A Reflective Personal History' in G. Griffin, M. Hester, S. Rai and S. Roseneil (eds), *Stirring It: Challenges for Feminism* (London: Taylor & Francis).

Rich, A. (1978), *The Dream of a Common Language: Poems 1974–1977* (New York: W.W. Norton).

Roiphe, K. (1994), *The Morning After: Sex, Fear and Feminism* (London: Hamish Hamilton).

Stanley, L. (ed.) (1990), *Feminist Praxis: Method, Theory and Epistemology in Feminist Sociology* (London: Routledge & Keegan Paul).

Steinham, G. (1993), *The Revolution Within: A Book of Self Esteem* (London: Bloomsbury).

Wolf, N. (1993), *Fire with Fire: The New Female Power and How it will Change the 21st Century* (London: Chatto & Windus).

5 Genital Identities: An Idiosyncratic Foray into the Gendering of Sexualities

Tamsin Wilton

MEAN-ING AND SEX-ING

Until recently, sociology has been guilty of ignoring or erasing the body (Turner, 1991; Frank, 1992), while post-structuralism has tended to reduce it to a text, a set of meanings constituted by and negotiated among discursive practices (Game, 1991; Zita, 1992). This flight from the flesh has been interpreted by some as evidence of the paranoid masculinist character of science:

> A fear of life and a disembodied approach to nature is an important characteristic of male history and scientific patriarchy. Man's 'paranoid somatophobia' ... can be traced to Descartes, who demonstrated the isolation of the male self,. the existence of a detached ego without connectedness to the natural world. *Cogito ergo sum* expressed the distrust of the body and the senses ... (Brodribb, 1992, p. 15)

It is perhaps ironic that the anti-enlightenment tendency of postmodernism, with its suspicion of meta-narratives, its refusal to hierarchize truth-claims and its concomitant de-centring of science, has written the body back into theory. Ironic, because general opinion is that postmodernism is the ultimate in anti-materiality. Many would sympathize with Jacquelyn Zita's gleeful assertion that, 'Against the intellectual anorexia of postmodernism, th[e] body stubbornly returns with a weight that defies the promises of postmodern fantasy and its idealist denial' (Zita, 1992, p. 126). Yet others insist that it is precisely the theoretical iconoclasm of postmodernism, the casting down of the throne of scientific rationalism, that enables the return of the body:

> It is with the postmodernist critique of the rational project that ...

the body is . . . brought back into . . . question. . . . The critique of reason as emancipation has resulted in an interest in the body, both as a source of opposition to instrumental reason and as the target of the colonization of the everyday world by the public arena of (male) reason. (Turner, 1991, p. 8)

The attention paid to the presumptively *gendered* nature of reason/ science in these accounts suggests that a feminist critique has been instrumental in the development of postmodernism, and that sex/gender itself has been accorded a new theoretical significance. Such is indeed the case, for questions of gender, sex and desire are among those that characterize current debates concerning the properties and meanings of bodies, and they are questions derived from the liberation movements of (primarily) feminism and queer.[1] Since those active in the liberationist movements were both materially oppressed and discursively constituted as 'other' by reason of their supposed bodily difference (having bodies that were female, Black or perversely desirous), it is not surprising that the postliberationist, postmodern intellectual agenda should thus foreground the body. Indeed, the postmodern cynicism towards the 'grand narratives' of progress and consistent self-hood has its roots in these same struggles. '[T]he liberation movements of the sixties and seventies emerg[ed] not only to make a claim to the legitimacy of marginalized cultures, unheard voices, suppressed narratives, but also to expose the perspectivity and partiality of the official accounts' (Bordo, 1990, p. 137).

In current discourses of the body, the question of *sex* has become central, and it is sex that I am concerned with here. And the problem of semantics confronts me immediately. For while sex is commonly used to refer to the biological attributes of male and female bodies – as distinct from the *social* scriptings of gender, seen as mapped onto, giving meaning to and deriving from that biological distinction – it is also used to speak about those desires, behaviours, acts and fantasies that coalesce (in the industrialized, millenial West at least) around the erotic. I have attempted to disentangle these two threads (largely inseparable in current common-sense understanding) by marking them clearly as either sex/erotic or sex/gender, since what I am engaged in here is an attempt to describe some current interpenetrations among the cultural (representations of bodies), the social (ascriptions of meanings to bodies and desires) and subjectivity (the reflexive narrative project of the 'self' and of identities), taking gender and sexual identity as my central problematics.

IDENTIFYING AGAINST OPPRESSION

In post-industrial Western societies, sexual desire, pleasure and identity are encoded within and by the apparently natural and yet powerfully policed duality of two sex/genders, understood as constituting
not only difference but *polarity*. Within the hegemonic narrative, sex/
gender and sex/erotic behaviour partake of the heterosexual imperative, such that deviant sex/erotic behaviour is elided with deviant sex/
gender identity, and both are enscribed onto specific bodily configu-
rations. There is a systematic distinction between those who possess
testicles and who perform the gender 'masculine', a performance that
includes penetrating others sexually, and those who possess ovaries
and who perform the gender 'feminine', a performance that includes
being available to be penetrated sexually.

This set of social scripts reflects the cultural/cognitive mapping of
the erotic onto the always already gendered body. Thus a body which
has a vagina and uterus is allocated meanings that include its being
for pentration/impregnation by a penis, while the meanings of a body
which has a penis include its being *for* pentrating/impregnating a va-
gina/uterus. The meaning of the body (perceived as intrinsically 'gen-
der/sexed') is a sexual/erotic one. At the level of flesh, that meaning
partakes of a naïve functionalism (penis is to vagina as plug is to
socket), that has been variously sanctified or naturalized according to
whether the scientific or religious paradigm is hegemonic in any particular time and place. It is this functionalism which gives rise to what
I here call *genital identities*; composite sets of sex/gender and sex/
erotic self-narratives precipitated by the heavy burden of signification
borne by the human genital organs. Of course gender and the erotic
are not the only organizing imperatives of sexual and body meanings.
Yet they do have a more immediate relation to the body than, say,
'race', class or age, factors whose significance is located more clearly
in the wider social arena, at a certain distance from matters of skin
and flesh. Both class and 'race' are relative: 'White' only acquires
meaning in relation to 'Black', 'working class' in relation to 'proper-
tied class' etc. It is perfectly possible to imagine a society (indeed,
such have historically existed) where there were only White people or
only Black people, or where material/economic relations were equi-
table. Although gender, too, is relative, there exists no society where
only men or only women are born. The meaning of gender is almost
instantaneously enscribed onto the new born infant's body, in a way
which is not universally the case for other significant stigmata.

Gender and sexuality, being co-dependent within the paradigm of genital identity, are subject to general elision. As historians and anthropologists of transvestism and of same-sex desire have shown, erotic object-choice and sex/gender have been contained within one paradigm in many cultures and at many historical moments (see, for example, D'Emilio and Freedman, 1988; Duberman *et al.*, 1989; Bremer, 1991; Garber, 1992). The *berdache* and the passing woman, the *kotoi* of Thailand and the *muskobanja* of the Balkans are expressions of and make sense only within such a paradigm.[2]

This naive heterobinarism has not gone unchallenged. 'Sex', as Rubin observes, 'is a vector of oppression' (Rubin, 1984, p. 293), and those oppressed within its terms – including feminists and queers – have been loud in exposing its idiocies. Gay philosopher Edward Stein cautions that 'A bipolar or binary view of sexual orientation cannot just be assumed' (Stein, 1992, p. 335); a sensible position, given the multiple and often contradictory interstices between sex/gender and the erotic which individuals (and indeed groups) may be seen to inhabit/ enact within the queer milieu. From lesbian boys to male lesbians, from leathermen and dykes on bikes to lipstick lesbians and queens, the performance of queer desire routinely makes hay with the anxious naivety of heteropolarity. Stein also cites psychologists Sandra Bem and Janet Spence who 'have pointed out that there is something seriously wrong with viewing masculinity and femininity, defined in terms of conformity to gender stereotypes, as opposite sides of a scale' (Stein, 1992, p. 336). For queers, whose sub-culture makes available to them a broad range of *self-consciously performative* sex/gender and sex/erotic positions, who may move from butch to femme or from Top to Bottom and still retain erotic and gender intelligibility, the heteropolar model is simply silly.

The elision of gender and the erotic is not restricted to the anxious unthinkingness of hegemonic discourse. An influential strand of radical feminism insists that to be a lesbian constitutes not simply deviant sexuality, but deviant gender behaviour: disobedience to patriarchal gender roles, gender rebellion (Vicinus, 1989) or even a complete escape from the female gender, seen as symbolically and materially constituted in obedience to male power (Wittig, 1992). Within this radical feminist paradigm there are at least three genders: man, woman and lesbian.[3] Although feminists have identified gender as a social institution oppressive to women, the most radically deconstructionist feminists tend, ironically, to reinforce heteropolarity, since 'woman' – inevitably – constitutes a privileged sign within feminist discourse, and since radical feminist constructions of gender tend to be organized around a definitional – albeit anathematized – *masculine* norm.

Some revolutionary feminists, such as Sheila Jeffreys, detach 'hetero-sexuality' from its gender base and reframe it within an alternative binary that takes power rather than bodily difference as its axis. Thus 'heterosexual desire *is* eroticised power difference . . . [it] originates in the power relationship between men and women, but it can also be experienced in same-sex relationships' (Jeffreys, 1990, p. 299). Although this apparent de-gendering of heterosexuality seems transgressively queer, it is flawed by the revolutionary feminist doctrine that 'homosexual desire' (which Jeffreys defines as 'eroticised mutuality') is unattainable by anyone with a penis. This apparently degendered heterosexuality is, in fact, merely an expansion of *masculinity*, a more academic presen-tation of the old notion of 'male identification'.

Queer activism and theory share radical feminism's project of ex-posing the political and constructed nature of gender. It is a tenet of queer that 'gender is apartheid' (Smyth, 1992), and queers valorize such execrated performers as drag queens and bull daggers for the challenge they pose to sex/gender *and* sex/erotic binaries simul-taneously. Indeed, one of the tensions between radical feminism and queer theory lies in their competing positions on the business of gen-der rebellion, a business which feminism approaches without the irony which characterizes queer (the natural child of camp). Feminism rec-ognizes – as queer notoriously does not – the material inequalities that both inform and are reproduced by the eroticization of gender. This position leads (understandably) to a feminist distrust of erotic playful-ness and parody. I would add, however, that queer and feminism can-not help interjecting into one another's speech. When, for example, Quentin Crisp describes his royal progress through the streets of Lon-don, 'blind with mascara and dumb with lipstick' (cited in Garber, 1992), his words resonate – albeit unselfconsciously – with radical feminist critiques of the feminine role as forbidding women both the gaze and speech.

Outwith the oppositional discourses of queer and radical feminism, the constructed relation between sex/gender and sex/erotic is main-tained for reasons of heterosexual paranoia. As Marjorie Garber puts it, 'the conflation is fuelled by a desire to *tell the difference*, to guard against a difference that might otherwise put the identity of one's own position in question' (Garber, 1992, p. 130; emphasis as in original). Garber suggests that much cultural anxiety about 'the borderline be-tween gender and sexuality' is invested in and shamanistically pro-cessed by the figure of the transvestite.

BODIES OF TEXTS: SEX, DEATH AND PLEASURE

Poststructuralism and queer theory offer a powerful lever with which to crack asunder the apparently seamless coherence of sex/gender and sex/erotic identities enshrined in hegemonic heterosexist discourse, a coherence located in and reproductive of oppressions around gender, desire, pleasure and 'race'. Early sociological theorists of sexuality, such as McIntosh, Plummer and Weeks, developed theories of sexual orientation that disengaged it from individualistic, psychological notions of identity and located it firmly within an early social constructionist model (McIntosh, 1981; Plummer, 1981; Weeks, 1985). More recently, Judith Butler's (1990) insights into the performativity of sex/gender have swept away for good the notion of an intrinsic or even stable sexual or gender 'identity'.

The stability of 'identity' had already proved politically and pragmatically fragile. The identity politics of the 1970s and early 1980s could not survive the wrath of the ideological children it spawned. Identities proliferated exponentially across communities and within individuals, and the usefulness of the concept for political organization wore thin as the demand for recognition stretched across an ever wider field of multiple identifications, a field marked by mutual hostilities and hierarchies. The body, recalcitrant and obstructive to incorporation within this paradigmatic enterprise, vanished. In the urgency of rescuing material bodies from oppressions engendered by social and cultural constructions, the body itself became a text. Liberationist rhetoric insisted that otherness and difference were social constructs. But if disability was located in the environment, 'race' in history and colonialist propaganda, 'sexual orientation' in the sexological imagination, what of the somatic markers of difference? What is the relation – if any – between a certain kind of body ('female'), the social role ('femininity') and the experience through time of being/inhabiting such a body (be-ing a woman)? As Jacquelyn Zita asks, in the context of a discussion of 'men' who claim they 'are' lesbians, 'You have to "body" lesbian in order to be one. However, what does it mean "to body" lesbian?' (Zita, 1992, p. 112).

There is a popular misconception that the postmodern proliferation of narratives and 'speaking positions' has played a similar vanishing trick with identity; a misconception that has fuelled heated debate among lesbian and gay communities who fear that the death of the self heralds the impossibility of political action in the face of homophobia (see Stein, 1992). Many feminists, too, harbour a lively suspicion that the deconstruction of gender represents a sophisticated defence against feminism on the part of the patriarchy – along the lines of 'if gender is only a social construct, "men" can't be oppressing "women"'. Roseann Mandziuk, who warns that, '[i]n casting its lot with postmodernism, feminism is, indeed, sleeping with the enemy' (Mandziuk, 1993, p. 170), is typical in her assertion that postmodernism is the enemy of social transformation. 'To give in to the allure of escape and ephemerality is', she warns, 'to become participants in the elimination of the possibility of social change' (p. 183).

Such fears are based on a misunderstanding of postmodernism. It is entirely inappropriate to critique postmodernism as if it were a politics. The deconstructive approach so characteristic of postmodernity is no more (and no less) than a paradigm shift, and as such does not cause anything to become more ephemeral or less 'real'. Recognizing 'woman' or 'gay man' as discursively contingent does not make them any less 'real', because there is nothing *more* real. In fact, it should prove extremely useful in the struggle against oppression to be able to focus attention on the social and cultural mechanisms whereby meanings (including meanings-of-the-self) are made, circulated and contested.

I would go so far as to say that for feminism the only alternative to the deconstruction and rewriting of gender – a rewriting that may take the form of *eradicating* gender altogether (Turner, 1991) – is to exterminate men! *Either* gender is an oppressive but manipulable construct *or* men are 'naturally' the oppressors of women – an equally 'natural' set of victims – and should be wiped out. For queers, the gentler option is of course seduction, but you cannot seduce a man into becoming a woman – not, that is, unless you accept a radically deconstructive paradigm for sex/gender that utterly denies the body. Tempting though this may be (and there are those, such as 'male lesbians' or certain transsexuals, who clearly do accept this), there is an important difference between recognizing that sex/gender is not intrinsic to or generated by the body and denying all significance to bodily differences. As Arthur Frank suggests, a working idea of the body needs to include the intransigence of corporeality:

> Bodies, of course, do not emerge out of discourses and institutions; they emerge out of other bodies, specifically women's bodies. . . . Empirical bodies do have real limits . . . corporeality remains an obdurate fact. . . . Thus what I am calling 'the body' is constituted in the intersection of an equilateral triangle the points of which are *institutions*, *discourses* and *corporeality*. (Frank, 1991, p. 49)

Frank's point about the emergence of bodies from bodies offers a timely reminder that reproduction is one facet of corporeality that both queers and feminists fail to take into sufficient account in theorizing sex/gender and sex/erotic identities and behaviours. Though, as Susan Bordo suggests, this may be the point at which theory needs to re-situate itself in relation to as yet non-existent empirical enquiry. She writes:

> In speaking of 'the practice of reproduction', I have in mind not only pregnancy and birth, but menstruation, menopause, nursing, weaning and spontaneous and induced abortion. I do not deny, of course, that all of these have been constructed and culturally valued in diverse ways. But does that diversity utterly invalidate any abstraction of significant point of general contrast between female and male bodily realities? The question, it seems to me, is to be approached through concrete exploration, not decided by theoretical fiat. (Bordo, 1990, p. 155)

Given that 'bodily realities' are yet to be adequately theorized, the relation of such social fictions as gender, sexuality and identity to the experiential/ontological matter of flesh and bone must here be identified as an open question. The naïve 'Russian nesting doll' model, which proposes a self located in its body, which is in turn located in the social, is clearly obsolete. What is certain is that the dynamic interface between discourse and subjectivity *is* the body. The body does not permit of discursive reductionism: bodily existence is not dependent on the production of texts and discourses about bodies. Discourse *is* however, dependent upon bodies: eyes, ears, mouths, hands and brains are prerequisite for all acts of textual production/reception, encoding/decoding.

STORIES TOLD ABOUT OUR SELVES

The origins and locations of the 'self' remain as contested as the origins and locations of gender. The postmodern position on identity/subjectivity is neatly summed up by Philip Mellor and Chris Shilling who write: 'self-identity is now something constructed through the continual re-ordering of self-narratives' (Mellor and Shilling, 1993, p. 413). Such narratives may not, of course, be entirely self-generating, rather they coalesce at the shifting interstices of culture and self, of social and psychological. A young man who wakes up one morning in, say, Preston to the realization that he feels sexual desire for men rather than women is not likely to interpret this realization as a call from the Great Spirit to become a *berdache*. This is not a set of meanings which are culturally available to him. His development of a 'gay identity' will entail making sense of a cacophony of cultural meanings for 'gay man' circulating in millenial Preston, among which effeminacy, contamination, unnaturalness and disease will figure more large than spirituality. The self-narratives available to any individual, the constitutive elements of subjectivity, depend on access to texts circulating in the wider culture.

My concern here is to question how textual address enables and encourages readers who position themselves either obediently or rebelliously in terms of that address to constitute their own gendered and erotic subjectivities. I am interested in the hermeneutic dynamics among sets of representations understood as addressing specific sex/gender or sex/erotic constituencies and the social identity *as* variously female/male, queer/non-queer that is constructed by means of such representations.

In particular, I am interested in the 'gay man', the 'lesbian', the 'heterosexual woman' and the 'heterosexual man' constructed by two specific sets of representational practice; HIV/AIDS health promotional material and telephone sex-line advertisements. I am interested in these sets of textual practices (rather than in pop videos, television soaps or fashion advertising) because they foreground specific issues which speak to current anxieties about gender/sex and erotic/sex. Sociologists often suggest that 'sexuality has . . . taken over many of the meaning-making functions of religion in modernity' (Luckmann, cited in Mellor and Shilling, 1993, p. 422), and certainly the erotic/sexual has been a privileged site of enquiry for both feminism and queer. Both HIV/AIDS health promotion and telephone sex-line ads address their reader *as sexual*, thus explicitly and overtly (if not always self-consciously) constructing a sexualized reading position in relation to which any reader must negotiate her own position.

This in itself should alert us to the inadequacies of any theoretical position which fails to take account of, or make sense of, the body, whether as erotic site or not. For sex/erotic and sex/gender meanings are mapped onto bodies, and, as Mellor and Shilling remind us, the body is integral to the postmodern project of constructing a stable sense of self:

With the decline of the religious frameworks which constructed and sustained existential and ontological certainties residing outside the individual, and the massive rise of the body in consumer culture as a bearer of symbolic value . . . there has been a tendency for people to place more importance on the body as constitutive of self. (Mellor and Shilling, 1993, p. 413)

Mellor and Shilling are concerned with the social sequestration of death, and especially with their insight that 'the presence of death appears especially disturbing in this context of reflexively constructed self-narratives which have at their centre a concern with the body' (p. 413). Death, although it is the inevitable end of all people, and hence may be understood as perhaps the only experience that partakes of an 'essential' humanity, is not something that currently concerns us all equally. Rather, living as we do in the time of AIDS, death is clearly regaining for the gay community (at least in the industrialized West) precisely that *social* significance that Mellor and Shilling claim it now lacks. Both HIV/AIDS health promotional material and telephone sex-line ads make explicit the strategies – variously of acceptance and denial, of incorporation and abjection – which different groups employ to survive the threat of AIDS[4] and of HIV, a potentially lethal virus.

Part of the significance of AIDS lies precisely in the seamlessness with which AIDS discourse stitches together questions of sex/gender and sex/erotics with the theoretically impervious corpo/realties of bodily disintegration and death. The heteropatriarchal elite has co-opted the perceived epidemiology of the pandemic as both reflection of and justification for its paranoid masculinist agenda whereby the feminine – seen as the shameful free-floating passivity/ penetrability of the thereby-gendered erotic body – is both fatal (the ultimate feminine passivity is in surrender to death) and potentially contaminating to an otherwise resistant (immune) masculinity. The meta-narrative of this queer-hostile discourse is precisely the fiction of genital identity: a sex/erotic, sex/gendered self that depends upon and is marked by its obedience or otherwise to the functionalist imperative of its genitals.

So, although I wholeheartedly agree with Butler that 'cross-gendered identification is not the exemplary paradigm for thinking about homosexuality' (Butler, 1994, p. 250) – it is clear by now that gender identification is not adequate for thinking about sexuality at all – this does not render anachronistic my interest in exposing the discursive/textual interstices between gender/sex and erotic/sex. Butler herself insists that the opposite is the case:

Precisely because homophobia often operates through the attribution
of a damaged, failed, or otherwise abjected gender to homosexuals,
that is, calling gay men 'feminine' or calling lesbians 'masculine',
and because the homophobic terror over performing homosexual acts,
where it exists, is often also a terror over losing proper gender ('no
longer being a real or proper man' or 'no longer being a real or
proper woman') it seems crucial to retain a theoretical apparatus
that will account for how sexuality is regulated through the policing
and shaming of gender. (Butler, 1993, p. 27)

I would add that the co-dependency of gender and sexuality within the
heteropolar paradigm requires that we also account for how *gender* is
regulated through the policing and shaming of *sexuality*. Such accounts
were, of course, developed long ago by radical feminists working on
issues such as the sexual harassment of girls and women and the lynching
of black men (Davis, 1982; Wise and Stanley, 1987; Jones and Mahony,
1989; Lees, 1993).

It is precisely because my two chosen iconographical lexica foreground sexualities-as-gendered that I am interested in deconstructing
their codifying regimes. In addition, a comparative evaluation of health
promotion (which has a self-consciously ethical objective) and sex-
line ads (which have an equally self-conscious transgressive objective)
may clarify the complex intersections of hegemonic and oppositional
group positions and discursive interpellations on sexuality-as-gendered.
Eve Kosofsky Sedgwick writes that she would:

like the concept of performativity to prove useful in some way for
understanding the obliquities among *meaning*, *being*, and *doing*, not
only around the examples of drag performace and (its derivative?)
gendered self-presentation, but equally for such complex speech-acts
as coming out, for work around AIDS and other grave identity-
implicating illnesses. (Sedgwick, 1993, p. 2)

I understand the text-sets that I am looking at here to partake of
performativity, in both gender/sex and erotic/sex senses, in that they
both come from and contribute to (variously reflexive) performance
praxes. They enunciate a whole range of anxieties, celebrations, repressions and rebellions, and in doing so they make intelligible the
self-narratives of the reader. This intelligibility does not come solely
from a reading position obedient to the address of the text, but just as
powerfully from disobedient positions. Thus, a gay man reading a text

addressed to a gay reader takes it as addressed to him, and hence is able not only to read the text, but to read *himself as gay*, and to negotiate his thesaurus of gayness in response to the meaning he makes of the text. Were he to read a text addressed to a non-gay reader, the intelligibility of the text may be compromized by his position of exteriority with regard to the codes and signs, but his own intelligibility of himself would be reinforced by his recognition that, as a reader, he is positioned *somewhere else*, and that he differs in specific ways from the assumed readership.

Butler notes that 'the subject only comes into intelligibility through the matrix of gender' (Butler, 1993, p. 22). In this, gender/sex has a more fundamental significance than erotic/sex. It is hardly the case that the subject only comes into intelligibility through the matrix of sexual orientation. Rather, we tend to see sexual orientation as something mapped onto pregiven genders. What is clear, however, is that heterosexual masculinity may well depend for its socio-cultural and psychological stability precisely on its declared non-gay status. Jonathan Dollimore reminds us that 'homophobia is often integral to a conventional kind of masculine identity' and, further, follows the trace of abject homosexual desire in homophobia, whose 'disgust always bears the imprint of desire' (Dollimore, 1991, p. 235). Heterosexual masculine gender identity depends upon a negative, upon being *not-gay*, and is generated by means of an ongoing process of disavowal which is inevitably painful, as Dollimore recognizes. He speaks of 'the classification of heterosexuality as the norm with homosexuality as its perverse other, and the splitting, displacements, and paranoia which accompany that division' (Dollimore, 1991, p. 233). Evidence of such splits, displacements and paranoia must be looked for in texts expressive of heterosexuality, especially of heterosexual masculinity.

THE CAMP AND THE NOT-SO-CAMP: THE LIMITS OF APPROPRIATION

My final concern is with camp. Safer-sex promotional materials targeted at gay men reveal an unprecedented leakage of queer/camp codes and signs from the margins to the mainstream, from the queer ghetto to central government agencies such as the Health Education Authority. Although such leakage is fairly common and widely recognized in entertainment (Dyer, 1992; Drewal, 1994), it is perhaps startling in health promotion.

My suggestion is that both safer-sex material and the ads for sex-lines reveal quite different anxieties around gender/sex and erotic/sex depending on their address to differently gendered sexual readers, and that this difference, although it divides along erotic/sexual lines into gay/not gay, remains located on the 'male' side of the gender/sexual divide. One consequence of this is that lesbians, while they have a presence as fetish on the non-gay side of the erotic/sex divide, are almost utterly invisible on the gay side. 'The lesbian' has no social existence, no discursive 'reality' outwith the psycho-functionalism of non-gay male fetish.

Camp is crucial to understanding the processes at work in these two sets of texts. Queer theorists have effectively challenged Susan Sontag's interpretation of camp as an essentially apolitical sensibility long as-similated into mainstream culture. Writers such as Cynthia Morrill in-sist on both the queerness and the political nature of camp:

> Camp discourse is the epiphenomenon of the queer subject's pro-scription in the dominant order; it is an effect of homophobia. . . . Camp results from the uncanny experience of looking into a nonreflective mirror and falling outisde of the essentialized on-tology of heterosexuality, a queer experience indeed.   (Morrill, 1994, p. 119)

Morrill's suggestion is that, denied access to the machinery of represen-tation (like women), gay male communities evolved camp as both queer signifying practice, a lexicography of the margin, and queer critique of the hegemonic. Jack Babuscio identifies in camp 'a heightened awareness of certain human complications of feeling that spring from the fact of social oppression' (cited in Kleinhans, 1994, p. 187), while Richard Dyer suggests that it 'holds together qualities that are else-where felt as antithetical: theatricality and authenticity . . . intensity and irony, a fierce assertion of extreme feeling with a deprecating sense of its absurdity' (cited in Kleinhans, 1994, p. 185). It is difficult for example to appreciate or even to understand the marvellous draw-ings of Tom of Finland without recognizing, as Chuck Kleinhans does, that 'Camp is an ironic and parodic appreciation of an extravagant form that is out of proportion to its content, especially when that con-tent is banal or trivial' (Kleinhans, 1994, p. 186).

The conflict between banality and extravagance is intrinsic both to sexual desire and romantic love. What is experienced by the subject as overwhelming, potentially anihilating, is at the same time pathetically commonplace, merely humdrum. Writers before and since Shakespeare have recognized that this conflict may be both tragic and comic, but it is a conflict which is peculiarly nuanced for queers. What is experienced as both overwhelming *and* mundane within the queer milieu is also discursively constituted as spectacularly dangerous and terrifying within the mainstream. A kiss may be just a kiss, but if it may also land you in jail, lose you your job or frighten the horses it becomes something else, an 'extravagant form that is out of proportion to its content'. The phallus, too, is just such a disproportionate extravagance of form, so indeed is gender itself. Camp, for all its shortcomings, makes use of this recognition to speak out against the cacophony of heterosexuality, a speaking out that incorporates a distinctive critique of gender. Kleinhans suggests that:

> Camp originates in the gay male perception that gender is, if not quite arbitrary, certainly not biologically determined or natural, but rather that gender is socially constructed, artificial and performed (and thus open to being consciously deformed). (Kleinhans, 1994, p. 188)

In both gay male sex-line ads and safer sex material addressed to gay men, camp enables a celebration of gay male desire and pleasure in the teeth of homophobia and the epidemic. Of course the eroticism is overstated, but that is intrinsic to materials which must bear the burden of igniting desire in the steady drizzle of heterosexual hegemony.

A quick glance at Tom of Finland's work will make clear how radical the disruptions of gender may be within the camp paradigm (see Plate 1). Commentators have argued that the importance of Tom's work to the gay community lies in the excessive masculinity of his representations of gay men, at a time when gay men had little with which to challenge the elision of homosexuality and effeminacy. Yet the drawings go further than mere celebration and parody of masculinity. Fetishized breasts, signifying sexually available femininity within the heteropolar paradigm, here grow on extravagantly hyper-masculinized torsos (see Plate 2). An icon of a nursing mother, perhaps a Victorian Caritas or a Monika Sjoo mother goddess, is here grotesquely virile, both masculine and feminine to excess.

If we look closely at sex-line ads we pick up on another characteristic which is unique to gay male culture. These ads are exclusive (see Plate 3), they have a dedicated address, constructing an hermetic semiotic universe which discursively mimics – and is almost certainly rooted in – the legislative fiat of privacy. In those rare instances where there is a lesbian presence it is dismissively de-sexualized. There is no Thomasina of Finland (see Plate 4).

In utter contrast, sex-line ads addressed to non-lesbian women reveal a quite remarkable lack of dedication. Their sexual constituency boundaries leak, appearing permeable and vague, constructing a 'heterosexual woman' that seems to incorporate both gay male and lesbian desires (see Plate 5). This is perhaps unsurprising, since the producers of these materials tend to be men, whose ignorance about female sexuality is legendary, but I suggest this is only part of the story.

Sex-line ads addressed to heterosexual men demonstrate a marked degree of heterosexual anxiety, revealing in their over-determined reductiveness a glaringly obvious anxiety to control female sexuality. Gay male ads feature black and white drawings of extravagantly sexualized gym bunnies, often accompanied by detailed 'shopping lists' of specific sexual activities (SM, water sports, spanking, fisting, etc). The delectable male flesh on offer is open to simultaneous consumption as both subject and object of the desiring male gaze.

Non-gay male ads, in contrast, depend on full colour photographs of female models in a somewhat farcical sequence of lordosis poses, eyes half shut and mouths half open in panting expectation of the lordly penis (see Plate 6). The accompanying text insists on the *reality* of the sexual experience to be gained from ringing the lines. Punters are assured that the girls at the other end of the phone will be *really* masturbating as they talk, that a recording of two women *really* 'doing it' will be played over the phonelines. The dissolving of subject into object is intolerable, because the subject/object binary is a unidirectional gender polarity in heterosexuality. So 'gay man' is resolutely absent from this paranoid vernacular.

'Woman' is here discursively constituted as sexual object. So deep-rooted is this construct that it seems impossible to imagine what the desires of a woman might consist of. Because the heteropolar model constitutes sexual agency as phallic, female sexual agency vanishes away into an erotic vagueness that might be lesbian, might be gay male, but cannot be comprehensible or representable within pre-existing semiotic codes unless it is for the phallus. 'Lesbian' is present only as reassuring male fetish, coded as a hyperabundance of female parts for male enjoyment (not one but two sets of enormous boobs, not one but two 'grinding pussies'). Jucy Lucy and Randy Mandy (see Plate 7) exist in order to reassure the paranoid phallic heteromale that what they *really* want is a mouthful of bedpost. The sexuality presented in these texts is what Irigary calls *hommosexuality*, a sexuality entirely produced and managed by and in the interests of men, whether its object of choice happens to be male or female.

This, I suggest, is why gay men have been able to develop camp as an oppositional discourse while women have not: because the privileged gender 'man' deflects to a significant extent the execrated (and concealable) sexuality 'gay'. Gay men may not have access to the machinery of representation qua 'gay', they certainly have qua 'men'. The mirror of culture may not reflect 'gay', it *does* reflect 'man'. It is the lesbian who, vampire-like, must look in vain for her reflection in that mirror, unseeable by reason of the gender that makes her desire impossible. Camp is not a product of *lack* of access, but of *compromised* access to that machinery.

If we turn our attention to safer-sex promotional material, a further dimension becomes visible. Material addressed to gay men constitutes 'gay man' as sexual and, moreover, as recreationally sexual. Rich, vivid, varied, this insistent oppositional semiotic obliterates 'gay man' as the sign signifying AIDS, disfigurement and death, and re-presents gay male sex as the eros that signifies health, beauty and life (see Plate 8). In utter contrast is the material addressed to women. Sexless, redolent of death and of responsibility, these materials construct 'woman' as devoid of desire, offended by pleasure, innocent of sexual agency (see Plate 9). As paradigmatic subject and agent, heterosexual man is seldom *overtly* addressed as at-risk from sexual transmission of HIV. His sexuality remains unproblematized, ungazed-upon, unobjectified. This is, truly, not the spectacular gender.

STRAIGHT AND NARROW

Both ethical and transgressive texts demonstrate an unquestioning obedience to heteropolarity. The heteropolar paradigm remorselessly genders sexualities and sexualizes gender. Its intellectual inadequacy, its paranoid fragility and its ruthless fundamentalism lie in its constitution of 'proper' identities as determined by genital functionalism. It is the fundamentalist doctrine of genital identity that mandates the subordination of women to men, queer to straight through the policing and shaming of sex/gender and sex/erotic behaviours. It also, within the textual interventions of safer sex promotion, constitutes women as powerless to prevent the sexual transmission of HIV (Wilton, 1992).

It is within the nebulous postmodern excesses of queer that resistance to genital fundamentalism can now most easily develop. Roland Barthes imagined homosexuali*ties* 'whose plural will baffle and constituted, centred discourse' (cited in Dollimore, 1991, p. 330). I would add, as one who espouses a queer feminist position, that we need to imagine a plurality of *genders* and to fracture the co-dependent heterobinarism of gender and sexuality. Jonathan Dollimore suggests that 'far from being an endorsement of discrimination, an excess of difference would disarticulate its very terms' (Dollimore, 1991, p. 330).

The transvaluation of gendered and erotic body-meanings demands that we shift focus from the textual and discursive body and develop a radically new sociology of the text-transgressive (rather than text-transcendent) body. Pain, ageing, sickness, reproduction and death mark the body not so much as time-bound but rather as a *function* of time and of change. Refusing the reductionist naivety of genital functionalism should not seduce us into failing to take account of corporeality. After all, it is by 'bodying queer' that the fictions of genital identity are exposed and transgressed.

Although it behoves us to recognize that transgressivity is not in and of itself necessarily radical (something which I think queer activism sometimes loses sight of), transgressive reinscriptions of (multiple, permeable) genders and of (multiple, shifting) sexualities onto and by perverse and disobedient *bodies* (not merely screens or pages) are the necessary strategy whereby we may discredit the ontological doctrine of heterobinarism.

ACKNOWLEDGEMENTS

I would like to thank Lisa Adkins for her useful and insightful comments on an earlier draft of this paper.

NOTES

1. The lesbian and gay liberation movement that sprang up in the industrialized West in the late 1960s did not, of course, call itself 'queer'. The word 'queer' has been adopted, as an anti-oppressive, anti-assimilationist self-naming strategy by a particular generation of lesbian, gay, bisexual and transgenderal activists, and also refers to a specific theoretical arena within the academy. I am using it here partly to signal my own involvement

in that theoretical arena, partly to align myself with the 'in your face' anti-assimilationism of the activists (although I disagree with much of the queer-activist position on gender), and partly because it is easier and quicker than the alternatives.

2. *Berdache* is a word coined by French colonists to describe Native American men who lived as women, a role sanctioned spiritually and socially in some tribal cultures (though not all). The *kotoi* are Thai male sex workers who are transvestite and often use hormones in order to develop breasts. Most are not castrated, and their gender ambiguity makes sense within Thai culture, so it is possible to make only a partial and inadequate comparison with the Western notion of gender dysphoria or transsexuality. *Muskobanja* refers to a woman of some Balkan tribal communities who takes on the role of male head of the family on the death of her father where there are no suitable male substitutes, and 'passing women' are women in European culture (though there have been examples in postcolonial North America) who, for various economic or erotic motives, passed as men.

3. It is significant that, as far as feminist writers are concerned, men are not permitted to escape their gender by being gay in the way that women may escape their gender by being lesbian. An oppressor is always an oppressor.

4. I am using AIDS here to refer to the social and cultural phenomenon which is the epidemic and all the prejudices, disavowals, repressions, oppressions and incorporations which have coalesced around it. When referring to the medical phenomenon rather than the medico-social, I use HIV/AIDS or more specific terminology.

REFERENCES

Bordo, S. (1990), 'Feminism, Postmodernism and Gender-Scepticism', in L. Nicholson (ed.), *Feminism/Postmodernism* (London: Routledge).

Bremer, J. (ed.) (1991), *From Sappho to De Sade: Moments in the History of Sexuality* (London: Routledge).

Brodribb, S. (1992), *Nothing Mat(t)ers: A Feminist Critique of Postmodernism* (Melbourne: Spinifex).

Butler, J. (1990), *Gender Trouble: Feminism and the Subversion of Identity* (London: Routledge).

Butler, J. (1993), 'Critically Queer', *GLQ: A Journal of Lesbian and Gay Studies*, 1: 1, pp. 17–33.

Davis, A. (1981), *Women, Race & Class* (London: Women's Press).

D'Emilio, J. and Freedman, E. (1988), *Intimate Matters: A History of Sexuality in America* (New York: Harper & Row).

Dollimore, J. (1991), *Sexual Dissidence: Augustine to Wilde, Freud to Foucault* (Oxford: Oxford University Press).

Drewal, M. T. (1994), 'The Camp Trace in Corporate America: Liberace and the Rockettes at Radio City Music Hall', in M. Meyer (ed.), *The Politics and Poetics of Camp* (London: Routledge).

Duberman, M. B., Vicinus M. and Chauncey, G., Jr (eds) (1989), *Hidden From History: Reclaiming the Gay and Lesbian Past* (Harmondsworth: Penguin).

Dyer, R. (1992), *Only Entertainment* (London: Routledge).

Frank, A. (1991), 'For a Sociology of the Body: an Analytic Review', in M. Featherstone, M. Hepworth and B. Turner (eds), *The Body: Social Process, Cultural Theory* (London: Sage).

Game, A. (1991), *Undoing the Social: Towards a Deconstructive Sociology* (London: Open University Press).

Garber, M. (1992), *Vested Interests: Cross-dressing and Cultural Anxiety* (Harmondsworth: Penguin).

Jeffreys, S. (1990), *Anticlimax: A Feminist Perspective on the Sexual Revolution* (London: The Women's Press).

Jones, C. and Mahony, P. (1989), *Learning Our Lines: Sexuality and Social Control in Education* (London: Women's Press).

Kleinhans, C. (1994), 'Taking out the Trash: Camp and the Politics of Parody', in M. Meyer (ed.), *The Politics and Poetics of Camp* (London: Routledge).

Lees, S. (1993), *Sugar and Spice: Sexuality and Adolescent Girls* (Harmondsworth: Penguin).

Mandziuk, R. (1993), 'Feminist Politics and Postmodern Seductions: Madonna and the Struggle for Political Articulation', in C. Scwichtenberg (ed.), *The Madonna Connection: Representational Politics, Subcultural Identities and Cultural Theory* (San Francisco, CA: Westview Press).

McIntosh, M. (1981), 'The Homosexual Role', in K. Plummer (ed.), *The Making of the Modern Homosexual* (London: Hutchinson).

Mellor, P. A. and Shilling, C. (1993), 'Modernity, Self-identity and the Sequestration of Death', *Sociology*, **27**: 3, pp. 411–31.

Morrill, C. (1994), 'Revamping the Gay Sensibility: Queer Camp and *Dyke Noir*', in M. Meyer (ed.), *The Politics and Poetics of Camp* (London: Routledge).

Plummer, K. (1981), 'Building a Sociology of Homosexuality' in K. Plummer (ed.), *The Making of the Modern Homosexual* (London: Hutchinson).

Rubin, G. (1984), 'Thinking Sex: Notes for a Radical Theory of the Politics of Sexuality', in C. Vance (ed.), *Pleasure and Danger: Exploring Female Sexuality* (London: Pandora).

Sedgwick, E. K. (1993), 'Queer Performativity: Henry James's *The Art of the Novel*', *GLQ: A Journal of Lesbian and Gay Studies*, **1**: 1, pp. 1–16.

Smyth, C. (1992), *Lesbian Talk Queer Notions* (London: Scarlet Press).

Stein, E. (1992), 'The Essentials of Constructionism and the Construction of Essentialism', in E. Stein (ed.), *Forms of Desire: Sexual Orientation and the Social Constructionist Controversy* (London: Routledge).

Turner, B. (1991), 'Recent Developments in the Theory of the Body', in M. Featherstone, M. Hepworth and B. Turner (eds), *The Body: Social Process and Cultural Theory* (London: Sage).

Vance, C. (1989), 'Social Construction Theory: Problems in the History of Sexuality', in D. Altman *et al.* (eds), *Which Homosexuality? Essays from the International Scientific Conference on Lesbian and Gay Studies* (London: Gay Men's Press).

Weeks, J. (1985), *Sexuality and its Discontents* (London: Routledge).

Wilton, T. (1992), 'Desire and the Politics of Representation: Issues for Lesbians and Heterosexual Women', in H. Hinds, A. Phoenix and J. Stacey (eds), *Working Out: New Directions for Women's Studies* (London: Falmer Press).

Wise, S. and Stanley, L. (1987), *Georgie Porgie: Sexual Harassment in Everyday Life* (London: Pandora).

Vicinus, M. (1989), '"They Wonder to Which Sex I Belong": The Historical Roots of the Modern Lesbian Identity', in D. Altman *et al.* (eds), *Which Homosexuality? Essays from the International Scientific Conference on Lesbian and Gay Studies* (London: Gay Men's Press).

Zita, J. (1992), 'The Male Lesbian and the Post-modernist Body', in C. Card (ed.), *Hypatia: A Journal of Feminist Philosophy Special Issue: Lesbian Philosophy*, 7: 4, pp. 106–27.

6 Irish Masculinities and Sexualities in England

Máirtín Mac an Ghaill

INTRODUCTION

This chapter explores the complex interplay between sexuality, ethnicity and masculinity. The main focus is the self-representation of young gay Irish men's sex/gender formations in England. There is a particular concern with the diverse range of sexual identities that they come to inhabit. Key cultural sites include the experience of recent immigration, including the pervasive influence of the Prevention of Terrorism Act (PTA), their over-representation in specific labour markets, the support of extended family/kinship networks, and their involvement in church and pub/leisure activities. At the same time, the young men offer a critical account of hegemonic English masculinity.

Currently, there is a theoretical concern with the interrelationships between different forms of social oppressions. This is still a largely under-theorized area, while at the same time there is little empirical work available to map out how these interrelationships are lived out within local cultural arenas (see McCarthy, 1990; Anthias and Yuval-Davis, 1992). This study brings together an examination of external social relations and internal psychic relations, providing a fresh perspective on the complex interconnections of different sets of power relations in the production of sex/gender subjectivities. As a white ethnic minority, young Irish men occupy a unique social location in which to explore the complexities, ambivalences and contradictions of contemporary forms of sexuality. On the one hand, they are ascribed masculine privileges as White men. On the other hand, as a subordinated masculinity, they experience a constant surveillance in public arenas, with their accent as a key signifier of social identification and cultural difference. I set out to go beyond a hierarchy of oppressions approach, emphasizing the multi-layered connectedness between different social categories. More specifically, I did not wish to privilege either anti-Irish racism or homophobia as the primary explanatory variable in these young immigrant gay men's experiences in England. Nevertheless, there were unexpected outcomes from the original research design.[1]

When I began the study on which this chapter is based, I intended to examine, from a phenomenological perspective, how young Irish men's experiences of living in England helped to produce a range of masculine subject positions that as White, sexual immigrants they came to inhabit. My original starting point was influenced by the need to gain a specific focus in researching the area of sexuality that with its complex interconnections is notoriously elusive and fluid. But a shift in my understanding of the research problem arose in interviewing the research participants. Focusing on their perspectives on the meanings and purposes of living in England, as young gay immigrants, I came to focus on a different question around the issue of Irish ethnicity, class cultural identity and nationalism in relation to the construction of masculine sexual politics (see Parker *et al.*, 1992). This is a complex story that is tentatively explored here.

METHODOLOGICAL ISSUES: INSIDER KNOWLEDGE AND ANTI-IRISH RACISM

The study was carried out from an insider position within a specific ethnic group. A number of writers have noted the advantages of researching a social group as a member of it. Less has been reported on the methodological difficulties that may arise from taking an epistemological stance that lays claim to 'insider knowledge' of a social group.[2] First, there are difficulties around the ethics of disclosure, in terms of making decisions about what to explore, what to report and what to keep silent about on Irish immigrants' lives to an English audience. It is equally dangerous, in locating the study in a conceptual framework that critically explores the complexity of anti-Irish racism, to adopt a reductionist approach that represents Irish experiences simply in terms of what English cultural imperialism *has done* and continues *to do* to the Irish, with specific reference to the military and political occupation of Northern Ireland. This is of particular salience at a time when race-relations theorists, much of the media and many English local authorities converge in an alliance of denial of anti-Irish racism.[3] Finally, in carrying out this research, I found that while I consciously attempted to emphasize the diversity of Irish immigrants' experiences, there were internal pressures within the study that shifted it in the opposite direction. A key constraint here was the fact that at times some of the research participants made claims to an ethnic absolutism.

This is a real tension in a study that works within a grounded methodological framework. However, it needs to be added that it is currently fashionable for progressive theorists to be highly critical of what they call 'essentialist identities', without giving sufficient consideration to the experience of oppressed social groups: that the construction of collective identities may act as an important political mobilizing force at specific historical moments.

All these tensions remained throughout the study and raise the issue of how academics represent research participants' accounts without claiming, as an 'expert insider', to *really know* the whole picture in contrast to the participants' incomplete, contingent part truths (Clifford and Marcus, 1986). I would agree with Evans (1992, p. 245), who has written of the need to rethink how we represent and describe research participants and how we conceptualize their thinking and subjectivity. He suggests that:

> This would involve some experimental writing; searching for different ways of describing the complexity, the multidimentionality, the organisation and disorder, the uncertainty and incongruities of the social worlds that we and others inhabit. It would also mean resisting the temptation to produce texts which contain 'flat' rather than 'rounded' characters.   (Evans, 1992, p. 245)

As for all social groups, the experiences of the Irish in England are heterogeneous and not reducible to specific social categories. The study involved a particular group of young gay men who had a Catholic, Southern Irish background. I originally met two of the research participants, Feargal and Robin, at an Irish conference in London. We quickly developed a close friendship, partly based upon our common regional origins in County Clare. There were many shared reference points with regards to our extended family and kinship networks. As our friendship developed, Feargal and Robin spoke of the absence of gay and lesbian perspectives among the Irish in England, as was highlighted in the different Irish social arenas that we visited. During the following two years, 1992–4, they introduced me to other Irish gay men, who in turn introduced me to their gay friends. This resulted in individual and group informal interviews taking place in a wide variety of settings and circumstances with 32 Irish gay men, aged between 16 and 27, all of whom were situated within London.

ENGLISH REPRESENTATIONS OF THE IRISH – A CRITIQUE OF ANGLO-ETHNIC MASCULINITY

As a result of 'taking' rather than 'making' research problems, English social scientists have tended to accept official state discourses of 'race' and ethnicity. Within this shared 'commonsense' framework, African Caribbeans and Asians have become the exclusive focus of 'race-relations' research, albeit providing caricatured representations of both groups. This reductionist conceptualization of racism to colour racism, serves to deny the existence of anti-Irish racism. In this process, England's largest immigrant group – the Irish – are made culturally invisible. In turn, English critical theorists' representations of racism serve to reinforce the categorization of racism in terms of a 'common-sense' dichotomy of 'Black victims' and 'White perpetrators', which they claim themselves to oppose (see Frankenberg, 1993; Bonnett, 1993).[4]

For example, in much 'race-relations' literature, the term ethnicity is employed as a politically neutral category, while serving as a racially coded euphemism for selected 'Black' communities with the English-born 'second generation', arbitrarily and contradictorily assigned the same immigrant status as their parents (Anthias and Yuval-Davis, 1992). These academic representations involve processes of converting fundamental political and moral questions into technical and administrative problems (Gramsci, 1971). In contrast to the Asian and black communities, the cultural attributes of the Irish are unproblematically of little interest or concern to multicultural or antiracist theorists and policymakers. As Jackson (1963) informs us, historically the cultural attributes of the Irish were of significance in England throughout the nineteenth and early twentieth centuries, when they were officially perceived as a subordinate 'race' (Miles, 1993). While more recently, Irish community workers and academics have been active in seeking to establish within local education authorities, the legitimacy of the Irish as an ethnic minority with specific needs. Equally important they have brought together a wide range of empirical evidence of the institutional and personal discrimination, around issues of work, health, education and welfare rights that the Irish experience in England (Hickman, 1986; Hazelkorn, 1990; Greenslade, 1992; Gribben, 1994). However, at present we have not developed theoretical frameworks that would enable us to analyse systematically and document coherently the material, social and discursive production of anti-Irish racism and Irish ethnic identity.

In response to the denial by English academics and policy-makers of anti-racism, there is a danger for the Irish of adopting limited defensive strategies. First, as is the case in many antiracist narratives that juxtapose a simple moral binary of immigrant 'goodies' and English 'baddies', there is a danger of adopting a 'roots approach' that serves to romanticize the Irish experience in England. At the same time there is also a danger in a critical account of making an appeal to the 'Irish community' on the basis of their shared experience of English racism and of subsuming differentiated experiences around gender, sexuality, age, geographical location, and 'first' and 'second' generation.

This is the background against which the research participants recalled their experiences of life in England. Most significantly, they shared a bewilderment about the current disinterest of English people in the Irish.[5]

> SEAN: One thing about the English is that they all know how to fix the situation in the North or they say its impossible to resolve. But I've never met one who really wanted to know what's going on. They know more about Bosnia or South Africa than Ireland.

> TONY: Its really confusing why English people aren't interested in us. Its funny because as soon as they hear your accent, they treat you as if you're a thick foreigner. But we seem to be the only foreigners who English people, even the liberal ones, feel they don't have to take serious how we're discriminated against.

In recent work (Mac an Ghaill, 1994) on the development of masculine subjectivities, I have explored the need to hold on to the tension between materialist, deconstructionist and psychoanalytic explanations of the interplay between racism, homophobia and ethnic/sexual identity formation.

In the first, racism and homophobia are viewed as a matrix of power relations, highlighted in the pervasiveness of state racial and sexual surveillance and regulation. As indicated below, some of these materialist concerns are clear in the young men's accounts. Although the young men are recent immigrants, they bring with them an acute awareness of dominant English representations of the Irish as an ethnically and sexually inferior 'race'. Most significantly, they point to the significance of the war in Northern Ireland as serving to maintain the English positioning of the Irish as the traditional colonial folk devils, with the accompanying negative categorization, typification and moral evaluation. Here, the emphasis is on England's cultural imperial domination of Ireland as an overarching explanation for the relations between the two countries; in short a narrative of 'nothing but the same old story' (Miles, 1982; Curtis, 1984; Cohen, 1988).

BRENDAN: The main way the English see us is as navvies. They always have and always will. Its the idea that they have the brains and we're just full of muscles. Its just common knowledge among Irish people that the English think they are superior to us.

JAMES: In the nineteenth century the English saw us as stupid, drunken Irish navvies and not much has changed. Its much the same now and of course we are all bomb-throwers and mad religious fundamentalists.

SEAN: I think to the English, we are seen as breeding like rabbits, because of our large families. Then again, they think we are religious nutcases because we are brought up not to believe in abortion or contraception. Probably, in sexual ways we are seen by the English as the most alien of all the immigrants here.

The research participants spoke of how anti-Irish racism and homophobia affected their lives when they described their own experiences of the State criminalization of the Irish and gay men. They linked the Prevention of Terrorism Act (PTA), Section 28 and the discriminatory age of consent for gays as attempts by the English state to enforce and codify a way of life. That is, these coercive legislative instruments of control are seen as being primarily concerned with prescribing and proscribing how people should live their lives. As they point out, of specific importance is that this current discriminatory legislation, as a contemporary form of control, involves imposing the self-policing of ethnic and sexual identities. At the same time, the young men provide an interesting contrast between the Catholic Church's religious instruments of sexual control that circumscribed their childhoods, and their more recent experience of the sexually repressive functions of the modern, secular state in England.[6]

SEAN: Well, it would take an Irish gay to see it, but the PTA threat, Section 28 and outlawing gay sex for young guys are all linked aren't they?

M. M.: In what ways?

SEAN: We're in the worst of all worlds aren't we? Like if a bomb goes off in London, you would be afraid that someone will hear your accent and attack you for being in the IRA. And it's the same with Section 28 and the age of consent for gays; you have to keep your head down all the time. It makes me think of in the North (of Ireland), the control is obvious, with the Catholics being threatened with the army. But it's worse in some ways here. You are forced to live with all this fear. It's brilliant from the English point of view, we end up policing ourselves.

CONNOR: Everytime you come off the boat and the police stop you (under the PTA), you think, do they know I'm gay. Remember the last time we came back? I thought they'll get me for being gay and say it's because I'm a terrorist. You always live with that extra fear, you know what I mean?

TONY: At home (in Ireland) we go on all the time about how awful the Catholic Church is to gays. All that shit about sin and going to hell if you play with your willy; and then there's a special place in hell, further down, if you play with other boys' willies. Then you come to England and you see that even if you get rid of religion, they have all these laws to persecute you.

In contrast to materialist accounts, deconstructionist theorists have emphasized that the living of ethnic and sexual categories and divisions is more contradictory, fragmented, shifting and ambivalent than the dominant public definitions of these categories suggest. The notion of discourse and discursive practices are of central importance here.[7] As Epstein (1993) makes clear in her recent study:

> We are positioned in various discourses as well as taking up positions ourselves. For example, we identify ourselves as heterosexual, lesbian or gay and could not do so if categorising discourses of sexuality did not exist. In this limited sense, we can be said to be 'produced' by discourses and discursive practices.   (p. 10)

Of particular interest here are the ways in which social relations and the accompanying discourses around gender, sexuality, class, 'race' and ethnicity combine and interact in contingent circumstances. As indicated below, the young Irish men in this study recalled similar experiences to those recorded in my earlier work where I found that particular social relations of 'race' simultaneously 'speak' gender and sexuality: to be a 'Paki' is also to be a 'poof', is to be a 'non-proper' boy' (Mac an Ghaill, 1994b).

> NOEL: If you go round the Irish conferences over here, everyone is going on about how we have been oppressed since the famine, as though stereotypes don't change. And its all about negative stereotypes of the English hating us. I don't agree. Its much more complex.

> MICHAEL: Yes, I would agree with that. Its easy to become paranoid about being Irish over here or being gay. Yes, sometimes there's a lot of bad pressure on you. But at other times English people will come up to you and be positive towards you. And its the same with being gay. Everyone, every straight person, is not against you. Like a lot of my family and some of my friends were very supportive when I first came out. I have some straight women friends who like me because I'm gay. So, prejudice and stereotypes are more complex, like Noel says. It really depends upon the situation, who you're with and whether they're sorted out themselves. So, sometimes you can relax and you don't have to think of yourself as just Irish or gay. You're also a friend or a work colleague or whatever in the particular circumstances.

A major limitation of much theoretical and empirical work on majority–minority relations in materialist and deconstructionist accounts has been a failure to incorporate critical social psychological and psychoanalytic perspectives (see Henriques, 1984; Cohen, 1987; Weedon, 1987; Greenslade, 1992; Nava, 1992; Davies, 1993). Anti-Irish racism and homophobia cannot be reductively conceptualized in terms of a simple binary social system, composed of a juxtaposed English straight superiority and Irish gay inferiority. The relations between the English and these young men involve a psychic structure, including such elements as: desire, attraction, repression, transference and projection in relation to a racialised 'sexual other' (Pajaczkowska and Young, 1992). In other words, there is a need to bring together social structures and inner dramas. Rutherford (1990) drawing on the work of Derrida, decribes the inner logic of the psychic relations of domination. He writes:

Binarism operates in the same way as splitting and projection: the centre expels its anxieties, contradictions and irrationalities onto the subordinate term, filling it with the antithesis of its own identity; the Other, in its very alienness, simply mirrors and represents what is deeply familiar to the centre, but projected outside of itself. It is in these processes and representations of marginality that violence, antagonisms and aversions that are at the core of the dominant discourses and identities become manifest – racism, homophobia, misogyny and class comtempt are the products of this frontier.   (p. 22)

There is much work to be done in this area in order to understand the ambivalent structure of feeling and desire embedded within different cultural sites (Fanon, 1970; Baldwin, in Troupe, 1989; Hollway, 1989). In the following accounts, the young Irish men discuss the range of split responses that were manifested in the interplay between racial fear and desire and the accompanying contradictory elements of repulsion, fascination and envy. Implicit in their accounts of life in England is the suggestion that ethnicity, sexuality and class can be seen as crucial points of intersection of different forms of power, desire and identity formation.

NOEL: At university I did a project on it [the English stereotyping of the Irish] and it really surprised me. Yes, the negative stereotypes hang on, the Irish drunk and the bomb thrower. And there is a lot of fear around these images. And it's true that they are projecting their fears onto us because any non-English person will tell you that in fact the English are a very violent people. They have been all round the world and they are today here. Just compare England's and Ireland's football teams. But this is mixed up with images of English people wishing they could be more like the Irish. Like they would talk about being on holiday in Ireland and that the Irish were the most hospitable people in the world. And again you can see that they are projecting things onto us. But you have to get away from the idea of simple stereotypes.

HUGH: I agree. There's too much emphasis on the negative stereotypes of the Irish. If you get to know English people, they would love to be like us or how they imagine us to be.

M. M.: Like what?

HUGH: They think we have a better outlook on life, more laid back and that we can enjoy ourselves more. I think they really envy the fact that we've held onto our culture, when they see theirs is disappearing. I think they envy the fact they are living in an old country and that we are a young one. What I'm saying is that you need to update how you see the English stereotypes of the Irish. And that means, yes, the negative ones are there but like Noel says these are mixed up with their deeper feelings that we have a better life than them.

ROBIN: Its funny when you think of straights. Because at one level everyone will say , oh they hate us for been poofters, benders and all that; but its more than that; its deeper.

M. M.: What do you mean?

ROBIN: Its like straight guys will always say that when they're after women, they're only interested in the chase. And that is really interesting, isn't it? Because what they are saying is that the sex bit is not important, which it is of course, but like all the straight women will tell you their blokes are hopeless in bed. Now the straight guys have this idea that gays are having sex all the time and they don't have to bother with all this chasing. So, I kind of think that when straights are putting the boot into gays, it's not only the fantasised anal sex that is the problem, but any sex. I really think that they are so confused and repressed about sex, and its really obvious with English straights, that in a mixed up way they wish they could be like us, or how they think we are. They wish they had our freedom and the fact that we can enjoy sex.

Furthermore, as the gay men pointed out at a time of crisis in dominant public forms of heterosexual arrangements, they as a sexual minority are forced to carry the burden of the sexual majority's sense of moral disorder (Dollimore, 1991).

FEARGAL: Like straights see us as all as fucked up. But they forget we come from straight families, we've been brought up in a straight world. And we know that its them that are fucked up. All the marriages breaking up, all the abuse, with kids telling the truth about their fathers. So what do they do? They blame us. We're the AIDS carriers, the perverts. They really need us, otherwise they would have to face up to the fact that their own lives are in deep trouble.

Most interestingly, the research participants contextualized the specificities of their highly contradictory immigrant masculine identity, emphasising how dominant English responses combine internal doubt and external anxiety that are projected onto them. At the same time, they discuss the implications of Irish gay men being able to 'switch' between ethnic and sexual minority/majority boundaries. In so doing, they serve to highlight, from the different perspectives of majority/minority cultural positions, the political investments in the maintenance of fixed collective identity boundaries, with the accompanying policing mechanisms.

CONNOR: You see the English are probably very confused about us. We're like them because we're White. It's easier to see Blacks as inferior immigrants. But then again they know we're different because we are still immigrants. The English are confused because they are supposed to be the ones with the brains and then we come along and show we are just as clever as them. And the pressure of this is really experienced by Irish professionals over here.

M. M.: In what ways?

CONNOR: I think any outsiders in a society are used emotionally, with all the bits that the insiders can't cope with thrown upon them. It's just like women are used by men. And I think it's probably more difficult if the women appear to be strong or don't fit into the role they're supposed to take. Well it's the same with Irish professional men, we don't fit into the usual stereotypes of Irish immigrants. So, I guess if you don't fulfil the insiders' emotional needs, there's a lot of conflict.

MICHAEL: You see Irish gay men are in a unique situation. As White immigrants you can switch from being Irish to people at least assuming you're English, in a way that Black people couldn't. And its the same with being an Irish gay in England. There are differences between Irish and English gays, and especially if you don't have a camp style, there can be situations when you can act straight, perhaps more easily than an English gay.

M. M.: And what do you think about that?

MICHAEL: Well, it's good in a way. It helps you to survive. But I think there's a lot of hostility from those who can't do that. Like straights will go mad if they find out that you're definitely not one way or the other, as they say over here. Even if you're not, you have to play the game, old man, and act it out. And my friends here [Irish gays] would say we shouldn't do it, but be proud of our own identity. I understand that. Switching from being gay to straight could be dangerous to other gays, with all the pressures that we are under. But in some ways I feel I'm personally being controlled at times. I think you can experiment a bit without it being a big defensive thing of being ashamed of who you are. And it's really difficult because we want to say to straights: we're as worked out as you are. But the other side of that is that we are probably as mixed up as well. Well, maybe not *as* mixed up!

There is a danger in examining minority–majority relations of un-intendedly reproducing images of fixed homogeneous groups. The young gay men suggest the importance of going beyond these false dichot-omies and examining the differences within subordinate and dominant groups. They provide another layer of the complex interplay between Irish ethnicity and heterosexual boundary maintenance. I have argued elsewhere that hegemonic modes of heterosexual subjectivity are con-stituted by cultural elements which consist of contradictory forms of compulsory heterosexuality, misogyny and homophobia. These are marked by contextual ambivalence and contingency (Mac an Ghaill, 1994). Of particular significance is the complex interplay of these cultural ele-ments as institutionally specific forms of gendered and sexual power operationalized to be key defining processes in sexual boundary main-tenance, policing and legitimization of male heterosexual identities. What emerges as of particular salience is the way in which heterosexual young men are involved in a double relationship: of disparaging the 'other', including women and gays (external relations), at the same time as expelling femininity and homosexuality from within themselves (internal relations). There is insufficient space here to provide a com-prehensive account of how these complex and contradictory processes are lived out, in relation to the dominant ethnic group among young Irish heterosexuals in England. However, the following quotation from Brendan provides evidence of the complexity within a minority com-munity in which ethnic boundary maintenance can be used to police dominant heterosexual boundaries.

BRENDAN: When I came out to some Irish guys over here, they just said I was becoming like the English. They just see homosexuality as unnatural. And that sort of thing happens here because the English have no religion or any proper family life.

FINTAN: It's Irish straights' way of controlling you, keeping you straight. It's like the way we export our abortions over here. We have this image of ourselves as if we're non-sexual and the English are seen as being obsessed with sex, with their tabloids and all that. So, if you come out as gay, it's like you're going through a phase. For Irish people, it's presented as an English phase you're going through. I swear that's true.

These young men, as economic immigrants, point to the need to locate current English sexual and racial politics in the present English socio-economic decline. An unexamined element of this decline is the crisis in Anglo-ethnicity and its interconnections with the construction of dominant English masculine identities. In other words, there is a need to shift the focus of academic inquiry to include English men as the ethnic majority alongside that of ethnic minorities.

The research participants made clear that a key aspect of immigrant life – the development of survival and coping strategies – is adopting a quasi-anthropological stance: observing the 'native majority'. In contrast to the English lack of interest in the Irish, the Irish know a lot about the English. These young men, as sexual immigrants, are particularly aware of the dominant institutional sex/gender regimes.

TONY: There are real differences between Irish and English men. The English have a real problem with being tough all the time and proving themselves. Like, if an Irish guy bumps into someone, he'll say sorry and walk on. But with English guys, especially the younger ones, if they bump into you, it's an excuse for a fight. Obviously, I don't mean all English guys, though the problem is you can't tell which ones will act this way. A lot of young English guys are very aggressive, very conscious of themselves. And there's this big territory thing they have. They've lost their empire, so they have to try and protect something to boost their egos. It's frightening. They have this big 'gang' thing, of attacking people if they think they're weaker than them. They keep on having to prove they're men.

SEAN: It's like what we were saying the other day. England is finished, and countries that are down aren't generous, especially to outsiders.

KEVIN: I think it's particularly difficult for English people. Remember their symbol is the bulldog. They have ruled the world and now they are just another little country. They are suffering shock. The Irish have always been an easy target as 'thick Micks'.

BRIAN: Well, English men have this superiority thing. You see it at work all the time. There's the lower class men who express it by being very aggressive. For middle-class English men it's expressed in different ways.

M. M.: Like what?

BRIAN: The way they have to put you down all the time. They are really competitive with each other. Like, if you did a good piece of work, they couldn't say, 'That's grand'. It's as if they lose something by you being successful. They have to boast about themselves, all the time. I think they express their superiority trying to be extra rational. It's this obsessive behaviour, like they can't show weakness by being emotional. They're incredibly stiff. You can see their repression in their whole body.

IRISH MASCULINITIES, ETHNICITY, CLASS AND NATIONALISM

As suggested above, the interconnections and interrelations between different forms of oppression are currently a major theoretical concern. While examining the social positioning of young Irish gay men in England, these interconnections and interrelations emerged in an unexpectedly specific form. In the absence of theoretical and empirical work on Irish masculinity, I examined the academic literature on Black masculinity. As Mercer and Julien (1988) have pointed out:

Whereas prevailing definitions of masculinity imply power, control and authority, these attributes have been historically denied to black men since slavery. The centrally dominant role of the white male slave-master in 18th and 19th century plantation society debarred black males from the patriarchal privileges ascribed to the male masculine role. ... Shaped by this history, black masculinity is a highly contradictory formation as it is a subordinated masculinity. (p. 112)

Young Irish gay men in this study reported that similar sex/gender dynamics of subordination operated in relation to them. However, the processes involved tend to be more covert, due to the contradictory subject positions that are made available to Irish immigrant men as white Europeans (Anthias and Yuval-Davis, 1992). Among the research participants, working-class young men provided accounts of the institutional marginalization they experience in England. They emphasized their employment experiences, which are located within low paid service-sector jobs and a rapidly declining construction industry, as part of the wider processes of deindustrialization currently taking place. The labour market is a key site for Irish working-class men, since work provides a primary immigrant identity. However, in response to structural discrimination in their workplaces which denies them the privileges ascribed to English masculinity, they appear not to have adopted predictable sex/gendered forms of contestation or resistance. Rather, their response was translated and lived out in terms of an increased sense of difference around their ethnic identity. Irishness, as a unifying fiction, appeared to operate as a collective strategy that served to contest their lack of masculine power in English public arenas. It was played out and developed in unofficially segregated subordinated work places that often had an Irish majority workforce; and separated settlement patterns that included over-representation in low status multiply-occupied residences and hostels. At the same time, their sense of social dislocation and institutional masculine subordination was eased within the cultural spaces provided by Irish pubs, clubs and leisure arenas, such as Gaelic games.

> BRENDAN: The main reason people have come over is to find work. Okay, for us it was also our sexuality; but also work. Your whole life when you arrive here is geared around work; where you live, the pubs you go to, the club, everything really. Even at Mass, you would meet up with the lads from work and go off from there.

> KEVIN: When you come over, even though you might have a trade, you know you'll probably end up doing the labouring jobs. There's

a lot who've come over with me as chippies [carpenters] and brickies [bricklayers] and they're still just labouring. It's always been like that for the Irish. But if you didn't work you'd be fucked, wouldn't you. You may as well be home.

M. M.: Even if it's bad work?

KEVIN: The only really bad work is no work. You get really bad money, you're treated like shit and the work is desperate, but at least you're among your own.

M. M.: Why is that important?

KEVIN: Well, like you are going to be looked down upon here. After all your training, this is low work. But at least you can relax more if you are with your own. If you work with a lot of English, they just treat you like you're a stupid Paddy, with all their fucking stupid jokes. And the thing is you're the skilled one and they are the real labourers.

SEAN: I came over mainly to get away, so I could be myself more, in a sexual way. But nearly as soon as I got here, it was completely different to what I expected. You think you're Irish in Ireland, but it's only when you get over here that you realize what it really means. My family at home aren't strongly nationalist, but anyone living over here sees what the English are really like. You're different, so you have to stay together.

M. M.: And what about being gay over here?

SEAN: I don't know really. I would say to other Irish gays coming from the country [in Ireland], go to Dublin or Galway rather than come over here. Then again there's no work. But on the gay scene here you're still a 'thick paddy'. So, how can you be yourself? So in the end you have to choose. You can't come out with the Irish you work with, but you're totally on your own on the English gay scene.

One reading of these young men's responses to their masculine subordination, which I initially shared, is to assume that ethnic belonging is more important than sex/gender relations as an explanatory variable of how these young men construct their lives. An alternative reading is to see Irish ethnicity, and for them its accompanying nationalism, as a form of sexual politics which has specific implications for the construction of Irish masculinities. As Enloe (1989) has argued:

> many of the nationalisms that have rearranged the pattern of world politics over the last two centuries have been patriarchal nationalisms. They have presumed that all the forces marginalizing or oppressing women have been generated by the dynamics of colonialism or neo-colonialism, and hence that the pre-colonial society was one in which women enjoyed security and autonomy. Thus simply restoring the nation's independence will ensure women's liberation. . . . Repeatedly male nationalist organizers have elevated unity of the community to such political primacy that any questioning of relations between women and men inside the movement could be labelled as divisive, even treacherous. (p. 62)

The masculinity of Irish nationalist politics is displayed by a wide range of cultural signifiers, including the pervasive playing of the national anthem at public gatherings and the obligatory response in terms of a military-style stance; the high visability of the Irish flag, the tricolour, within the Irish community in England; the consumption of traditional Irish music, recalling the sacrifices of male Irish heroes; the celebration of male literary figures; and, more recently, the celebration of the ubiquitous Irish soccer team, albeit managed by an Englishman. Most significantly, the militarization around the armed struggle, encapsulated in the Irish Republic's national anthem, (translated as *The Soldier's Song*) serves symbolically to maintain a public collective consciousness of what it means to be a man. In turn, this historical legacy is a central element that informs the production of specific masculine subjectivities among young Irish men. It should be noted that this version of Irish nationalist politics may be read as adopting a rather atavistic stance. Nevertheless, it is also a potentially powerful political mobilizing force in a nation for whom a 'normal' mode of citizenship is that of immigrant status.

In exploring how the research participants' come to inhabit a range of masculine subject positions, it is necessary to examine sexual politics in Ireland. In the above male fantasy narrative, women tend to be written out.[8] However, this is not to suggest that women do not contest this marginalization and exclusion. For example, there has been a

rapid growth of Irish women's groups which have been very successful in publicly challenging the highly prescriptive sexual politics of
the Irish state and the Catholic Church. Irish society has changed rapidly in the last thirty years; but what is under-reported is that feminism has been one of the major social forces in bringing about this
change. It is well established that a fundamental economic contradiction in Irish society is that it projects a modern European urban identity while having the key defining characteristics of a developing economy,
such as high levels of structural unemployment, mass emigration and
a high national debt (Smyth, 1993). The working-class young men in
this study felt that this contradiction was lived out most overtly by
those who emigrate.

In contrast to public awareness of the economic situation, the contradictions of Ireland's sexual politics are less commented upon. For
example, there is a long history of state and Catholic church discrimination against women and gays, while at the same time there has recently been progressive legislation on gay rights (Rose, 1994; O'Loughlin,
1994). Most recently, these contradictions around sexual politics have
been played out in the contrasting responses in Ireland and England to
the sexual lives of public figures (Keane, 1994).[9]

CLASS CULTURAL AFFILIATIONS

It is against this background that I explored the young Irish gay men's
accounts of their subordinated masculine status in England. My primary conceptual framework was to locate how they made sense of
their lives within the constraints of anti-Irish racism and homophobia.
Unexpectedly, diverse class cultural affiliations among the young Irish
men emerged as a key variable in their explanations of the development of their sex/gender subjectivities. This serves to illustrate the
contextual contingency of identity formation, located within the interconnections between social and psychic relations.

The significance of class cultural affiliations was made explicit in
the young Irish middle-class gays' accounts of life in England. In contrast to the working-class young men's sexual identity that can be seen
to coalesce around nationality, middle-class Irish young gay men's
experiences as sexual immigrants appeared to take a more expected
form. For example, although the latter were critical of the English gay
scene, they claimed that they 'felt at home' there. The anti-Irish racism

that they experienced among English gay men was less of a problem for them than the homophobia of the Irish community in England. In the following accounts they develop their explanations of the diverse class cultural affilations of recent Irish sexual immigrants and the range of masculine subject positions that are made available to them. Most significantly, they point to their involvement in the English gay scene as part of a broader contemporary identity politics based on middle-class values and lifestyle. In contrast, it is suggested, working-class gays may identify more easily with Irish Republican politics in England based on traditional working-class values of community and collectivism.

FINTAN: I'd say it's easier for us middle-class Irish to fit into the gay scene here. You see, even though you get others on the scene, it's definitely a middle-class atmosphere. A lot of working-class Irish wouldn't be able to cope, so they might end up staying with their own, where they feel comfortable.

FEARGAL: When the working-class guys were talking the other night, they had this big anti-English thing about being discriminated against. And I'm not saying it doesn't exist. But I agree with Fintan. What they're really talking about is differences in class, I mean in different life-styles.

M. M.: Like what?

FEARGAL: Just about everything. Middle-class people have basic different values, different expectations, of what they want out of life.

M. M.: So would you feel closer to English gay people than Irish straight people?

FEARGAL: You can't put it as simple as that. You couldn't live your life like that. Like you would get on with your family and friends at home. But one thing the guys didn't comment upon the other night was the homophobia among the Irish. And, yes, I would feel I could be more myself with any gay people than all the pressure of the straight world, whether in Ireland or here.

CONCLUSION

In exploring the complex interplay between sexuality, ethnicity and masculinity, I found the study very difficult to carry out. The under-theorized social position of Irish immigrants in England adds to the difficulty of making sense of these young men's lives. Nevertheless, their accounts find a resonance in Rutherford's (1990) suggestion, that we are currently:

> caught between the the decline of the old political identifications and the new identities that are in the process of becoming or yet to be born. Like Laurie Anderson's 'urbanscape' in her song 'Big Science' the imagery traces of the future are in the present, but as yet have no representation or substance.   (p. 23)

As is suggested above, the Irish immigrant experience has its own trajectory, with a specific incorporation of the Irish into the English state, specific labour and housing locations, and specific experience of the state and civil society, including immigration, the courts and the police. At the same time, the Irish have developed their own forms of accommodation, contestation and resistance. These latter strategies are exemplified most graphically in the long campaigns, such as the Birmingham Six and the Guildford Four, as part of the wider contestation of state processes in the criminalisation of the Irish community.

In short, the Irish are in search of counter-discourses that are not simply derivative of discourses of anti-Black racism. At the same time it is important to stress the internal divisions, around social relations of class, gender and sexuality, within the 'Irish community' in England (Anthias and Yuval-Davis, 1993).

This chapter suggests that in order to develop a critical comprehensive explanatory framework, these counter-discourses need to draw upon materialist, deconstructionist and psychoanalytic accounts of the interplay between racism, homophobia and ethnic/sexual identity formation. At the same time it suggests the critical importance in exploring Irish masculinities of acknowledging the complexities of social and psychic relations and the interrelationship between them. The young gay men in this study may provide some of the clues to move forward theoretically and politically.

ACKNOWLEDGEMENTS

A special thanks to the young men, who collaborated in the production of this study. The paper has benefited from the comments of Mairead Dunne, Chris Haywood and Iestyn Williams, and conference organisers' detailed reading.

NOTES

1. As I have noted elsewhere (Mac an Ghaill, 1989), qualitative methodology is relatively autonomous from wider interrelated theoretical and substantive issues, and the dialectical relationship between these research elements is highly productive.
2. Such epistemological issues have been debated within feminist methodology, see for example, Ramazanoglu (1989).
3. There are notable exceptions to this trend, such as Phil Cohen and Robert Miles who write of the range of historical and contemporary forms of racisms. See also Conner (1985), Curtis (1985), Hickman (1986), (1993), Hazelborn (1990), Brah (1992) and Rattansi (1992).
4. See Frankenberg's (1993) study of the social construction of whiteness. Her study is premised on the idea that white people as well as people of colour are racialized.
5. All names of participants have been changed to maintain confidentiality.
6. See Connell and Dowsett (1992, pp. 50–1) on religious/cultural nativism.
7. Discourse refers to the specialized and common-sense regulated systems of meaning through which we make sense of the world, which are constructed in and through particular practices, which make available social identities or subject positions, and which simultaneously entail relations of power (Foucault, 1977; Redman, 1994).
8. Interestingly, Irish women have outnumbered men as immigrants in England.
9. An Irish junior minister, who was linked to a 'gay scandal', received positive support from the media and the wider public, enabling him to hold onto political office.

REFERENCES

Anthias, F. and Yuval-Davies, N. (with Cain, H.) (1993), *Racialized Boundaries: Race, Nation, Gender, Colour and Class and the Anti-racist Struggle.* (London: Routledge).

Bonnett, A. (1993), *Radicalism, Anti-Racism and Representation* (London: Routledge).

Byrne, C. and Rayment, T. (1993), 'Irish Desert Britain for 'Good Life' Overseas', *The Sunday Times*, 21 November, p. 7.

Clifford, J. and Marcus, G. (eds) (1986), *Writing Culture: The Poetics and Politics of Ethnography* (Berkeley, CA: University of California Press).

Cohen, P. (1987), *Racism and Popular Culture: A Cultural Studies Approach*, Working Paper no. 9, Centre for Multicultural Education (London: Institute of Education).

Cohen, P. (1988), 'The Perversions of Inheritance', in P. Cohen and H. S. Bains (eds) *Multi-Racist Britain* (London: Macmillan).

Connell, R. W. and Dowsett, G. W. (1992), '"The Unclean Motion of the Generative Parts": Frameworks on Western Thought on Sexuality', in R. W. Connell and G. W. Dowsett (eds), *Rethinking Sex: Social Theory and Sexuality Research* (London: Melbourne University Press).

Curtis, L. (1984), *Nothing But the Same Old Story: The Roots of Anti-Irish Racism* (London: Information on Ireland).

Davies, B. (1993), *Shards of Glass: Children Reading and Writing Beyond Gendered Identities* (St Leonards, NSW: Allen and Unwin).

Dollimore, J. (1991), *Sexual Dissidence: Augustine to Wilde, Freud to Foucault* (Oxford: Clarendon Press).

Enloe, C. (1989), *Bananas, Beaches and Bases: Making Feminist Sense of International Politics* (London: Pandora).

Epstein, D. (1993), *Changing Classroom Cultures: Anti-racism, Politics and Schools* (Stoke-on-Trent: Trentham Books).

Evans, J. (1992), 'A Short Paper about People, Power and Educational Reform. Authority and Representation in Ethnographic Research. Subjectivity, Ideology and Educational Reform: The Case of Physical Education', in A. C. Sparkes (ed.), *Research in Physical Education and Sport* (London: Falmer Press).

Fanon, F. (1970), *Black Skin, White Masks* (London: Paladin).

Frankenberg, R. (1993), *White Women, Race Matters: The Social Construction of Whiteness* (London: Routledge).

Foucault, M. (1977), *The History of Sexuality*, vol. 1 (Harmondsworth: Penguin).

Greenslade, L. (1992), 'White Skins, White Masks: Psychological Distress and the Irish in Britain', in P. O'Sullivan (ed.), *The Irish in New Communities* (Leicester: Leicester University Press).

Gribben, P. (1994), 'Discrimination Study at Last', *The Irish Post*, 29 January, p. 1.

Hall, S. (1990), 'Cultural Identity and Diaspora', in J. Rutherford (ed.), *Identity: Community, Culture and Difference* (London: Lawrence & Wishart).

Hazelkorn, E. (1990), *Irish Immigrants Today: A Socio-Economic Profile of Contemporary Irish Emigrants and Immigrants in the UK*, Irish Studies Centre Occasional Paper series No. 1 (London: Polytechnic of North London Press).

Henriques, J. (1984), 'Social Psychology and the Politics of Racism', in J. Henriques, W. Hollway, C. Urwin, C. Venn and V. Walkerdine (eds), *Changing the Subject: Psychology, Social Regulation and Subjectivity* (London: Methuen).

Hickman, M. J. (ed.) (1986), *The History of the Irish in Britain: A Bibliography* (London: Irish in London History Centre).

Hollway, W. (1989), *Subjectivity and Method in Psychology: Gender, Meaning and Science* (London: Sage).

Jackson, J. A. (1963), *The Irish in Britain* (London: Routledge and Kegan Paul).

Johnson, R. (1992), 'Radical Education and the New Right', in A. Rattansi and D. Reeder (eds), *Rethinking Radical Education: Essays in Honour of Brian Simon* (London: Lawrence & Wishart).

Keane, F. (1994), 'The Public Pain of Emmet Stagg', *The Sunday Tribune*, 13 March, pp. A12–13.

Mac an Ghaill, M. (1989), 'Beyond the White Norm: The Use of Qualitative Methods in the Study of Black Youths' Schooling in England', *Qualitative Studies in Education*, **2**: 3, pp. 175–89.

Mac an Ghaill, M. (1994), *The Making of Men: Masculinities, Sexualities and Schooling* (Buckingham: Open University Press).

Mac an Ghaill, M. (1994a), '(In)visibility: Sexuality, Race and Masculinity in the School Context', in D. Epstein (ed.), *Challenging Lesbian and Gay Inequalities in Education* (Buckingham: Open University Press).

Mac an Ghaill, M. (1994b), 'The Making of Black Masculinities', in H. Brod and M. Kaufman (eds), *Theorizing Masculinities* (London: Sage).

McCarthy, C. (1990), *Race and Curriculum* (Lewes: Falmer Press).

Mercer, K. and Julien, I. (1988), 'Race, Sexual Politics and Black Masculinity: A Dossier', in J. Rutherford and R. Chapmen (eds), *Male Order: Unwrapping Masculinity* (London: Lawrence & Wishart).

Miles, R. (1993), *Racism after 'Race Relations'* (London: Routledge).

Miles, R. (1982), *Racism and Migrant Labour* (London: Routledge).

Nava, M. (1992), *Changing Cultures: Feminism, Youth and Consumerism* (London: Sage).

O'Loughlin, E. (1994), 'Cruising as Part of Culture', *The Irish Times*, 11 March, p. 8.

Parker, A., Russo, M., Sommer, D. and Yeager, P. (1992), *Nationalisms and Sexualities* (London: Routledge).

Pajaczkowska, C. and Young, L. (1992), 'Racism, Representation and Psychoanalysis', in J. Donald and A. Rattansi (eds), *'Race', Culture and Difference* (Milon Keynes: Sage/Open University Press), pp. 11–48.

Ramazanaglu, C. (1989), *Feminism and the Contradictions of Oppression* (London: Routledge).

Redman, P. (1994), 'Shifting Ground: Rethinking Sexuality Education', in D. Epstein (ed.), *Challenging Gay and Lesbian Inequalities in Education* (Buckingham: Open University Press).

Rose, K. (1994), 'Moving Hearts and Changing Minds: Lifting a Burden from Gay Men', *The Irish Reporter*, **14**: pp. 16–26.

Rutherford, J. (1990), 'A Place called Home: Identity and the Cultural Politics of Difference', in J. Rutherford (ed.), *Identity: Community, Culture and Difference* (London: Lawrence & Wishart).

Smyth, J. (1993), 'Nationalist Nightmares and Postmodernist Utopias: Irish Society in Transition', *History of Education Ideas*, **16**: 1–3, pp. 157–63.

Troupe, Q. (1989), *James Baldwin: The Legacy* (New York: Simon & Schuster/Touchstone).

Weedon, C. (1987), *Feminist Practice and Post-Structuralist Theory* (Oxford: Blackwell).

Weeks, J. (1986), *Sexuality* (London: Norwood and Tavistock).

Westwood, S. (1990), Racism, Black Masculinity and the Politics of Space', in J. Hearn and D. Morgan (eds), *Men, Masculinities and Social Theory* (London: Unwin Hyman).

7 Beyond the Predatory Male: The Diversity of Young Glaswegian Men's Discourses to Describe Heterosexual Relationships

Daniel Wight

INTRODUCTION

The literature on sexual relationships has expanded rapidly in recent years as a result of different interests. Public health concern with HIV has prompted much empirical research, but this was predated by more sociological work on gender, heterosexuality and homosexuality. More recently, writing on the emotions has built on feminist analyses of relationships, and has developed largely independently of HIV-related research.

There are now extensive survey data on young people's sexual behaviour which allow comparisons between groups in the general population (e.g. HEA, 1990; Ford, 1991; West *et al.*, 1993; Johnson *et al.*, 1994). However, there is little detailed information on specific groups that allows analysis of the variations existing within them, apart from studies of certain people particularly vulnerable to HIV. Such analysis of variation seems important if we are to get a better understanding of the factors that shape young people's sexual behaviour.

This paper focuses upon variation in the sexual behaviour of young men from working-class homes, and more specifically on the various discourses they used to talk about sexual relationships. Hollway's study of heterosexual relationships (1984) has been particularly influential in this analysis. It is in her sense that the term 'discourse' will be used, to mean a cohesive set of written or spoken ideas that are shared socially but not necessarily held in their entirety by any one individual. These ideas seem to promote particular kinds of behaviour, although the extent to which discourses and practice actually match up is a theme I will return to at the end of the chapter.

Emotions within intimate relationships, rather than in occupational contexts, have of late become a respectable subject of sociological enquiry (e.g. Jackson, 1993; Duncombe and Marsden, 1993), with perhaps the most ambitious attempt to theorize sexual relationships in late modern society being Giddens' *The Transformation of Intimacy* (1992). In this book three kinds of love are distinguished: the fairly universal passionate love, the romantic love that emerged with industrialization and 'confluent love' which is peculiar to late modern society. Confluent love depends on mutual intimacy and is the basis of the 'pure relationship', one that is self-consciously contingent on both parties finding it rewarding. The separation of sexual activity from reproductive and kinship functions in the twentieth century allowed the emergence of 'plastic sexuality' which is at the heart of pure relationships.

Giddens draws on an eclectic range of evidence, largely from North America, and he implicitly acknowledges how large his generalizations are. The extent to which relationships in Britain are actually transforming to his ideal type, rather than merely have the potential to do so, is not addressed. Preliminary findings from a study of interrelationships between the emotions and economic aspects of couples' lives (Duncombe and Marsden, 1993) suggest that an enormous imbalance still exists in the gender division of 'emotion work'. However, women's dissatisfaction with this asymmetry, and their demands for emotional reciprocity, suggest they share something of Giddens' ideal of a 'pure relationship'. Nevertheless, the recent literature on emotions tends to rely on data from middle-class people in their 30s or older; its relevance to the experiences of young people from working-class homes has received little attention.

One of the only other qualitative studies in Britain specifically of young men's heterosexual beliefs and behaviour is the 'Men, Risk and AIDS Project' (Holland *et al.*, 1993). This interprets data from a largely self-selected sample of forty-six 16–21-year-old men in London from a feminist perspective, and it has usefully informed my analysis. In their initial paper, Holland *et al.* analyse the various ways in which young men deal with their first experience of sexual intercourse. Both these authors and Hollway emphasize the often predatory character of male sexuality, described as arising from the 'dominant or hegemonic masculinity' (Holland *et al.*, 1993). In this chapter I aim to build on their analyses, but will argue that more diverse concepts of masculine sexuality exist, even within a sample that is fairly homogeneous in terms of age, locality, parents' social class, housing and sexual orientation (cf. Morgan, 1992).

One of the most striking things to come out of my study was the diversity of sexual experience that young men reported at the age of 19, in terms, for instance, of number of partners and length of relationships. This is all the more remarkable given the homogeneity of their family backgrounds. The variation in sexual histories can be understood as resulting from three main factors, all of which are interrelated:

(1) how the men positioned themselves within different discourses relating to sexuality;
(2) their confidence in initiating physical relationships; and
(3) the behaviour of their potential or actual partners.

It is the relationship between sexual behaviour and discourses around sex that is the subject of this chapter.

METHODS

In order to study the social context of sexuality the research was based in one specific locality, an area on the edge of Glasgow broadly similar to the city's other peripheral council housing estates. The population is predominantly manual working-class and overwhelmingly White. A sample of fifty-eight 19-year-old men were recruited by sub-sampling from a longitudinal cohort study of health and wellbeing, the 'West of Scotland Twenty-07 Study'. Largely due to survey loyalty a response rate of 85 per cent was achieved.[1]

Respondents were interviewed by myself (a male, married heterosexual) for two to three hours about their leisure activities, friendships, how they learnt about sex, their sexual histories and, finally, the salience of HIV in their lives. The primary focus on HIV-related risk *behaviour* meant that, regrettably, detailed information was not systematically sought on associated but broader issues of heterosexuality. Nearly all respondents chose to be interviewed in their homes rather than in the local health centre, community centre or my office; the vast majority still lived with their parents.

It has to be stressed that the data presented here come from young men's *accounts* of their behaviour in a single interview, and they provide only partial information on the way discourses relate to practice. It is difficult to establish whether the discourse used in the interview to describe particular behaviour was the same as that through which the behaviour was understood at the time. More fundamental, however, is the difficulty in clarifying whether the discourse within which someone located himself prompted certain actions or whether, having acted in a particular way, the person adopted a particular discourse through which to interpret those actions. The following analysis can therefore only be tentative.

The term 'sexual intercourse' will generally refer to penetrative vaginal intercourse, which is how respondents understood it (Wight, 1994a), and 'sexual relationships' will refer to relationships in which sexual intercourse occurred.

HETEROSEXUAL ACTIVITY AND RELATIONSHIPS

The sexual histories of the respondents varied considerably. Some men reported no sexual partners by the age of 19 while others reported over twenty, and some men's sexual relationships consisted entirely of one-night stands while others' were exclusively long-term. Between these poles there was considerable diversity.

Of the fifty-eight young men interviewed, four reported not having had sexual intercourse with anyone of either sex. One of these four described his homosexual orientation. Another respondent's account of his sexual history was so implausible I have assumed it was entirely fabricated. For the other fifty-three respondents age at first heterosexual intercourse ranged from 12 to 19, the median and modal age being 16. There was a predictable positive association between early sexual activity and number of sexual partners. The modal number of partners was one, three-fifths of the total sample reported less than four partners, while the maximum reported was about thirty.

However, in order to gauge the extent of these young men's sexual experience, it is important to note that in half of the sexual relationships described, sexual intercourse only occurred once. Only half the respondents reported that they had ever had more than one partner with whom they had had sex more than once, which supports Giddens' characterization of men's sexuality as episodic (Giddens, 1992). Both American and British surveys have documented this low frequency of intercourse amongst teenagers, both in absolute terms (West *et al.*, 1993; Johnson *et al.*, 1994) and in relation to adults (Zabin and Haywood, 1993), but it is often overlooked due to the focus of both public health officials and moralists on age at first intercourse and number of partners.

1. Tom of Finland (1963).

2. Tom of Finland (1986).

3. Advertisements from *Gay Times* (June 1993).

4. Advertisements from *The Pink Paper* (1989).

5. Phone lines for women: *Women Only* (1992).

6. Phone lines for men: *Knave* (1992).

7. 'Lesbians' from phone advertisements for men: *Knave* (1992).

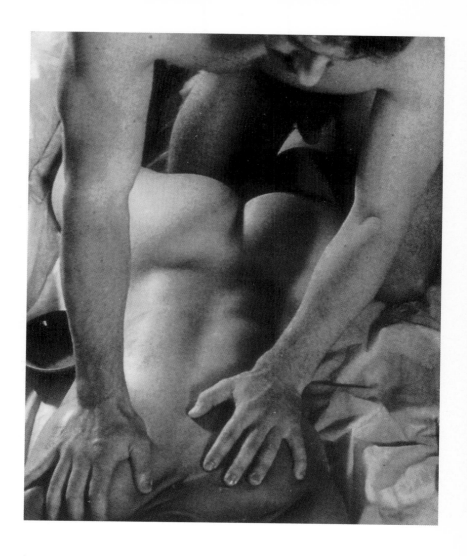

8. From a safer-sex leaflet produced by the New Zealand AIDS Foundation (n.d.).

9. Cover of leaflet produced by San Francisco AIDS Foundation and San Francisco Department of Public Health Jail Medical Services (n.d.).

As these figures suggest, many of the young men's sexual relationships were short-lived: about half lasted less than a fortnight. A third of the men had never had a sexual relationship that lasted more than six months. While six of these men only reported one sexual partner, similar numbers reported three or more.

Amongst the two-thirds who had had a sexual relationship lasting at least six months there was an even greater range in reported number of partners. It is possible, however, to characterize their sexual histories as in general moving from short-term relationships to long-term ones. There are two main elements of diversity in this general pattern: the relationships were not always sexual, and the respondents were at different stages in this career by the age of 19.

At the time of the interview a third of the whole sample were in relationships that had lasted more than a year, six of them in relationships lasting more than three years. Three were engaged to be married, two were married and six had children.

PEER GROUPS

In order to explore how these young men's sexual careers were shaped, my initial approach was to see how they were associated with four interrelated factors: family composition, occupational history, income and peer groups. With this small sample it was only possible to discern a relationship between sexual histories and the young men's peer groups.

To investigate this it is useful to contrast two polar ideal types of peer group that began to emerge around the age of 12 or 13: those who expected to stay on at school after 16 to do 'O' Grades and Highers, and those involved in local gangs, who would leave at 16 and rejected their education (akin to Willis's (1977) 'lads'). Around this age there would have been considerable agreement in the sample about who belonged to these groups, the former being referred to as '*bright guys*' and the latter being referred to by others as '*neds*' (a Glasgow term for hooligan). It is important to stress that only about a dozen of the 58 respondents were in each of these peer groups, the others having far less clearly identifiable peers, and there was movement in and out of friendship groups which meant the boys were subjected to varying influences through their teens.

The 'bright guys' tended to coalesce in friendship groups before the age of 16 and, in contrast to most of the other young men, their friends were not entirely male. Once in the sixth forms they became further integrated with their female counterparts. Most 'bright guys' left school after taking Highers, but some before that. The former went into higher education and most of the others into apprenticeships or, in one case, a junior manager's job in a large store. They lost touch with most of their school friends within a few months of leaving, but, by and large, their new friendship groups still included young women.

I have defined gang members as those who had been actively involved in gang fights, mainly in local territorial gangs but for a few with Rangers or Celtic football fans as well. In their last years at school they were, typically, also using illicit drugs (mainly cannabis and solvents), drinking, and truanting. These activities, however, were for many a stage in a particular life course. As they grew older, which for many coincided with developing long-term relationships with girlfriends, their fighting and intense drug use had modified. On leaving school those involved in gangs went in and out of Youth Training Schemes, unskilled employment and unemployment, and most developed new friendship groups. However, there was more continuity between their friends pre- and post-leaving school than with other peer groups, and their friends were more likely to come from the local area. These friends, other than sexual partners, were almost entirely male. Over half of this group were unemployed at the age of 19.

The 'bright guys' fit Morgan's characterization of Protestant masculinity (1992). Their sense of internal control had been most fully developed, illustrated by their commitment to their careers and their self-concept as responsible people, both to themselves and, in the future, to others. Gang members, on the other hand, approximated to the stereotype of *machismo* masculinity, concerned with externally, communally determined criteria of honour and shame which often revolved around control over women (Morgan, 1992, p. 64). Notions of masculine honour frequently featured in the gang members' accounts of their lives, usually in relation to fighting or women, and they were also generally keen to gamble, the antithesis of sober Protestant control.

There was a distinct contrast between the reported age at first intercourse of those involved in gangs (14 or 15) and the 'bright guys' (between 16 and 18), but there was no obvious link between peer group and reported number of partners or length of relationships. There was, however, a clear association between the young men's peer groups and the way they talked about their sexual relationships. The moral dichotomizing of young women and predatory norms of male sexuality were most pronounced amongst those involved in gangs. The 'bright guys', in contrast, tended to have ideals of companionate relationships and were more likely to describe some of their relationships in terms of mutual commitment.

DISCOURSES AROUND SEXUAL RELATIONSHIPS

In her analysis of talk about heterosexual relationships, Hollway (1984) argues that people's roles arise from the way they position themselves within particular discourses related to sex. The discourse involves more than language, 'it also organizes meaning and action' (Gilfoyle *et al.*, 1993, p. 182). At any specific time 'several coexisting and potentially contradictory discourses concerning sexuality make available different positions and different powers for men and women' (Hollway, 1984, p. 230). Although in principle both men and women can locate themselves as subjects in three of the four discourses identified below, in practice taking up subject or object positions (*vis-à-vis* one's [potential] partner) within these discourses is not equally available to both genders. Consequently men (and women) often understand their heterosexual relationships according to different discourses from those of their partners and, importantly, they assume their partner occupies a different position or different discourse from themselves.

Hollway stresses that the classification of different discourses and the boundaries between them is fairly arbitrary, and that her typology of three discourses could be augmented by many more. The analysis of these young men's accounts suggests it is appropriate to delineate four discourses, which I will refer to as the 'uninterested discourse', the 'predatory discourse', the 'permissive discourse', and the 'have/hold or romantic discourse'. The permissive discourse corresponds closely with that described by Hollway under the same name, while the predatory and have/hold discourses approximate to her other two.

These four discourses were all simultaneously available to the young men, although some discourses were more familiar or more legitimate to certain sub-groups than others. The discourses in which the young men positioned themselves changed over time and with different partners, and several respondents drew on different discourses at different stages of the interview. Furthermore, whatever the discourse through which a man might generally understand his behaviour within a relationship, different discourses could be drawn on in conversation as socially appropriate. Thus when 'chatting someone up' the have/hold romantic discourse would often be used, but when describing behaviour to a fellow male the predatory discourse might be drawn on. This is illustrated in Joe's account of how he seduced his first sexual partner:

DW: Did she know how old you were?

JOE: No. I actually told her I was 16. We went to the dancing and that and I told her everything she wanted to hear.

DW: Like what, what do you mean by that?

JOE: You know what I mean: 'See when I saw you in there, I was like that, oh just . . .' [expression of joyous wonder].

DW: Going through all the patter?

JOE: And then I managed to get her to come home with me one night and that was it: Eureka!

Conversely, sometimes the meaning sexual relationships had for a young man restricted him from joining in the discourse current in particular social contexts. In such cases, peer group influence clearly did not override the prior adoption of a particular discourse:

JAMES: They [young women] would be sitting in a crowd and a lot of the guys would be talking about it [sex], and I couldnae. I am funny when it comes to things like that. Now I have changed. I don't mean I am talking about it and joking about it.

I will now discuss in turn the four discourses relating to sexual relationships.

The Uninterested Discourse

This discourse is an extreme expression of homosociality in that contact with the opposite sex is claimed to be of no concern at all. 'It was just basically that I wasn't interested.' In the following extract I was questioning Barry about his first sexual experience of any kind, including fondling girls:

BARRY: A waste of time.

DW: How do you mean?

BARRY: Better wait until you are married and then naebody can say anything to you about it.

DW: When you say naebody can say anything to you about it, who are you referring to?

BARRY: Like your pals and that, like they see you walking about with a lassie and they say, like, 'Are you feeling her up?' and all that.

Frequently expressing lack of interest involves an implicit or explicit devaluing of the opposite sex. For instance, girls might be described as 'pains in the neck' or traditional divisions of labour asserted, as when I asked about the absence of women in the pub:

BARRY: They should be in the house watching the weans and making the dinner.

DW: How do you ever get to meet girls if they all stay in the house?

BARRY: I don't want to meet them.

The uninterested discourse is reproduced within the gender-segregated world that characterizes young people's school and street life until the age of at least 14. It might be viewed as emerging from the rigid gender boundaries that are central to traditional working class culture which, as Martin (1981) argues, are potentially dangerous to cross. Typically boys (and girls (Thorne, 1993)) go through a long stage from pre-school to around second year at secondary school in which this is the predominant discourse. Only a few of the 19-year-olds still understood their relationship to women in terms of this discourse, though they could draw on it when appropriate to distance themselves from female company.

The uninterested discourse was nicely encapsulated in a cartoon of two skinheads shown in Figure 7.1.

'You ever had sex?'
'Na! That's for lassies.'

Figure 7.1   The uninterested discourse (with apologies to the unknown original cartoonist).

The Predatory Discourse

The predatory discourse also comes out of a profoundly homosocial culture, but it engenders opposite practices to those of the uninterested discourse. It involves the stereotype of masculine sexuality, in which men gain esteem from their male peers by having as many sexual partners as possible. Here Danny, who positioned himself in a have/hold discourse, was generalizing about most other young men:

> I think guys like to have respect aff their pals, and if [for example] I go out and get a different girlfriend every week my pals respect it.

Within this discourse heterosexual intercourse is fundamental in asserting one's masculinity, and physical sexual pleasure is of less importance than the opinions of one's male peers (see also Holland *et al.*, 1993). A boy's interest is 'to do with gender not sex' (Hollway, 1984, p. 240). The enormous pressure teenage boys experience to lose their virginity (cf. Wight, 1994b) is one aspect of this discourse. Another is the view of sex as a hunt. The challenge is to seduce a woman, and the less accessible she is the greater one's esteem if successful. Several of those who reported the highest numbers of partners explicitly referred to this idea:

> ANTHONY: Basically, if you're going out, right, and you're looking at somebody, right, and you say 'She looks easy, she'll have sex no problem', fine, that's it. You can go up and say 'Do you want to have sex?' and they could just turn round and say 'Aye' – and that's it, there's nothing to it, you're not getting to know this person. At least you maybe see somebody else, there might be a bit of a challenge there, you overcome barriers, break down barriers.

> DW: So is that half the fun of it?

> ANTHONY: That's the major part of it, aye.

Joe expressed the same view, although it was contradicted by his stories of sexual relationships with very willing partners:

> JOE: I like a challenge, I'd rather go with somebody they'd say: 'You've got no chance with her', rather than go with some daft slut that anybody could go with – I've never done that. Anybody like that I've always said 'No way, I'd rather go withoot', know what I mean? I'd rather have a bit of a challenge.

There is little value in continuing a sexual relationship once one has 'had it', and consequently the predatory discourse gives rise to short-term relationships with minimal commitments intended by the man (whatever he might profess when seducing his partner). Avoiding commitments was a recurrent theme, as illustrated by a man remembering his first sexual partner four years earlier:

> TOMMY: She thought like she owned me totally, you know. That is what like put me off her and that. Like she started like as if she owned us and that because the two of us had done it and that. Like that was us sort of thing.

Many young men expressed this sort of resentment of demands on their time or restrictions on their relationships with other women. Whether behind these social concerns there was also a psychological vulnerability to relationships that might engage their emotions, as others have argued (e.g. Hollway, 1984; Reibstein and Richards, 1992; Holland *et al.*, 1993), cannot be resolved from these data.

Within the predatory discourse, the woman is sexually passive, relationships generally do not last long enough to develop much physical intimacy and trust, and there is an overwhelming focus on penetrative sex (Wight, 1994a). Consequently men's sexual repertoires are often limited.

In most respects what I have named the predatory discourse is similar to Hollway's 'male sexual drive discourse' (1984). The important difference, however, is the idea that men's sexuality is directly produced by a biological drive which is a key tenet in the discourse Hollway identifies. Although there were some references to such biological essentialism, this notion featured little in the young men's accounts, beyond the view that men would desire sex much more if there was a long interval between encounters. By contrast several men emphasized the variation in their peers' sexual attitudes and behaviour and recognized that they are influenced by social factors: 'the way you're brought up . . . sort of stereotyped' (cf. Wight, 1994b).

> MICHAEL: This is a good time for guys like me, because over the next few years all the role models on TV, it is hard to describe. It is no longer these guys out of shaving adverts and coke adverts, like the clean shaven and that. These are not any more sex symbols. See, the nineties for me is the guy with a wee bit of grey matter upstairs. I think that is what a lot of girls are going to be looking for.

It is possible that the lack of a clearly expressed biological drive explanation reflects how young Glaswegian men actually think about sex in the 1990s, which would give some support to Giddens' idea of 'plastic sexuality'. Alternatively, the absence of biological explanation might be an artefact of either inadequate questioning or careful self-presentation by the respondents within the interview.

The predatory discourse was most pronounced among those involved in gangs, nearly all of whom positioned themselves in it through much of their accounts. The public contesting of their masculine esteem was reflected in the early reported age of first intercourse. The 'bright guys', in contrast, were far less likely to refer to predatory norms. While only a minority of the whole sample seemed to see their current relationships in terms of this discourse at the age of 19, many described their roles in early sexual relationships in this manner. Research with 14–16-year-old boys in the same locality suggests that the predatory discourse predominates at that age (Wight, 1994b). Several of the 19-year-old men seemed to have moved from the predatory to the have/hold discourse in the course of their sexual careers.

The Permissive Discourse

The permissive discourse values sex as a worthwhile end in itself, locating it with the individual rather than seeing it in terms of a relationship. It is therefore similar to the predatory discourse, but there are two fundamental differences. First, in the permissive discourse sexual encounters are valued for their own sake, not primarily in order to confirm one's masculinity with one's male peers, and second, ideally women should play the same role as men, initiating encounters for their own sexual gratification.

> ROBERT: I think it's sexist and unfair that it's always the guy has to go up and ask [someone out].

In reality, of course, permissiveness affects women and men differently (Campbell, 1980), particularly given the enduring importance of women's sexual reputation in working-class culture (Kitzinger, 1995; Holland *et al.*, 1994). Following the statement above, Robert's double standards quickly became apparent when he talked of a long-standing female friend trying to change the nature of their relationship:

> ROBERT: I got on with her and we were having a laugh, you know, you could talk to her, but as soon as she started coming on like that I didn't find her attractive . . . she was trying to chase me and I just got annoyed at the fact that you couldn't have a friendship with a girl without her trying to change it. I was happy just being pals with her, but she wasn't and she was trying to put a bit of pressure on and she knew I wasn't wanting to go out with her.

Since the focus of the permissive discourse is on erotic pleasure, one might expect it to give rise to more adventurous sexual practices. However, within the whole sample the greatest sexual experimentation occurred within long-term relationships, probably due to increasing trust and intimacy, and the young women's growing awareness of their own sensuality (Gagnon and Simon, 1974); the lack of commitment to relationships in the permissive discourse meant they were nearly all short-lived.

The permissive discourse is a construct of, or at least gained legitimacy through, the libertarian ethics of the 1960s. The discourse suggested in these young men's accounts is much the same as that described by Hollway (1984), apart, again, from the emphasis she puts on the biological sexual drive. This description of sexual encounters has one of the very few references to such a drive:

> ANTHONY: Basically, what you're doing there is, the animal instinct is coming through and you and this person just want one thing, right. You want each other, and you want each other now, and that's all you're going for, and you might not realise it [about HIV] until later on.

The permissive discourse has similarities to Giddens' (1992) notion of 'confluent love'. He argues that this arose from the emergence of 'plastic sexuality' and the democratization of personal life, which are historically specific to the changing status of women in the twentieth century. Mutual sexual satisfaction is at the core of the new kind of relationships, and there is no commitment to make them last, both of which fit with the permissive discourse. However, the intimacy and mutual vulnerability of confluent love are not part of the permissive discourse. Furthermore, whatever their practice, none of the Glaswegian young men abandoned the principle of (usually serial) monogamy, which is neither part of confluent love nor Hollway's permissive discourse.

Only Robert positioned himself consistently within the permissive discourse, but a few young men drew on it to describe most of their sexual relationships. It is notable that all of them were 'bright guys', or had been part of this peer group prior to leaving school at 16. They deviated markedly from the majority of this peer group in their use of discourses. Night clubs featured prominently for two of them as locations to meet most of their partners, illustrating how choice of leisure activities can cut across school-based social groups. These two young men reported far more partners (twelve and twenty-three respectively) than the other 'bright guys'. All those using the permissive discourse had, by the age of 19, extensive friendship networks that almost entirely excluded their own locality. This distancing from parochial norms might have been a necessary condition for them to be exposed to the influences of late modern society that give rise to Giddens' confluent love, in so far as the permissive discourse is akin to it. However, broader social contacts were evidently not sufficient for this: other young men had similarly dispersed friendship networks but subscribed to the have/hold romantic discourse.

The Have/Hold Romantic Discourse

This refers to the set of ideas and practices associated with monogamy, partnership and family life, though it does not necessarily involve companionate relationships. Hollway names this simply the 'have/hold discourse' and argues that women take up a position as subjects within it, actively attracting and trying to keep their men, in contrast to the other discourses in which they are positioned as objects (except, sometimes, in the permissive discourse). From the accounts collected in this study and from my own experience, however, it is clear that men can also occupy a position as subject within this discourse.[2] This is a crucial modification to Hollway's analysis, with profound implications for the relative power women and men have within relationships, hence I have amended the name of the discourse. The term 'romantic' highlights what is often, at some stage, the key subjective experience of women and men who see their relationships in terms of this discourse: love (see Jackson, 1993).

For young women to attain the conventional feminine goal of attracting men (primarily to establish their own gender identity, as with men attracting women), they can either adopt an object position within the predatory discourse or a position as subject within the have/hold romantic discourse. It was in the latter position that my respondents generally viewed their partners: 'she'd do anything for me'.

> JOE: She loves me a lot, I know that, and when I was in hospital she helped me a lot, know what I mean? She was up every night and . . . she'd been crying and that, like when I was in pain and all that. She didnae want to go away from me and all that.

> DW: How often do you usually see her in a week?

> JOE: I was oot with her last night in fact and the night before, too much recently. I'd better get a grip of things.

DW: Why's that? Why do you think you ought to get a grip of things?

JOE: I think she's trying to get one of they wee rings on my finger as well.

The danger for a woman who tries to attract and keep a male partner is that this strategy grants him enormous power: she is always vulnerable to him letting her down.

DANNY: I think the guy usually gets his way, especially, like, if the lassie wants to keep the guy and she really likes the guy, and most lassies will think he'll go out and get somebody else if they don't keep them happy, that's what I think anyway.

In so far as could be discerned from their accounts, perhaps half of my sample wanted to be 'held' in a long-term monogamous relationship, so long as it was with the right woman. This included those involved in gangs, half of whom talked of particular relationships in terms of long-term commitment, though they more clearly located themselves as the object within this discourse than did the bright guys. In respect to Duncombe and Marsden's (1993) exploration of the relationship between women's emotional and men's economic work, it is worth noting that locating oneself as the object within this discourse was not patterned by employment status. Some men reported their only sexual relationship in terms of the have/hold discourse, while others described short-term relationships early in their sexual careers in predatory or permissive terms and contrasted these with their current long-term relationship which they talked about using the have/hold discourse. Here Andrew reflects on his perspective changing from a permissive viewpoint:

ANDREW: I don't want to settle down, I just want to have – I've never had a really long relationship with anybody and I'd like to sort of try and have a long-term one. I always seem to get bored dead quick, you know.

Nearly all respondents not currently in a long-term relationship envisaged 'settling down' at some point, the expected age for this being between 23 and 28. Very few expressed long-term aspirations for something approximating to Giddens' 'confluent love'. Most imagined they would get married, and those who wanted children (the majority) only wished to do so within stable two-parent families. This ideal of parenthood seemed to be largely borne out in practice, for the seven children born to men in the sample had all been conceived within long-term relationships and the fathers intended to stay with the mothers. The one exception was a man who had had a second child with another woman and was living with this second mother.

With several young men I could not ascertain whether they took up a position as object or subject within the have/hold romantic discourse when they described their long-term relationships. There were a number of possible reasons for this: they were not pressed enough, were not clear in their own minds about the nature of their relationship, were insufficiently articulate, or were too inhibited by the predominance of the predatory discourse. It is likely that both they and their partners actively wanted to maintain the relationships, though it might be rare for the feeling to be mutual at any one time. For instance Tommy told me how he had a phase with his girlfriend of 'more fighting than anything else', which involved her smashing a bottle on him and him retaliating physically, but nevertheless:

TOMMY: She thinks I don't love her and I do. . . . She thinks I am using her because she has got the house and I am getting my dinners here, but it is no'.

DW: And do you tell her that you love her?

TOMMY: Aye. You feel like a prick, like, you feel that stupid and that. I don't feel stupid like, but I want to tell her and that.

Later I asked him if he hoped the relationship would last a long time.

TOMMY: I hope so, aye. I really do hope; I have got this feeling I am not going to last because sometimes we have arguments too much and that. But I would like to stick with her as long as I could. For the wean's sake and all.

These men's accounts were characterized by expressed concern about their partner's feelings in relation to, typically, pressurizing her to have sex, her sexual reputation and unwanted pregnancies. Sexual behaviour was generally referred to as a dimension of a pre-existing relationship, rather than the rationale for the relationship.

MARK: It was strange because we were not really seeing each other

for the sex, it was more for the friendship. I was not actually
bothered about having sex. That is probably why I left it so long.
I did not try again. I tried once, I don't know if it was nerves or
the pizza I had earlier, because I was almost sick over her!

Several men who reported loving their partner said they could not tell
her this directly, and they explained this as an unwillingness to appear
emotional. Here Tony described talking with male friends about being
in love:

> TONY: Aye, me and my pals and that. They would sit and say things
> like 'I really like her' and that. They would say it to me but they
> would not say it to the lassie at all.
>
> DW: Why do you think that is?
>
> TONY: . . . I think the problem with guys is that they don't know
> how to show it. They think it is too soppy or that.

Yet the fact that some could talk about their emotions with their male
peers suggests their underlying reason not to express their love to their
partner was to avoid revealing their vunerability, which would increase
their partner's power.

Perhaps half the sample wanted to be in the object position within
the have/hold romantic discourse: to be 'held'. Some alternated positions as object and subject with their partner according to the dynamics
of the relationship. A smaller number of young men described some
of their sexual relationships, or their only one, clearly from the position of subject within this discourse.

> DW: Would you say you're in love?
>
> COLIN: Aye.
>
> DW: Have you been in love before?
>
> COLIN: I've been in love but I've never been sort of – I'll say that
> she is, she is the one I've been looking for for a long time, know
> what I mean?

These men wanted to hold someone in a long-term, monogamous relationship, and first sexual intercourse with that woman often had enor-

mous symbolic importance as the culmination and confirmation of a steadily developing relationship (see Kent *et al.*, 1990).

Men who positioned themselves as subjects hoped their feelings would be mutual but sometimes knew that they were not. Some showed they were aware that being in love gave their partners power over them:

MICHAEL: If I ever experienced love it was with Christine. . . . I could never understand why she was going out with me; she always had the pick of the bunch with guys. . . . When I was with her I lacked in self-confidence. When I was with other girls I felt great, she sort of brought out the worst in me in many ways . . .

From the start of their physical relationship Christine:

. . . did everything, like, she took control. If I had been clever at the start I would have just nipped it in the bud. I should have just nipped it in the bud, took control of it, but I didn't and I suffered. I feel if I had taken control in the beginning she would have bombed me out anyway.

The young men were not very articulate about their emotions (and in comparison with Hollway's self-reflexive respondents almost mute), but it seemed that the intensity of their love tended to weaken if the relationship became established and they would shift from a subject to object position within the have/hold romantic discourse. Other relationships described in romantic terms ended when the woman left, or the love was never requited, all of which illustrates Jackson's argument (1993) that insecurity, restriction and unattainability are fundamental to romantic love.

This kind of romantic love can be traced back to the late eighteenth century when, as a consequence of industrialization, women became increasingly subordinated to the home and orientated to their families (Giddens, 1992). The appeal of romantic love to women has been widely considered, for instance in the way it satisfies a need for nurturance and helps deal with anxieties about masculinity without fundamentally challenging it (Radway, 1989). What reason, then, could young men have to position themselves as the active subject in the have/hold romantic discourse, particularly when being overly emotional challenges conventional masculine identities? In contrast, it is clear why they might position themselves as subjects in the other discourses, or as objects in this one.

Radway (1989), Giddens (1992) and Jackson (1993) all refer to the idea of personal fulfilment invested in romantic love. Giddens argues that it is linked to a degree of self-reflection, in that it requires an understanding of one's own feelings and a personal narrative in which 'self-identity awaits its validation from the discovery of the other' (1992, p. 45). It follows, therefore, that it was amongst the bright guys that the have/hold romantic discourse was most prevalent, since one might assume that they were most reflexive about their future itineraries.

Dichotomizing Women: 'Slags' and 'Nice Girls'

Group discussions in this locality with 14–16-year-olds found that the traditional moral distinction between 'slags' (or more commonly 'cows') and 'nice girls' (mistress and wife, whore and virgin) was widely subscribed to by boys of that age (Wight, 1994b). Interviews with young women from the same locality established that they too actively reproduce these categories (Kitzinger, 1995). The extent to which these findings support previous analyses of the regulation of female sexuality (e.g. Cowie and Lees, 1987) is dealt with in these publications.

The dichotomizing of women might be seen as an overarching or proto-discourse (illustrating how arbitrary the identification of particular discourses and their boundaries is), since it is compatible with three of the four discourses identified here and links the predatory and have/hold discourses. Within the uninterested discourse, degrading women as 'slags' gives further reason to distance oneself from them. Within the predatory discourse easily seduced women are 'slags' and difficult ones 'nice girls', thus more challenging and more prestigious to catch. However, 'nice girls' would also be assumed to see the relationship from a have/hold perspective and therefore demand commitment. Within this have/hold romantic discourse a man would only have a long-term relationship with someone he perceived as 'nice', though he might be unfaithful to her in a clandestine relationship with a 'cow'. If the man locates himself in the position of subject within this discourse and romanticizes his relationship then the 'purity' of his partner is often an important element of his idealization:

JAMES: If I was going out with someone that I had any doubts about then I don't think I would be going out with them for too long. If I knew, like, it was somebody that had quite a few partners. . . . If it [sex] was going to happen then it would need to be when I wanted it to be with somebody that I cared about and that.

Only the permissive discourse clearly contradicts the moral categorization of women, since it legitimates women seeking sexual gratification outwith a committed relationship; it is perhaps significant that this was the discourse least clearly articulated by my sample.

Nevertheless, despite the compatibility of the 'slag/nice girl' distinction with most of the discourses identified above, the 19-year-olds, interviewed individually, referred to it far less explicitly than the 14–16-year-olds. This could be because they were more aware of my liberal, middle-class sensibilities or, perhaps, because by that age they had modified such simple moral categories for women.

Those who referred most frequently to the 'slag/nice girl' dichotomy were those involved in gangs, who were also most likely to draw on the predatory discourse. The vague criteria used to define unfeminine sexual behaviour and the role of reputation in this process allowed partners to be classified in keeping with the respondent's sense of honourable conduct. Young women who could be persuaded to have sex on the first night, and were then avoided, had acted like 'slags', while those who resisted early pressure for intercourse and with whom the relationship endured were 'nice'. There was also considerable scope for retrospective re-evaluation of their partners to maintain their self-esteem, thus a woman who ended a relationship when they wanted to prolong it might subsequently be regarded as a 'cow':

MICHAEL: When she finished with me she said, 'Oh, by the way, I had more than two partners.' Like as if she was trying to put the knife in. . . . My reaction was: 'Do you think I did not know that, you slut.'

Conversely, a partner who had agreed to sex at an early stage might come to be seen as 'nice' when the relationship was prolonged. Dave had been 'a bit sceptical' about his current girlfriend's claim that she was a virgin when she had agreed to have sexual intercourse on the third occasion they met. However, after going out with her for ten months he wanted to think of her as respectable and gave her the benefit of the doubt: 'like, there was not any bleeding, but that does not go for much: I might be wrong.'

CONCLUSION

There was great diversity in the patterns of heterosexual relationships reported by this sample at the age of 19, despite the homogeneity of their social backgrounds. Family composition, occupation/educational level and income did not shape the young men's sexual histories in any discernible way, and the influence of peer groups seemed to be largely through the discourses available within them, which in turn affected age at first intercourse.

The discourses through which the young men thought about their relationships, and the positions they adopted within them, constitute one of the main factors by which we can understand the variation in their sexual histories. The discourses they drew on tended to change in the course of their sexual careers, often from the uninterested discourse, through the predatory discourse to the have/hold romantic discourse. However, it is impossible to show in a categorical way how the use of discourses resulted in particular practices because this relationship was mediated by two further main factors: the degree of confidence the young men had in initiating physical relationships and the behaviour of their potential or actual partners. There has not been scope in this chapter to discuss either.

Identifying discourses as a key influence on sexual relationships begs the further question: what shapes the position men took in discourses? My data suggest that there was not a simple relationship of discourse to practice, but that practice (such as that shaped by one's partner or one's prior psychological state) could affect which discourses young men drew on. Involvement in particular peer groups made certain discourse positions more available and legitimate than others. However, preference for particular discourses probably influenced selection of, and selection into, friendship groups, which undermines any simple notion of causation. Several young men talked of how they had consciously chosen their friends:

> ANDREW: . . . I knew quite a lot of people because, sort of, I came from hanging about with, I suppose you would call them neds, . . . to sort of deciding I think this is a wee bit wrang, I think I should try and get something and sort of like change roon'. . . . I just sort of changed company . . .

Furthermore, once in a peer group its influence did not always determine how respondents positioned themselves within discourses. Other factors seemed to play a part, possibly the family culture within which the young men were brought up and their access/exposure to romantic literature (cf. Jackson, 1993), but my data do not allow me to do more than speculate.

The focus on sexual relationships in this paper might have obscured the limited importance that sex as an erotic activity had in these young men's lives. Most respondents reported a low level of heterosexual activity, and three of the four discourses through which they thought about sex embedded it in other social concerns. The uninterested discourse reproduces the boundary between genders and discourages heterosexual contact; the predatory discourse is concerned primarily with establishing masculine gender identity, while in the have/hold romantic discourse the main significance of sex is as an expression of one's relationship with someone of the opposite sex. It is only the permissive discourse that privileges sex as an erotic pleasure and this was the discourse least subscribed to.

With respect to Giddens' thesis, there is scant evidence from this study that the 'transformation of intimacy' has proceeded very far amongst Glaswegian young men, although respondents' lack of reference to a biological sex drive might indicate a move towards 'plastic sexuality'.

The predatory character of male sexual behaviour is often taken to typify male sexuality, and heterosexual intercourse is theorized as a prime site for establishing masculinity. However, the young men in this study who located themselves in the predatory discourse could express their masculinity in many ways other than through sexual intercourse, for instance through fighting, drug use, theft, powerful dogs and so on. Furthermore, I have argued that the predatory discourse is only one of several discourses through which young men think about sexual relationships. The others also allow masculinity to be expressed, but in different ways, such as by devaluing women or meeting family responsibilities.

Much feminist analysis of heterosexuality privileges heterosexual sex as the key place where gender power relationships are reproduced (e.g. Hollway, 1984). The findings discussed here suggest that this might not always be appropriate. Sexual relationships were often subordinated to gender identity; frequently this led to sexual encounters in which the woman's interests were callously disregarded, but it could also lead to sexual encounters being discouraged altogether. In other circumstances gender identity did not seem to be of great importance in the heterosexual relationship. Although the woman's investment in maintaining this relationship was usually greater than the man's, thus making her more vulnerable, the opposite situation was sometimes the case.

ACKNOWLEDGEMENTS

I am very grateful to the fifty-eight young men who agreed to be interviewed in this study and to Sarah Cunningham-Burley, Gill Green, Jenny Kitzinger, Sally Macintyre, Caroline Ramazanoglu and Rory Williams for providing valuable comments on earlier drafts.

NOTES

1. Very few qualitative studies of sexual behaviour in Britain have attempted to recruit a representative sample of a particular population. This is very important if we are concerned with variation in sexual histories. In large scale surveys on sexuality there is a non-response bias towards those with least sexual experience (Catania *et al.*, 1990), and those who declined to participate in this study were significantly more likely than participants to have reported no sexual partners at the age of 18 in the previous sweep of the Twenty-07 Study. This bias, however, was probably modified by survey loyalty to a longitudinal health survey that was not sex-specific, and the sample was almost certainly more representative than it would have been if it were self-selected.
2. It is interesting that, in a recent study of 843 15–16-year-olds, when asked to rank 'the most important things in life for you', 'love' came second to 'happiness' for most young men, but unfortunately this is not explored (Brannen *et al.*, 1994, p. 71).

REFERENCES

Brannen, J., Dodd, K., Oakley, A. and Storey, P. (1994), *Young People, Health and Family Life* (Buckingham: Open University Press).

Campbell, B. (1980), 'A Feminist Sexual Politics: Now you see it, now you don't', *Feminist Review*, 5: pp. 1–18.

Catania, J. A., Gibson, D. A., Chitwood, D. D. and Coates, T. J. (1990), 'Methodological Problems in AIDS Behavioral Research: Influences on Measurement Error and Participation Bias in Studies of Sexual Behavior', *Psychological Bulletin*, 108: 3, pp. 339–62.

Cowie, C. and S. Lees (1987), 'Slags and Drags', in Feminist Review (eds), *Sexuality: A Reader* (London: Virago).

Duncombe, J. and Marsden, D. (1993), 'Love and Intimacy: The Gender Division of Emotion and "Emotion Work"', *Sociology*, 27: 2, pp. 221–41.

Ford, N. (1991), 'The Socio-Sexual Lifestyles of Young People in the South West of England', the South Western Regional Health Authority, King Square House, 26/27 King Square, Bristol BS2 8EF.

Gagnon, J. H. and Simon, W. (1974), *Sexual Conduct: The Social Sources of Human Sexuality* (London: Hutchinson).

Giddens, A. (1992), *The Transformation of Intimacy: Sexuality, Love and Eroticism in Modern Societies* (Stanford, CA: Stanford University Press).

Gilfoyle, J., Wilson, J. and Brown (1993), 'Sex, Organs and Audiotape: A Discourse Analytic Approach to Talking about Heterosexual Sex and Relationships', in S. Wilkinson and C. Kitzinger (eds), *Heterosexuality: A Feminism and Psychology Reader* (London: Sage).

Health Education Authority (HEA) (1990), 'Young Adults' Health and Lifestyle: Sexual Behaviour', prepared for the HEA by MORI (London: HEA).

Holland, J., Ramazanoglu, C. and Sharpe, S. (1993), *Wimp or Gladiator: Contradictions in Acquiring Masculine Sexuality* (London: The Tufnell Press).

Holland, J., Ramazanoglu, C., Sharpe, S. and Thomson, R. (1994), 'Reputations: Journeying into Gendered Power Relations', paper presented at BSA Annual Conference 'Sexualities in Social Context', University of Central Lancashire, 28–31 March.

Hollway, W. (1984), 'Gender Difference and the Production of Subjectivity', in J. Henriques, W. Hollway, C. Urwin, C. Venn and V. Walkerdine (eds), *Changing the Subject: Psychology, Social Regulation and Subjectivity* (London: Methuen).

Jackson, S. (1993), 'Even Sociologists Fall In Love: An Exploration in the Sociology of Emotions', *Sociology*, **27**: 2, pp. 201–20.

Johnson, A. M., Wadsworth, J., Wellings, K. and Field, J. (1994), *Sexual Attitudes and Lifestyles* (London: Blackwell Scientific).

Kent, V., Davies, M., Deverell, K. and Gottesman, S. (1990), 'Social Interaction Routines Involved in Heterosexual Encounters: Prelude to First Intercourse', paper presented at Fourth Conference on Social Aspects of AIDS, South Bank Polytechnic, London, 7 April 1990.

Kitzinger, J. (1995), '"I'm Sexually Attractive but I'm Powerful": Young Women Negotiating Sexual Reputation', *Women's Studies International Forum*, **18**, 2: pp. 187–96.

Martin, B. (1981), *A Sociology of Contemporary Cultural Change* (Oxford: Basil Blackwell).

Morgan, D. (1992), *Discovering Men* (London: Routledge).

Radway, J. (1989), *Reading the Romance* (London: Verso).

Reibstein, J. and Richards, M. (1992), *Sexual Arrangements: Marriage, Monogamy and Affairs* (London: Mandarin).

Thorne, B. (1993), *Gender Play: Girls and Boys in School* (Buckingham: Open University Press).

West, P., Wight, D. and Macintyre, S. (1993), 'Heterosexual Behaviour of Eighteen-Year Olds in the Glasgow Area', *Journal of Adolescence*, **16**: 4, pp. 367–96.

Wight, D. (1994a), 'Assimilating "Safer Sex": Young Heterosexual Men's Understanding of "Safer Sex"', in P. Aggleton, P. Davies, and G. Hart (eds), *AIDS: Foundations for the Future* (London: Falmer Press).

Wight, D. (1994b), 'Boys' Thoughts and Talk about Sex in a Working Class Locality of Glasgow', *Sociological Review*, **42**: 4, pp. 703–37.

Willis, P. (1977), *Learning to Labour* (Farnborough: Saxon House).

Zabin, L. S. and Hayward, S. C. (1993), *Adolescent Sexual Behavior and Childbearing* (Newbury Park, GA: Sage).

Part III
Sexual Exchange

8 Organized Bodies: Gender, Sexuality and Embodiment in Contemporary Organizations

Anne Witz, Susan Halford and Mike Savage

INTRODUCTION

A defining feature of the Weberian ideal-type is that bureaucracies are governed by a formal set of rules and procedures which ensure that operations and activities are carried out in a predictable, uniform and impersonal manner. Within this rational-legal model 'personal' (i.e. non-bureaucratic) relationships are excluded from organizational life, and only bureaucratically legitimated forms of power can operate. The model has been widely debated since its first appearance (see Albrow, 1970; Jackson, 1982, for reviews) but in recent years two particularly stringent critiques have emerged.

First, feminist writers suggest that Weber's account of rationality in modern organizations is underlain by a gendered sub-text (Acker, 1990). It is argued that whilst the rational-legal model *presents* itself as gender-neutral it in fact constitutes a new kind of patriarchal structure. In this vein Pringle (1989) argues that the concept of rationality itself is built on a particular form of masculinity which excludes the personal, the sexual and indeed the feminine which, in turn, is associated with chaos and disorder and thus clearly placed in opposition to Weberian notions of rationality. In this critique, then, the emphasis is on the way in which gender interests are obscured by the apparent neutrality vested in bureaucratic rules and procedures. Rather, it is argued that gender relations are *embedded* within organizational structures and practices.

Second, and simultaneously, a debate has emerged which questions whether in fact modern bureaucratic forms *have* banished sexuality from organizational life. Focusing attention on the pervasiveness of sexualized relationships in the organizational arena, this account draws particularly on the work of Foucault to suggest that sexuality and power are intertwined in everyday social interactions in bureaucratic organizations (Burrell, 1984; Pringle, 1989). This account argues that male sexuality is routinely privileged within organizational practices.

Both accounts have made important contributions to thinking about gender and organization (see, for example, Hearn and Parkin, 1988; Cockburn, 1991). However, at present, it seems to us that the precise nature of the *interrelationship* between these two developments is unclear. Whilst the former 'gender paradigm' emphasizes the notion of a corporate patriarchy, or systemic sets of relations of male dominance and female subordination within organizations, the latter 'sexuality paradigm' focuses on the localized and strategic deployment of power and sexuality through organizational discourses. Some feminist writers have criticized the diffuse conceptualization of power in the 'sexuality paradigm' (Walby, 1990; Adkins and Lury, this volume), whilst the 'gender paradigm' itself has been criticized for an over-emphasis on structural and universalized forms of power and for a lack of attention to human agency and the diverse forms which this can take (Pringle, 1989; Callas and Smircich, 1992).

In this paper we draw upon insights from both paradigms in order to explore everyday interactions between women and men in contemporary organizations and, in turn, understand the construction of organizational hierarchies. However, integrating analysis from both accounts is not a straightforward matter given that the differences between them run to fundamental questions of epistemology and philosophy. In addition, we remain wary of the tendency within the 'sexuality paradigm' to either subsume gender within the category of sexuality (cf. Witz and Savage, 1992, for a development of this argument) or to 'retire' gender as part of the social or economic, whilst valorizing sexuality as part of the 'cultural' (see Adkins and Lury, this volume, for an argument of this point). On the other hand, the gender paradigm tends to 'retire' the issue of sexuality. Like Acker (1992), we see sexuality as *part of* the ongoing production of gender. One way of retaining a focus on both gender and sexuality without 'retiring' either is to operationalize a notion of the 'lived body' as the materiality of both gender and sexuality. So it is by introducing insights from a third area of social theory – writing on human embodiment – that we seek to develop an embodied perspective on gender and organizations as an exciting and fruitful way of building on the strengths of both paradigms.

Explorations of the significance of human embodiment for social relations have proliferated in recent years (cf. Turner, 1992; Shilling, 1993; Morgan and Scott, 1993) and several writers have begun to draw attention to the significance of embodiment in organizations (Hochschild, 1984; Cockburn, 1991; Adkins, 1995). It is perhaps in Joan Acker's recent work that the argument is most developed in relation to organizational processes. Acker (1990) argues that the embodied nature of organizational work has been obscured by the gender-neutral, asexual discourses of organizational structure, processes and logic which derive from Weber's model. The rational–legal model presents a radical denial of human embodiment (Morgan and Scott, 1993) yet, Acker argues, the bureaucratic form of organization is actually premised on a type of embodiment associated with the male body: 'it is the man's body, its sexuality, minimal responsibility in procreation and conventional control of emotions that pervades work and work organisations' (1990, p. 152). These masculine characteristics are normalized and presented as gender-neutral desirable characteristics of 'organization' (thus shaping organizational design and practice) and of organizational employees (thus shaping organizational expectations of those workers). This gender-embodied sub-text underlying organization means that men are more likely to (and/or more likely to be *perceived* to) match the (embodied) requirements of bureaucratic organization far more closely than women do.

Thus, Acker's work displaces the notion of organization work or labour as an abstract disembodied capacity or accomplishment, carried out by a universal worker, and emphasizes instead that real workers, and indeed real jobs, are embodied and that this embodiment is gendered. We part company slightly with Acker where she suggests that this gender embodied sub-text of organization privileges 'the' male body. Instead we prefer to suggest that it is a particular version of the male body which is privileged, corresponding to what Frank (1991) calls the disciplined body: highly controlled or regimented, lacking in desire, isolated in it's own performance and disassociated from itself. Clearly the material from which bureaucrats should be made!

Once we 'see' bureaucracies as embodied systems of social relations the articulation of gender and sexuality becomes clearer. Both gender and sexuality are inscribed on, marked by and lived through the body. Indeed, it is because real jobs and real workers are embodied that workplace interactions are infused by both gender and sexuality. Both everyday interactions *and* the structural design of organizations are informed by, draw on and work through dynamics of gender, sexuality and embodiment. We would argue, then, that there is a recursive and dynamic relationship between organizational structures and cultures, as we seek to avoid conceptualizing 'sexuality' as exclusively occupying the domain of the cultural, or using 'gender' only to evoke the more systemic properties of the structural. The recursive nature of the structural context and interactional content of organizations works through participants knowledge and understanding of organizational rules, procedures and injunctions. Because these participants do not 'leave their bodies behind' when they 'go' to work, part of this understanding is an embodied one.

Our paper is not explicitly structured around an exploration of 'embodiment' in these organizations but is led by the major issues which our interviewees raised when asked about sexuality in everyday workplace life. Through this presentation of our material it is clear that organization sexuality is always discussed as gendered. We can also see how hierarchies of authority and mechanisms of control can, in various ways and to different degrees, evoke the boundaries of the body through sexualized and gendered markers to 'position' and 'control' organizational men and women. Further, we begin to see the ways in which organizational members use gendered heterosexual and gendered familial/kinship discourses to regulate workplace interactions between embodied men and women, thus providing grist to the mill for Pringle's (1989) argument that the boss–secretary relation is discursively constructed by familial/kinship as well as by sexualized discourses.

In the remainder of this paper, we use new empirical material to investigate how gendered hierarchies and interactions are underpinned by discourses of gender, sexuality and 'the body'. We examine three organizational arenas: the hospital ward, the local authority office and the bank branch. The material presented here is drawn from 90 in-depth interviews with roughly equal numbers of women and men, drawn from different points in organizational hierarchies, across the three sectors. In order to capture the ways in which gender and sexuality 'operate' within the apparently gender-neutral and de-sexualized arena of workplace organizations, we use the notion of a 'politics of the body' (Cockburn 1991) in the course of our data analysis. Cockburn continues to operate within a feminist structuralist paradigm, maintaining a focus on the corporate patriarchy and the systemic patterning of male dominance and female subordination, but also explores new agendas emanating from post-structuralist concerns, identifying male discourses of difference (as negative representations of women in terms of their problematic relation to power and authority – 'women can't manage') and differentiation (as positive representations of women as tractable and willing subordinates), and linking a sexual politics of the workplace to body politics. In the concluding section of our paper we build on the themes which emerge in the discussion of our empirical material and suggest an analytical framework which might enable us to, literally, 'flesh out' a concept of a politics of the body.

WARD WORK AND WARD TALK

Turning first to the hospital ward, nurses described two rather different ways in which gender, sexuality and a politics of the body underscored workplace interactions and hierarchies. One set of relationships was described between nurses, and another between doctors and nurses.

Looking first at work relations between nurses, the fact that most nurses are still female means that a striking feature of the hospital ward is that there is a feminized culture centering on a female homosociability. This is unusual, contrasting with other studies which have exposed the dominance of masculinist cultures in offices and factories (e.g. Kanter, 1977; Collinson and Collinson, 1989). This was evident when nurses described the problems that might be experienced by male nurses entering a female work environment, as well as the ways interactions were altered by the presence of a male nurse:

> Having worked in a lot of my career in just single sex groups, you get on. I mean a certain amount of bitching goes on, but I don't think it's meant in a malicious way, because people just get on with it, but if you've got men working with you then you might be a little bit more cautious of what you're saying. (Female Nurse Manager)

Single sex female workgroups were often described as being emotional, intense, and even 'bitchy', but also as fairly open, sharing environments, within which women shared information about non-work matters, but which could also tip into 'backbiting'. Differences between female and male workplace cultures were often evoked by nurses:

> I think that if you have a predominantly male environment with one female the swearing would be reduced, and I think it's the same in a predominantly female environment with a male, then the conversation

would change. They wouldn't be talking about female subjects all the time. (Female Staff Nurse)

Thus, the hospital ward is a workplace where male nurses are, in the words of one nurse, 'strangers in a female world'. Some nurses were incredulous that men would want to be nurses at all and invoked strong associations between physical caring and femininity. There was also a widespread suspicion of men's motives for becoming nurses in the first place, criticisms of male working style and a strong feeling that the embodied presence of male nurses necessitated alterations to established female sociability on the ward, and especially to the sexualized elements of ward talk. Whereas talk around (hetero)sexuality was a common source of pleasure and camaraderie between women on female-only wards, and women nurses were described as capable of having 'quite raucous conversations', the embodied presence of men transformed sexual talk into a potential source of danger. This sense of danger relates to women's perception that they might not be able to control sexualization of the ward where men are present. If female sociability is replaced by a masculine sex-drive disourse (Collinson and Collinson, 1989) women may find it harder to adopt authority positions, instead being routinely positioned in ways subordinate to men, and sexual harassment becomes a greater possibility.

Thus, the physical entry of a male nurse into this feminine space is not automatically welcomed. However, nor are male nurses automatically excluded *unless* they deploy unacceptable forms of masculinity, particularly sexism or sexual harassment. There is a clear onus on male nurses to refute the suspicions raised by their presence on the ward by negotiating non-hegemonic and more acceptable forms of masculinity. To this end it seems male nurses are prepared to carry out considerable amounts of 'relational work' and that, in return, female nurses will also work to ease the accommodation of men into ward life.

For both male and female nurses, although especially female nurses, one common way of negotiating a successful working relationship was to invoke familial and kinship discourses. The nurses we interviewed provided numerous instances of workplace relationships built on familial relations such as brother/sister, mother/son, uncle/niece and so on. These roles provide a range of 'subject positions' through which women can position themselves in relation to men, as equal and/or authoritative; and through which men can position themselves in non-hegemonic masculine roles, both subordinate to female authority, and in positions of authority over female nurses. It was the gay male nurse in particular who represented a non-hegemonic form of masculinity and was described by nurses as 'getting on better with women' and 'like a brother to us'. A male charge nurse also described how his position of authority over female staff nurses was understood by all concerned in kinship terms: 'I'm not their dad. . . . I have been known as Uncle for a long time.'

This use of familial imagery to represent work relations between embodied women and men is one way in which female nurses facilitate the integration of male nurses into a female ward culture, carefully containing the heterosexualized elements of ward life. Sexual banter still occurs, but more commonly with women 'ribbing' male nurses who in turn are expected to accept sexual banter at their expense. This contrasts with (hetero)sexualized discourse in organizations dominated by male sociability which routinely privileges men's sexuality and in which women find it more difficult to locate subject positions, especially those of an authoritarian or egalitarian nature (Collinson and Collinson, 1989).

The pattern of relationships between nurses and doctors is strikingly different, but again we can see how gender, sexuality and a politics of the body are implicated in workplace interactions and hierarchies.[1] Unlike nurse–nurse relations where, as we have seen, nurses sought to limit and contain the sexualization of ward life, drawing on non-hegemonic forms of masculinity, it was widely agreed that the nurse–doctor was routinely (hetero)sexualized and drew both on hegemonic forms of masculinity and emphasized femininity.

At its most benign this was described in terms of doctors being 'friendly', or as doctors and nurses 'playing each other up' and was tinged with Mills and Boon type notions of romance. But this could also be experienced as undermining, humiliating or threatening, tipping into either verbal or physical sexual harassment. In particular, female nurses described the ways in which male doctors used heterosexualized language and conversation – usually to draw attention to nurses' physical appearance – and also used physical acts to establish their power and authority. Female nurses gave many examples of such treatment by male doctors, with *senior* medical staff often cited as the worst problem. One nurse vividly remembered her shocking initiation into the routine eroticization of nurses' bodies by senior members of the medical staff:

My very first day, I went and worked in a theatre, and the Senior Registrar stopped the whole theatre to admire my legs, and I was mortified . . . he made all the students stop. . . . I felt acutely, acutely embarrassed, because I'd had attention drawn to me and I was new, I was very new, . . . I could not believe it.'   (Female Nurse Manager)

Even after this the same nurse went on to describe how although this doctor always talked about her legs whenever they worked together, she 'eventually got used to it', accommodating it as 'just his way'. Similarly, male medical staff would routinely deal with nurses deemed to be too assertive (i.e. challenging medical authority) with verbal reference to the nurses' bodies, for example 'you're being arsy because it's the time of the month' or the description of one nurse as 'needing her tits twisted', invariably said in a room full of people.

In contrast then to the use of familial discourses which enable female nurses to hold authoritative and equal relationships with male nurses, the nurse–doctor relationship is characterized by hegemonic forms of masculinity, and the heterosexualization of nurse–doctor relationships is accepted as a routine part of everyday life, as this comment clearly demonstrates:

When doctors think they have a right to touch you, I think still that if you tend not to notice, that's good, but if you actually go into hysterics and draw attention, I think that makes you feel as bad yourself. But I don't know how many other people react to being touched, because we're all touched by doctors. But I wouldn't have said that's a big problem. It's part of everyday life, as far I'm concerned.   (Female Staff Nurse)

Thus, nurses accommodate themselves to an imposed masculinist hierarchy by adopting an 'emphasized femininity' (Connell, 1987, p. 183) in their relationships with doctors. The central feature of this 'emphasised femininity' is an orientation towards accommodating the interests and desires of men, including the accommodation (to a degree) of the sexualization of women by men.

Nurses rarely made formal complaints and the boundary between acceptable and unacceptable heterosexualization was blurred. When nurses tried to articulate the point at which they became uneasy they found it difficult:

it's when it just goes over, and it's very difficult to pin-point. I think it's body language more, and the expression and it's how close they stand, . . . all those little nebulous things . . . the arm slipped round the waist, or the shoulder, or the standing close behind you. (Female Staff Nurse)

Thus when female nurses attempt to differentiate sexual harassment from the routinely accommodated 'politics of the body', which underpins the nurse-doctor relationship, they could be said to be describing the breakdown of this routinely accommodated bodily order. In the case above, it is violation of the spatial politics of the body – bodily integrity – which is constituted as harassment.

What emerges from this brief discussion of nurse–nurse and nurse–doctor relations is a wholly different 'politics of the body' governing these two relationships. Where sexualized comments on the appearance or body or unwanted touching of a female nurse by a male nurse would absolutely not be tolerated the same actions by a male doctor would be accepted as part of the bodily order of their relationship. The tacit parameters of heterosexuality in nursing (in terms of what was deemed acceptable or unacceptable behaviour) were drawn quite narrowly and clearly, and much more on terms set by women, so were more likely to be formally resisted if contravened. The tacit parameters of heterosexuality in doctor–nurse relations, by contrast, threw the net of acceptable sexualization much more widely, and there were no examples of formal resistance cited by the nurses we talked to.

LOCAL GOVERNMENT: THE BODY POLITICS OF THE OFFICE

Despite the persistence of gendered occupational segregation at the structural level in Housing and Finance large, open-plan offices are the norm and it is common to find men and women working side by side.

Widespread preference was strongly expressed for this mixed-sex environment. Single-sex groups were almost universally associated with distinct forms of sociability. Left to themselves, it is claimed, men tend to be 'laddish', characterized by overtly sexualized and often crude conversations which impeded concentration on work. Equally, groups of women, it is claimed, talk incessantly about non-work related issues often relating to bodies and self-presentation i.e. diets and clothes:

With women they're all sort of comparing themselves all the time. Women always feel in competition with each other. . . . 'Oh, she's prettier than me' that sort of thing. . . . It's just clothes in our office, that's the be-all-and-end-all of their lives. And *weight*. They're all on bloody diets. (Ms 26, junior clerical worker)

As well as personal relationships. Men characterize this female sociability as domestic compared with their own heterosexualized sociability, to the amusement of women who describe similar forms of (hetero)sexualized talk as in female-only groups as in nursing (above).

Either way, these gender-specific forms of sociability are widely rejected by junior staff and managers alike. Female staff reject what they see as the 'bitchiness' of women-only groups (also raised in nursing and banking) whilst male staff appear to welcome relief from a masculine sociability which is characterized as obsessively sexual, yet also lacking in mutual support and friendship:

I used to work in an all male section and it was all male talk. Everything was pushed and catered towards the male way of life so to speak . . . Down the pub and a few bevvies and talk about women and what you'd like to do and talk about what you wouldn't like to do etc. etc. But when you come into a male/female situation a lot of that goes out of the window, you know. You change the way you talk and the attitude you have towards people. . . . I've changed as a person working with women and men rather than just being in an all male section. (Mr 23, junior clerk)

Managers explicitly saw mixing women and men as a way of curbing unruly single sex groups. Contrary to popular suggestions that mixed groups won't get on with their work, managers claim this as a problem with single-sex groups:

Q: Are there any problems with single-sex groups?

Probably lack of control. At the end of the day you're here to do a job of work, not enjoy yourself. (Mr 5, junior clerk)

Thus, it is *mixed-sex groups* which are characterized as enhancing organizational productivity and control. This conception appears to rest on the forms of self-discipline which come into play when embodied women and men work alongside one another. It is suggested that both women and men will tone down sexual banter when faced with the real, embodied presence of the opposite sex. As in nursing, the physical presence of men may make sexual banter a potential source of danger for women. It also seems that women are less likely to 'bitch' in front of men, not least because of a perception that men find this behaviour unattractive. Men working in mixed-sex groups articulate a strong sense of 'not in front of the ladies' and we also detect a more concealed anxiety about working with real, embodied women rather than abstracted or fantasized ones. Whilst this may, on occasion, result in sexual harassment, it also places individuals in a more uncertain and practical relationship to one another which seems to curtail excesses of abstract sexualized discussion.

Thus, the presence of women is thought to 'tone down' the unruly sexuality of men transforming a subterranean, non-productive and disruptive male sexuality into an organizationally legitimate mode of heterosexualized interaction in office spaces. There is then the notion of an acceptable level of heterosexualization of office culture resting on a heterosexualized discourses of difference and complementarity which articulates a mode of managerial control.

Evidently this self-censored sociability is far from de-sexualized and both sexes claim to derive pleasure from the sexualization of workplace interactions. This is usually referred to as 'banter' and characterized as a harmless pleasure. This raises an important and complex issue. How can we distinguish pleasure from danger: the two sides of the coin of workplace sexuality (Pringle, 1989; Cockburn, 1991). Women may claim enjoyment, but the authenticity of this is denied by some writers who claim that workplace sexuality is male defined and controlled therefore denies women any real power or pleasure (Adkins, 1995). We do not wish to deny women's pleasure in this way, although there is certainly evidence that women's participation in sexual banter may be defensive on occasion:

When I'm pushed too far I can be very aggressive back. . . . I mean like they used to have the lads' chat or whatever about sex or whatever, and they used to say 'Whoops, sorry Helen' and I'd say 'Oh, I've heard worse', or I'll come out with something worse and they're like 'Oh, alright' [shocked into silence].   (Ms 26, junior clerk)

Women in the local authority offices tended to describe the flip over point between the pleasure and danger in terms of a verbal politics of the body, i.e. the calling up of embodiment and sexuality in conversations. Harassment is perceived at the point where men call up women's embodiment in ways which diminish their competence and authority.

The only two experiences described to us explicitly as sexual harassment took precisely this format. A woman building inspector described how:

> I was trying to do an inspection and the guys were in there putting in the windows and they were giving it all 'get your tits out, blah, blah, blah' you know. So I said 'just shut up and get on with your work'. So this piece of mastic comes flying over and hits me in the face'.

By contrast, the nurses accepted this verbal politics of the body in their relationship with doctors and described the flip-over into harassment through reference to a spatial politics of the body, whereby tacit spatial boundaries were transgressed.

BANKING: HETEROSEXUAL OFFICE CULTURE

There are some strong similarities between banking and local government. Here too, mixed sex groups were the norm and were preferred by both staff and managers and the discourses of sexual difference and complementarity are even stronger. We came across numerous instances where managers advocated mixed sex groups as a way of overcoming what they saw as the intrinsic problems of single-sex sociability. For example, a female manager commented:

> if you get a whole bunch of women together it could be absolute chaos and you probably wouldn't get anything done for hours. They need a little bit more discipline. . . . I think they [women and men] complement each other. I think men stop women talking all day.   (Ms 8: Manager)

In many ways this managerial endorsement of heterosexual sociability is extraordinary in the context of banking. Traditionally, personal relationships at work were prohibited – mainly on the grounds of a threat to security – and as soon as any sexual liaison (or even sexual interest) was known about the bank would move one partner, usually the woman. In recent years, this policy has clearly relaxed and the bank even produced advertisements showing it's staff going out on dates together.

There are however two crucial *caveats* here. First, bank management still expects to *control* sexualized interactions in the branch to its own specifications and to this end still conducts surveillance over 'inappropriate' sexual liaisons in the bank:

> it [a relationship] can cause issues amongst other staff that there is a bit of lovey doveyness going on. Then, as manager, you have got to speak to them.   (Mr 10: Senior Manager)

Managers continue to deploy strategies which enable them to manage sexual liaisons amongst staff. Further, since the majority of managers are male, there is a tendency to place such relationships within the masculine sex drive discourse (Collinson and Collinson, 1989):

> I had a manager about two years ago. . . . he rang me to tell me about one of the girls on his staff. He's a divorced guy. He says 'can you transfer her'. I said 'why?' He says 'I'm going out with her.' I said 'You dirty bastard, She's a nice young girl. In fact, she's leaving, she's going to university.'   (Mr 30: Manager)

This personnel manager clearly held the branch manager in some admiration and complied with his request.

Thus, bank management openly colludes in the sexualization of the bank environment only so long as it conforms to definitions of *productive* sexuality and is not perceived as a threat to bank 'organization'. Whilst the sexual dynamics of mixed sex groups was widely believed to contribute to bureaucratic control, the formation of consummated sexual relationships was still perceived negatively in banking and local government alike. Actual sexual relationships continue to be seen as violating the supposed impartiality of bureaucratic rules, in a way that friendships and non-consummated sexual relationships do not. Thus, managers will still impose the separation of bodies which transgress in this way in order to re-establish a *status quo* governed by rules defining appropriate spatial–sexual parameters of gendered workplace interactions. Although we found less open approval of men's sexual relationships in the workplace amongst our local government workers, managerial distinctions between productive and unproductive sexualization at work were also made.

The second limit on bank managers collusion in a heterosexualized workplace culture is it is only acknowledged amongst junior staff. Amongst managers, *management itself* is not seen in such terms, but is defined in a gender-neutral way. The result is a managerial discourse on heterosexuality which positions male and female clerks but which refuses to include itself. Thus, it seems that management deliberately evokes the heterosexualization of the clerical workforce, as the discourse of complementarity functions as a control mechanism.

To illustrate this point, it was striking how male managers claimed not to regard female bank managers as any different from themselves. In contrast to discussions about male and female clerks, which deployed discourses of sexual difference, male managers were unwilling, by and large, to state that female managers were any different to men in the workplace. Women managers were assumed (required) to fit in with a largely male defined set of management attributes and, to employ Kanter's (1977) phrase, into patterns of male sociability which characterized managerial culture in the banks. As one senior male manager stated:

> [women] are one of the [management] team and I do try and treat them as one of the lads, and I don't mean one of the lads in terms of male/female. But, look, if you want equality we are going to have to have equality. (Mr 10: Senior Manager)

This illustrates only too well that it is in fact embodied male rationality which marks the tacit norm to which women managers must approximate.

Whilst male managers may refer to this as 'gender-neutral', women managers were very aware of their position as women and talked at length about how they felt themselves to be 'strangers' in a male defined management culture (cf. Marshall, 1984). Sometimes these women managers felt able to deploy this 'difference' with positive effect:

> I think women do stand out more. As I say, like at this dinner last week, I mean we were bound to stand out. There were five long tables, and there was one woman on each. I mean, we are going to stand out, aren't we. But you see, I try and take advantage of that, so I wore a red suit on the basis that all the men I knew would be in grey and dark. So I did stand out and, yes, the speaker did come over and speak to me at the end . . . that is part of playing the game, isn't it? (Ms 8: Manager)

The practice of sharing the women out amongst the men by seating one at each table is in itself significant, but the overt manipulation of the physical dimension of organizational body politics is interesting. It serves to illustrate how embodied organizational participants can call up their embodiment through ways of presenting the body. The choice of a red dress is evoking a number of associations between red and the womanly body. In addition, the contrast between the evocation of the distinctive womanly body in the red dress with the mass of manly bodies similarly clad in dark suits introduces a moment of female 'jouissance' into the social situation, albeit largely in male defined terms.

However, such deliberate actions as this have to be handled carefully. The flip side of this assertion of embodied difference in a context where women are required to accommodate to male norms, i.e. be the same, is that it can be turned back upon the woman in such a way as to disempower her.

'ORGANIZED BODIES': CONCLUSION

Gender relations between embodied women and men at work are regulated through heterosexualized discourses, which mark out legitimate and illegitimate modes of sexualization in the workplace and which are underpinned by a bodily politics. But there are two quite distinct heterosexualized discourses that come into play. Both refer to difference, but in one case this is constructed as complementary, whilst in the other the difference is seen as disruptive and negotiation is required.

It was notable how, in local government offices and bank branches, the heterosexualized discourse of complementarity was unequivocally endorsed by managers and subordinates alike as a feature of workplace culture amongst subordinates. This was not so much the case in nursing, because the prevailing discourse of sexuality implies a hegemonic masculinity and emphasized femininity (cf. Connell 1987) which empowers men and disempowers women and hence, is inimical with female patterns of authority and control on the hospital ward. We observed how interactions between female and male nurses were conducted within familial or kinship discourse, rather than sexualized discourse, and suggested that this was because the former enables women to position themselves as authoritative and competent 'subjects' in relation to men, whilst the latter does not. However, the gendered parameters of authority relations between male doctors and female nurses were routinely sexualized, and it was a heterosexualized discourse of difference which served to mark out authoritative subject positions for doctors, and subordinate positions for nurses.

The notion of a 'politics of the body', introduced at various points of our analysis, has enabled us to excavate further the ways in which sexualities in organizations are deployed through and with reference to gendered bodies. People in organizations participate daily in hierarchies that are visibly gendered, in that men and women are doing certain organizational tasks, and part of the experience of the power relations underscoring these hierarchies is an embodied experience. There is a sense, then, in which hierarchies can be understood not simply as ordered spaces between jobs, but also as spaces between bodies.

We propose that there are, in fact, a number of experiential dimensions of a politics of the body in organizations; a number of different ways of understanding the tacit rules governing interaction between embodied, gendered participants. First, there is a *spatial* dimension to an organizational politics of the body, which describes the rules governing spaces between bodies. This may refer quite literally to spatial proximity between embodied organizational members or to the spatial distribution of men and women in organizations. The notion of 'personal space' and especially the invasion of that space by others is also an aspect of the first, whilst an aspect of the second is the spatial segregation of men and women into different offices or work stations. Sometimes, contact between bodies is incorporated into the routine of the job, such as in the relationship between nurses and their patients, and doctors and their patients. This spatial dimension of a bodily politics in organizations has also been included under the definition of sexual harassment, as an explicitly sexualized, unwanted and threatening form of contact initiated largely by men and violating women's bodily space. Lastly, the spatial dimensions also refers to the symbolic space between bodies as they are arranged into hierarchies within organizations. Hierarchical work relations, then, are underpinned by a politics of the body and one of the ways in which differences in power and authority may be expressed and experienced is as spaces between bodies.

Second, there is the *verbal* dimension or the 'calling up' of embodiment in the language of organizational life. This is particularly so for women, as the womanly body is routinely called up in some jobs, especially where part of the bargain women strike with employers is to respond to or initiate 'sexual banter' with customers (Adkins, 1995). Almost always this means the calling up of women's embodiment by men in organizations through indirect or direct reference to clothes or, more usually, to eroticized parts of women's bodies. And, of course, sexual harassment has been defined in such a way as to incorporate 'verbal harassment', which describes the threatening or unacceptable verbal sexualization of women by men (cf. Stanko, 1988).

Thirdly, there is the *physical* dimension of a politics of the body. Routinely, this is politics of the presentation of the body – how we dress and what this signifies. Some women's jobs demand explicitly sexualized presentation of the body, others a desexualized, if implicitly sexualized, presentation. But this is also experienced in terms of body size, shape, etc. and an awareness of this, as well as bodily comportment and acceptable or unacceptable ways of carrying and using our bodies in organizational encounters. This dimension draws attention to the internal work done by organizational members when 'conducting' their bodies in their workplace.

We are suggesting, then, that analyses of gendered interactions and hierarchies in organizations might, quite literally, be 'fleshed out' by a concept of a politics of the body consisting of three dimensions: the verbal, the spatial and the physical. However, these dimensions are not discrete but interrelated, and throughout our analysis we have sought to introduce these various dimensions of 'organized bodies' in such a way as to analyse the interplay of the institutionalization and discursive construction of gender and sexuality in workplace organizations.

NOTE

1. We deal here with interactions between male doctors and female nurses – still the most common pattern in hospitals. For discussion of situations where the genders are reversed (see Halford, Savage and Witz, 1996, forthcoming).

REFERENCES

Acker, J. (1990), 'Hierarchies, Jobs, Bodies: A Theory of Gendered Organisations', *Gender and Society*, 4: 2, pp. 139–58.

Acker, J. (1992), 'Gendering Organisational Theory', in A. Mills and P. Tancred (eds), *Gendering Organisational Analysis* (London: Sage).

Adkins, L. (1995), *Gendered Work: Sexuality, Family and the Labour Market* (Buckingham: Open University Press).

Albrow, M. (1970), *Bureaucracy* (London: Pall Mall Press).

Burrell, G. (1984), 'Sex and Organisational Analysis', *Organisation Studies*, 5: 2, pp. 97–110.

Callas, M. and Smircich, L. (1992), 'Using the "F" Work: Feminist Theory and the Social Consequences of Research', in Mills, A. and Tancred, P. (eds), *Gendering Organisational Analysis* (London: Sage).

Cockburn, C. (1991), *In the Way of Women: Men's Resistance to Sex Equality in Organisations* (London: Macmillan).

Collinson, D. and Collinson, M. (1989), 'Sexuality in the Workplace: The Domination of Men's Sexuality' in Hearn, J. *et al.* (eds), *The Sexuality of Organisation* (London: Sage), pp. 91–109.

Connell, R. W. (1987), *Gender and Power* (Oxford: Polity Press).

Frank, A. (1991), 'For a Sociology of the Body: An Analytical Review', in Featherstone, M., Hepworth, M. and Turner, B. S. (eds), *The Body: Social Process and Cultural Theory* (London: Sage), pp. 36–102.

Halford, S., Savage, M. and Witz, A. (1996, forthcoming), *Gender, Careers and Organisations* (Basingstoke: Macmillan).

Hearn, J. and Parkin, W. (1987), *Sex at Work: The Power and Paradox of Organisation Sexuality* (Brighton: Wheatsheaf).

Hochschild, A. (1983), *The Managed Heart* (Berkeley: CA: California University Press).

Jackson, P. (1982), *The Political Economy of Bureaucracy* (London: Phillip Allen).

Marshall, J. (1984), *Women Managers: Travellers in a Man's World* (Chichester: John Wiley).

Moss Kanter, R. (1977), *Men and Women of the Corporation* (New York: Basic Books).

Morgan, D. and Scott, S. (1993), 'Bodies in a Social Landscape', in S. Scott and D. Morgan (eds), *Body Matters: Essays in the Sociology of the Body* (London: Falmer Press).

Pringle, R. (1989), 'Bureaucracy, Rationality and Sexuality: The Case of Secretaries' in Hearn, J., Sheppard, D. L., Tancred-Sheriff, P. and Burrell, G. (eds), *The Sexuality of Organisation* (London: Sage).

Pringle, R. (1989b), *Secretaries Talk: Sexuality, Power and Work* (London: Verso).

Shilling, C. (1993), *The Body in Social Theory* (London: Sage).

Stanko, E. (1988), 'Keeping Women in and out of Line: Sexual Harassment and Occupational Segregation', in S. Walby (ed.), *Gender Segregation at Work* (Milton Keynes: Open University Press).

Turner, B. (1992), *Regulating Bodies: Essays in Medical Sociology* (London: Routledge).

Witz, A. and Savage, M. (1992), 'The Gender of Organisations', in M. Savage and A. Witz (eds), *Gender and Bureaucracy* (Oxford: Blackwell), pp. 3–64.

9 Feminist Debates on Prostitution

Mary McIntosh

However nicely our meetings begin, there always comes a crunch point where feminists cannot accept women providing sex for men.[1]

The first feminist conference on prostitution was called in December 1971. . . . The conference was both an enlightenment and a disaster. The first day began sedately enough. . . . The afternoon was devoted to workshops where all hell broke loose – between the prostitute and the movement . . . the confused animosity of the prostitutes' attack, the uneasy guilt and muddled answers given back by the movement women – both were predictable. After hours of heated and fuzzy argument we had drawn lines, stated positions, denounced each other – or rather the prostitutes denounced the movement, some of whose members would occasionally stop defending themselves long enough to listen or vie with each other for approval from the prostitutes, who were enthralled to find themselves the center of attention in a group of women they were free – even encouraged – to insult. An S and M trip. The specter of sexual freedom, the real issue, was palpable in the room. Who knows most about sex? Who gets more? What is most? Who is cool? Money is fun. What's pride? What's prudery? Everyone was deeply ambivalent about everyone else: unconscious envy and resentment operated like steam engines – one felt them throb. We quarrelled and were reconciled, then quarrelled again – but at least we had come together. And in the interminable 'just let me finish my point' versus 'baby you don't know where it's at' that prolonged itself in doorways and staircases or over the post-mortem drinks in bars, we were at least becoming persons to each other. There was a gulf, but it was closing. It was all possible. On the second day things exploded. An inadvertent piece of tactless precipitance, the title of the day's program was inscribed on leaflets for our benefit: 'Towards the Elimination of Prostitution.' The panel of experts included everyone but prostitutes. A few of them arrived late and after some hesitation were permitted to sit on

191

the platform. As the last in turn to speak on the panel, I was delighted to turn over the discussion to the real experts. But it was too late. . . . Things rapidly degenerated into chaos. Prostitutes had gathered their still-nebulous rage against their own lives and summarily redirected it toward movement women who appeared to be quite as summarily 'eliminating' prostitution, the very means of their livelihood. Beyond the absurdly hypothetical threat posed by the term 'elimination,' since the first step toward elimination was agreed by all to be decriminalization – an obvious benefit to the prostitutes who would no longer be arrested, fined and imprisoned – beyond this was the far greater threat of adverse judgment by other women. For if large number of 'straight' women congregate to agree that there is an absolute benefit in the elimination of prostitution – what does this convey to the prostitute? That she is despised and rejected by her sister women. . . . The accusation, so long buried in liberal good will or radical rhetoric – 'you're selling it, I could too but I won't' – was finally heard. Said out loud at last. The rejection and disapproval which the prostitutes have sensed from the beginning, and with the unerring instinct of the unconscious have directed all their energy toward exposing, is now present before us, a palpable force in the air. The prostitutes are justified at last. There is fighting now in earnest. Someone is struck, the act obscene, irreparable. Attempts at reconciliation are futile. Order and direction are out of the question in what is now an encounter group of more than five hundred people. The afternoon lies in shambles.   (Millett, 1973, pp. 18–26)

That was New York at the dawn of the second wave of feminism. The style of the confrontation – and the telling of it – are pure New York and pure 1971, but the self-same issues have plagued feminism around the world before and since.

In London a couple of years later another conference was the setting for more decorous but equally divisive debates. Here again, the women's movement activists were pitted against prostitutes and against each other. This time, the most clearly articulated feminist position was 'we are all prostitutes'. It came from the Wages for Housework[2] supporters whose critique of unpaid housework covered sexual servicing as well as cooking and cleaning for men. In their view, all women have to trade sex for financial support. 'Prostitute women' differ only in being more frank about what they are doing and suffer degradation and exploitation in consequence. Predictably, the prostitutes present did not agree. They did not feel exploited but spoke proudly of their colour televisions and fitted carpets. And they certainly did not feel the same as straight women: 'I'll give you a packet of rubbers and we'll go up Kings Cross and see how you get on', was the way one of them taunted the Wages for Housework leader.

A hundred years before, in the heyday of Victorian prostitution, feminists had also claimed a sisterhood with prostitutes, which for a brief moment seems to have been reciprocated by some. Those who campaigned against state regulation of prostitution, which was intended to check venereal disease, argued that it enabled male clients to degrade women and gave control over women's bodies to male doctors, police and magistrates. As one prostitute put it:

It is *men*, only *men*, from the first to the last, that we have to do with! To please a man I did wrong at first, then I was flung about from man to man. Men police lay hand on us. By men we are examined, handled, doctored and messed on with. In hospital it is a man again who makes prayers and reads the Bible for us. We are up before magistrates who are men, and we never get out of the hands of men. (*The Shield*, 9 May 1870, quoted in Walkowitz, 1980, p. 128)

The members of the Ladies' National Association for the Repeal of the Contagious Diseases Acts in the 1870s would never have used the same language, but their ideas are not a million miles from those of Kate Millett in the 1970s:

Prostitutes are our political prisoners – in jail for cunt. Jailed for it, for cunt, for the offence we all commit in just being female. That's sexual politics, the stone core of it. (Millett, 1973, p. 114)

The strange thing about the similarity is that Millett wrote this in an era with a much more positive attitude to sex, and an era relatively unshadowed by venereal disease – before AIDS – or unwanted pregnancy – after The Pill. She was severely critical of the male-dominated heterosexual permissiveness of the 1960s, but not of sexual freedom itself. The Ladies' National Association mounted a very specific campaign against 'laws that punish the sex who are the victims of vice and leave unpunished the sex who are the main causes both of the vice and its dreaded consequences' (quoted in Walkowitz, 1980, p. 93). They never doubted the orthodoxy of the day, that sexual licence was evil as well as hazardous to health, but they reserved their moral obloquy for men rather than for the 'fallen women' who were usually held to blame. Theirs was the feminism that was to be summed up in the 1913 slogan, 'votes for women, purity for men'.

The nineteenth-century alliance between prostitutes and feminists was short-lived. With the repeal of the Contagious Diseases Acts in 1886, the common ground of the unfairness of police regulation and concern with the economic plight of working-class women disappeared and the feminists turned their energies to a social purity crusade aiming to protect young girls and attack the 'white slave trade' but in practice serving to intensify the policing of prostitutes' lives.

The central feminist criticism of prostitution is that it epitomizes and reinforces men's oppression of women. Sex appears as something that men desire and women can supply or withhold, but women's own desires are irrelevant. Women's economic powerlessness leads them to trade one of their few assets. It is almost socially acceptable for a man to be a client, but a woman who is a prostitute is morally condemned or at best seen as sick or a pitiable slut. Prostitution is the epitome, the extreme expression, of the asymmetrical male-defined and male-dominated heterosexuality in which women are sexually used and then despised by men.

But around this central and distinctively feminist criticism revolve a number of others, one of them is the old-fashioned view, based on a repressive sexual morality, that condemns any sex outside a loving relationship of marriage. These days, this is seldom just a blanket rejection of all sexual expression; everyone seems concerned not to be seen as anti-sex. Mary Whitehouse (1977), famous for her campaign to clean up television, values sex as an expression of love in an intimate monogamous marriage and bewails the way that public portrayals of sex in the media are necessarily impersonal and purely physical. There is a feminist version of this argument, which sees impersonal, genitally focused sex as being a male-defined perversion of the true possibilities of sexual relations; men should learn from women that sex can be more diffuse and more emotionally expressive. In this view, prostitution reflects a distorted and stunted form of sex.

Feminism today is racked by the 'tension between sexual danger and sexual pleasure', as Carole Vance (1984, p. 1) put it. It is clear that the predominant ways in which sexual life is organized work in favour of men rather than women. And there is often a close association between sex and male violence, both in public forms like sexual harassment and rape by strangers and in the private intimacy of the couple. But it is also clear that many women have relished the sexual enlightenment of the twentieth century and that one strand of feminism has been the 'sexual enthusiasm' of the modernist approach to sex (Robinson, 1976, p. 3), and especially the challenge to the double standard and the claim to sexual parity with men. Another strand of feminism – of which Andrea Dworkin represents an extreme example – has emphasized the danger for women of male-dominated sex.

But it is not clear where either of these strands leads us in the politics of prostitution. Recognizing the danger and exploitation involved in all heterosex could lead to a defence of prostitution as more honest and as redressing the imbalance to some degree. As we shall see, some feminist prostitutes argue that they at least insist on being paid for being used – other women just submit. More often, though, this emphasis leads to a view of prostitution as the epitome of all that is wrong with male-dominated sex. On the other hand, sexual enthusiasts can seek to cast the prostitute as the ultimate 'liberated lady', as Margo St James, a vocal American prostitute, has rather improbably done. Or they can champion women's free pursuit of autonomous and self-defined sexual pleasure and condemn prostitution as capitulation to men's ideas. One writer who has emphasized the importance of sexual expression in defining our whole identity is Carole Pateman.

'SHE IS SELLING *HERSELF* IN A VERY REAL SENSE'

Carole Pateman (1988) presents the most sustained philosophical discussion of prostitution from a feminist perspective, in a chapter entitled 'What's Wrong With Prostitution?'. Her particular concern is to refute what she calls the 'contractrian' defence of prostitution. This is the argument that the prostitution contract is exactly like any other employment contract: the prostitute offers her labour power for sexual services for a given period in exchange for money. In this view the problems with prostitution are the same as those with any other labour contract. Prostitutes need trade union rights and a degree of control over their working situation just as other workers do. But the idea that prostitution in itself is peculiarly degrading is seen as part of the patriarchal hypocrisy about sex that feminism rejects. So contractarians argue that 'sound prostitution' is possible, with a free market in sexual services in which anyone, male or female, may have the opportunity to be a buyer or a seller.

Against this view, Pateman argues that prostitution is not just another branch of commodity capitalism but is 'part of the exercise of male sex-right, one of the ways in which men are ensured access to women's bodies' (1988, p. 194). Part of her argument rests upon her conjectural history of the origins of modern patriarchy, the story of the sexual contract, the fraternal agreement between men to ensure their mastery as a sex including their right of sexual access to women. In the light of this story she analyses three kinds of contract involving women – the marriage contract, the prostitution contract and the surrogacy contract – to show that what is at issue in each case is the body of a woman. Women, she says, can never become the disembodied 'individuals' of classic social contract theory. Because there is an integral relationship between the body and the self, 'women's selves are involved in prostitution in a different manner from the involvement of the self in other occupations' and a woman cannot contract out the use of her body without 'selling *herself* in a very real sense' (1988, p. 207).

One issue here, then, is about the body: how far is it separable from the self? Can 'you' be said to be the owner of your body, to use or hire out like any other form of property? The body forms part of the contract in many forms of employment, but Pateman distinguishes the factory owner's, or even the slave owner's, interest in what the body can produce from the prostitute's client's interest in the women's body as such. An employer or slave owner would be just as happy with a robot if it could do the job as well; but a man goes to a prostitute precisely as an embodied woman. The fact that men often go to prostitutes for 'hand relief' is often cited to show that prostitutes provide a service rather than passively offering their bodies; but Pateman argues that, on the contrary, it shows that it is the woman herself who is being bought since her clients could easily masturbate for themselves or get another man or a machine to do it for them.

In contrasting prostitution with productive employment or slave labour, Pateman is not really comparing like with like. A more testing analogy would be with personal service occupations. People are willing to pay to have restaurant meals served at their table by personable waiters; on the whole you pay more to have it brought by men than by women; to be able to command a man as a servant in the house or as personal assitant in the office is more statusful than to command a woman. In the caring professions, too, the person is as important as the task. Day nurseries and old people's homes are staffed by people, not by closed-circuit television monitors and automated food dispensers. Perhaps more importantly, many occupations increasingly involve harnessing personality and emotions, which are surely as integral to the self – and indeed to the gendered self – as the body is. We all collude in this when we deride the 'plastic smile' of British Airways and laud the 'genuine friendliness' of Quantas. As Arlie Hochschild has shown in *The Managed Heart* (1983), stewards are trained to smile with feeling: emotions are part of the job.

As well as involving bodily and emotional work, these service occupations often play a part in the constitution of specifically gendered selves for women. Rosemary Pringle has analysed the way in which secretarial colleges provide their students with the basis for the construction of adult femininity. Office skills are combined with 'a well-groomed appearance, a well-modulated voice, maturity, poise and grace and the ability to converse intelligently with managers' in the making of the 'office "lady" with its dual overtones of gender and class' (Pringle, 1988, p. 133). Many occupations, of course, tend to gender their workers: Cynthia Cockburn, for instance, has discussed how the masculinity of printers is constructed in the workplace and how deeply their sense of self is rooted in their craft (Cockburn, 1983). But the service sector seems to be particularly linked to femininity, both in the sense of requiring the engagement of already formed feminine selves and in the sense that the day to day work relations constitute added aspects of femininity.

Is prostitution *logically* different, as Pateman insists, from these other service occupations?

Socially, at least, they are very similar. The further up the market you go the more the prostitute is expected to give of herself. The more she charges, the less she can be brusque and matter-of-fact like a cheap streetwalker and the more she must talk and use a sophisticated range of interpersonal skills. But just as schoolteachers or undertakers have individual and collective ways of distancing themselves from the feelings they must deploy in their jobs, so prostitutes often have clear ways of distinguishing their relationships with clients from those with friends and lovers. They may change their clothes, their hair, their manner; they may mix with people of a different race, age or subculture from their clients; they may have women as lovers.

Another issue in Pateman's argument is about the connexion between 'the sex act' and gendered identity:

men can also affirm their masculinity in other ways, but in relations between the sexes, unequivocal affirmation is obtained by engaging in 'the sex act'. Womanhood, too, is confirmed in sexual activity. (1988, p. 207)

So it is not just the body that is integral to the self, it is the body in the [hetero]sex act. She goes on to argue that surrogate motherhood involves the self in an even more profound way, on the grounds that: 'The 'surrogate' mother contracts out rights over the unique physiological, emotional and creative capacity of her body, that is to say, herself as a woman' (1988, p. 215).

The difficulty about this is that it is hard to know at what level of generalization to take it. Is it an empirical sociological statement about the centrality of heterosexual sex (and of pregnancy) to gender and of gender to self in our culture? And if so, does it recognize that individual gendered subjectivities are much more various than this? Some men can feel weakened and feminised by sex with a woman; some young women can feel empowered and freed by their first experience of sex with a man. Many lesbians feel fully feminine and many gay men feel fully masculine, even if they never go in for heterosex. It is not clear how important it is to Pateman's argument that the cultural and subjective levels of gender should coincide here. It is not clear, for instance, whether a lesbian in prostitution would sell *herself* any less than a straight woman would. Pateman has fallen into the same trap as a lot of feminist theory: the description and critique of a deep empirical gender divide becomes transmuted into a logical disjunction that has necessary consequences.

One difficulty here is that Pateman is using a very wooden notion of self. Sociologists would tend to see selves as more fluid, more situational; some would see them as essentially fragmented and the 'unitary self' as a performative or perhaps a discursive construct, an accomplishment rather than a pre-given. Arlie Hochschild herself has an extended discussion of the various uses of the concept of self.

Nevertheless, regardless of what may be happening with gendered selves in individual acts of prostitution, it is clear that the existence of prostitution as an institution is significant at the level of culture. Pateman's philosophical argument that prostitution is bad because it essentially involves the prostitute selling herself may be dubious. But there is a good empirical sociological point that prostitution is a central instance of patriarchal heterosexuality.

Pateman's philosophical approach, resting as it does on a conjectural history of an original social contract, is absolutist in its implications. The problem for her is, are we 'for' prostitution as an essence or 'against' it? The answer is equally absolute: we are against it because it is 'part of the exercise of male sex right'. But what are the political implications of this? Pateman herself states that you can condemn prostitution without condemning the prostitute, just as you can condemn capital-ism without condemning the worker. However, her own argument is not a critique of the institution but of the *act* of prostitution. If its essence is that the prostitute sells herself, then anyone who chooses prostitution is condemned for what she does, not just for its effects. Many feminists who take a similar position to Pateman's, though, do condemn prostitutes for participating in this essentially patriachal set-up. They take the view that women should have no truck with the patriarchy and live as far as possible in post-patriarchal ways. Against this, some prostitutes have argued that you can take part in prostitu-tion in such a way as to undermine men's power.

'STRIPPING DOESN'T PERPETUATE THE STRUCTURE OF OUR WORLD, IT CASHES IN ON IT'[3]

From the mid-1970s onwards the voices of feminist prostitutes began to be heard. Margo St James founded COYOTE (Call Off Your Old Tired Ethics) in San Francisco in 1973; prostitutes occupied churches in Lyons and elsewhere in France in 1975, in protest against police harassment and failure to protect them against violence coupled with government attempts to tax their earnings; they were followed by pros-titutes in London and Canada.

Their main emphasis has always been on immediate issues around the laws and the overall goal of decriminalization. Their ideal is simi-lar to what Pateman would call 'sound prostitution'. They believe that if there were no laws specifically concerned with prostitution, but the ordinary laws to protect people from force, fraud and exploitation were actually enforced in their case, the business could run smoothly and cause no social problems. Two features of their argument are distinc-tively feminist. One is that the stigma of the label 'whore' affects all women and serves to keep all women under control.

> Even the wives of company directors can't go to the Hilton Hotel unescorted because they can be taken for prostitutes; and teenage girls are told by their mothers how not to dress or put make-up on because they might 'look like a tart'. (Valentino and Johnson, 1980, p. 21)

Prostitutes were not the first feminists to see that the distinction between good and bad women works to divide and rule. The madonna and the magdalen of the Victorian imagination (Trudgill, 1976) and the 'slags' and 'drags' of modern teenage culture (Cowie and Lees, 1981) have long been recognized as providing a restricting range of meanings for all women's sexual lives.

The second distinctively feminist feature is the idea of prostitution as sex work, meaning that it is an occupation, an activity with its own skills and ways of operating, rather than an identity or a selling of the self, as Pateman would have it. The claim is that prostitutes are paid for what they do, rather than for what they are or what they have. They are a kind of entertainer and have affinities with strippers, pornographic models and actresses, and peep-show workers. One prostitute organisation in Atlanta, Georgia took as its name the acronym HIRE – Hooking Is Real Employment (French, 1989). They disclaim the identity of 'common prostitute' or 'known prostitute', which are written into legal methods of control. Indeed, they emphasize how much they are like other women. 'We were not born prostitutes' (*Nous ne sommes pas nées prostituées*) was the title of one book that came out of the French prostitute movement of the mid-1970s. 'We are women, mothers, human beings. . . . We have become prostitutes. Why?' ('Chantal' and Bernad, 1978, p. 13). The answer always has something to do with the limited range of choices open to women. Some point to the way in which all women are liable to get labelled as slags or whores unless they restrict their sexual activities according to a subtle but effective social code. Those who have been most influenced by socialist ideas stress the fact that low pay and restricted opportunities make it hard for a woman to support herself, especially if she has children to look after.

This emphasis on prostitution as work – as an occupation like any other – has affinities with the early feminist recognition that being a housewife is a job[4] and that mothering and caring for the old, the sick or the disabled are also work. 'Every mother is a working mother', as a slogan of the late 1970s put it. It also echoes the feminist recognition that many of women's abilities, such as manual dexterity, sewing, or a good telephone manner, are not classified as skills in the world of employment, so that women's work is less highly valued than men's, and less well paid (Phillips and Taylor, 1980; Elson and Pearson, 1981). The old-fashioned terms 'working girl' and 'pro' are pre-feminist in this respect. They suggest a contrast with the 'amateur', seen from a men's point of view, who gives sex away for nothing. So what marks the prostitute as a pro, or as working, is that she charges for it. From this pre-feminist perspective, an unpaid activity does not count as work.

In a feminist context, then, the term 'sex worker' carries a double load: it means that these are women who are paid for what they do, who earn their living by sex, but it also means that, as with other women, what they do should be respected as a skilled and effortful activity and not considered simply as a natural capacity of every woman.

This brings us back full circle to the 'Wages for Housework' position on prostitution. For the idea that all women are prostitutes in the sense that all heterosexual relations involve trading sex for financial support, leads to the idea that women should be paid for it in money, rather than in a more nebulous exchange for dependence. Just as housework is only respected if it is paid a wage, so having sex with men can only be respected if it is paid for. So in this view, prostitutes are more admirable than other women because they are more frank about what they are doing and never sell themselves cheap.

But this analogy also reveals a weakness in this hard-line pro-prostitute position. The 'Wages for Housework' position was early criticized for freezing the division of labour and condemning women to cleaning, cooking and childcare as their occupation. From the perspective of feminist households that were trying to share these tasks equally among all their members, the 'Wages for Housework' solution would prematurely foreclose on what they saw as a progressive move towards abolishing sexual difference. In addition, in so far as these households had a communal ethos, they encouraged the idea of mutual interdependence and doing things for the social good rather than for monetary reward. Similar criticisms can be applied to prostitution, from the perspective of a feminism that sees a future in a greater freedom and women's pursuit of sexual pleasure, as well as recognizing that the sexual arena is at present one of danger and exploitation for women (Vance, 1984).

Paid prostitution freezes the sexual division of labour in relation to heterosex and condemns women to doing sex as a service to men rather than for themselves. In recognizing, and perhaps rather exaggerating, a current reality it forecloses on more progressive efforts to transform the heterosexual world.

Prostitution is a deeply paradoxical issue for feminism. Whether we see the desirable transformation of the heterosexual world in a reactionary way – curbing men's desires: 'purity for men' – or in a progressive one of empowerment for women, prostitution implies at once a challenge and an acceptance of the doudle standard of the *status quo*. As such, it can neither be condemned nor embraced wholeheartedly. One thing is certain, however, given that prostitution does exist on a wide scale: that feminists should listen to the voices of organized prostitutes and other sex workers (van der Gaag, 1994) and support campaigns that help protect them against violence, disease, abuse and exploitation.

NOTES

1. Helen Buckingham, a London call-girl and outspoken campaigner for the decriminalization of prostitution, speaking at the Second World Whores' Congress at the European Parliament in Brussels, 1–3 October 1986, quoted in Pheterson (1989, p. 150).
2. 'Wages for Housework' groups were set up in a number of countries – notably in North America, Italy and the United Kingdom – following the publication of Maria Dalla Costa and Selma James's book *The Power of Women and the Subversion of the Community* in 1973. The analogy between the home and the factory and the recognition that housework was like any other work but unwaged led to the demand that women's work in the home should be rewarded and respected. In London, the 'Wages for Housework' group gave birth to 'Wages Due Lesbians' and also to the 'English Collective of Prostitutes' which shared their base in the Kings Cross Women's Centre and has run effective campaigns, such as that against tightening up 'kerb crawling' legislation.
3. Jessica, a stripper, quoted in Mimi = Freed (1993, p. 51).
4. Ann Oakley (1974) applies the sociology of work to this occupation which has normally been considered simply as a part of women's 'role'.

REFERENCES

'Chantal' and Bernad, J. (1978), *Nous ne sommes pas nées prostituées* (Paris: Les Editions Ouvrières).

Cockburn, C. (1983), *Brothers: Male Dominance & Technological Change* (London: Pluto).

Cowie, C. and Lees, S. (1981), 'Slags or Drags?', *Feminist Review*, 9, Autumn, pp. 17–31.

Dalla Costa, M. and James, S. (1973), *The Power of Women and the Subversion of the Community* (Bristol: Falling Wall Press).

Dworkin, A. (1987), *Intercourse* (London: Martin Secker & Warburg).

Elson, D. and Pearson, R. (1981), '"Nimble Fingers Make Cheap Workers": An Analysis of Women's Employment in Third World Export Manufacturing', *Feminist Review*, 7, Spring, pp. 87–107.

French, D. (1989), *Working: My Life as a Prostitute* (London: Gollancz).

van der Gaag, N. (1994), 'Soliciting for Change', editorial in *New Internationalist*, no. 252, pp. 7–8.

Gorham, D. (1978), 'The "Maiden Tribute of Modern Babylon" Re-examined: Child Prostitution and the Idea of Childhood in Late-Victorian England', *Victorian Studies*, **21**: pp. 353–79.

Hochschild, A. (1983), *The Managed Heart: Commercialization of Human Feeling* (Berkeley, CA: University of California Press).

Millett, K. (1973), *The Prostitution Papers* (New York: Avon).

Mimi = Freed (1993), 'Nobody's Victim', *10 Percent*, **1**: 3, pp. 48–53.

Oakley, A. (1974), *The Sociology of Housework* (London: Martin Robertson).

Pateman, C. (1988), *The Sexual Contract* (Cambridge: Polity Press).

Pheterson, G. (ed.) (1989), *A Vindication of the Rights of Whores* (Seattle: Seal Press).

Phillips, A. and Taylor, B. (1980), 'Sex and Skill: Notes Towards a Feminist Economics', *Feminist Review*, **6**, pp. 79–88.

Pringle, R. (1988), *Secretaries Talk: Sexuality, Power and Work* (London: Verso).

Robinson, P. (1976), *The Modernization of Sex: Havelock Ellis, Alfred Kinsey, William Masters and Virginia Johnson* (London: Paul Elek).

Trudgill, E. (1976), *Madonnas and Magdalens: The Origins and Development of Victorian Sexual Attitudes* (London: Heinemann).

Valentino, M. and Johnson, M. (1980), 'On the Game and On the Move', in C. Jaget (ed.), *Prostitutes – Our Life* (Bristol: Falling Wall Press).

Vance, C. S. (ed.) (1984), *Pleasure and Danger: Exploring Female Sexuality* (London: Routledge & Kegan Paul).

Walkowitz, J. (1980), *Prostitution and Victorian Society: Women, Class, and the State* (Cambridge: Cambridge University Press).

Whitehouse, M. (1977), *Whatever Happened to Sex?* (London: Wayland).

10 The Cultural, the Sexual, and the Gendering of the Labour Market

Lisa Adkins and Celia Lury

In this chapter, we want to explore the complex relations between culture, sexuality and gender in feminist theorizations of the labour market. To begin to do this, we turn first to early feminist analyses of the labour market, including Barrett (1980) and Cockburn (1981). We explore what we see to be their restricted understandings of the social as an analytic category in the explanation of gender, restrictions which, in later work made possible the hollowing out of the social, and led to its abandonment and replacement by the cultural. We see this trajectory as having led to limited understandings of the gendering of the labour market, especially visible in the investigation of the significance of sexuality in the organization of the labour market.

EARLY FEMINIST ANALYSES OF THE LABOUR MARKET: RESTRICTED UNDERSTANDINGS OF THE SOCIAL

Among the first to explore the relationships between the social, the cultural (including the ideological) and gender in the labour market was Michèle Barrett. In *Women's Oppression Today*, Barrett summarizes her own argument in the following terms,

> Although I will argue against the view that women's oppression is solely ideological, the role of familial and domestic ideology is considerable. Also it is important to stress that no clear separation can be made between the economic and the ideological. Relations of production, grounded as they are in a deeply ideological division of labour, cannot be investigated through economic categories alone. (1980, p. 40)

As Barrett herself and many others have noted, this analysis, while making a formidable advance in understandings of women's oppression, proved better able to deal with some aspects of women's position in the labour market more than others. There are, for example, recognized difficulties in evaluating the significance of sexuality in the constitution of women's oppression in the labour market within this framework. We suggest that these difficulties arose, in part, because of *how* the relationship between Marxism and feminism was itself defined, and the consequences this definition had for understandings of 'gender' and the aspects of oppression it revealed.

On the relationship between Marxism and feminism, Barrett herself writes,

> The problem faced by [Marxist feminism] can be put simply in terms of the different objects of the two perspectives. Marxism, constituted as it is around relations of appropriation and exploitation, is grounded in concepts that do not and *could not* address directly the gender of the exploiters and those whose labour is appropriated. A Marxist analysis of capitalism is therefore conceived around a primary contradiction between labour and capital and operates with categories that, as has recently been argued, can be termed 'sex-blind'. Feminism, however, points in a different direction, emphasizing precisely the relations of gender – largely speaking, of the oppression of women by men – that Marxism has tended to pass over in silence. (op. cit., p. 8; our emphasis)

In retrospect, three aspects of this statement appear especially problematic. These are, first, the shift in the focus of study from the 'relations of appropriation and exploitation' to the relations of production of capitalism. Second, the assumption that the relations of appropriation and exploitation within capitalism are gender-neutral. Third, the assumption that feminism is to be understood in relation to the analysis of gender, where the meaning of gender itself is held to be self-evident, and is equated – 'largely speaking' – with (one particular kind of) oppression of women by men. We will concentrate on this last point since we think that Barrett's lack of attention to gender as an analytic category leads her, at times, to adopt a common-sense, and socially restricted understanding of the term (see Delphy and Leonard, 1986, 1992; Acker, 1990).

To develop this last point: while, for Barrett, the problem for feminist theory is the supposed ahistoricism universalism, and essentialism of the concept 'patriarchy', what seems more problematic from our point of view is the adoption of the category of gender as the difference between 'men' and 'women', especially since she treats these differences as if they were pre-given. Gender is largely equated by Barrett with the oppression of women by men, which she defines as independent of relations of production and appropriation (they are seen as gender-neutral). For Barrett, this means that feminism may have to show how gender is to do with oppression – that is, how the differences between men and women are rendered unequal – but it does not have to show how these differences are constituted. Instead, such differences are assumed, at least in certain crucial respects. The 'fact' that there are differences is assumed, and that these differences can be understood in terms of a single binary opposition, that is, that there are two genders is assumed; so is, the 'fact' that these two are men and women, masculine and feminine.

What we hope to show is that this restricted understanding of gender actually limits the kind of oppression and thus the dimensions of the social that can be identified. In order to do this, we explore how Barrett herself uses the term gender. At the time Barrett was writing, Marxist feminism was itself frequently defined (and defined itself) in opposition to radical feminism – in this particular case, represented for Barrett by Millett and Firestone, who are held to invoke an 'apparently universal and trans-historical category of *male* dominance' (op. cit., p. 12). The use of the term 'male' as an invocation of 'sex' is identified by Barrett as problematic; it is equated with the radical feminist emphasis on the bodily, the biological. It is held to be ahistorical, essentialist, and reductionist. Radical feminism regresses to a time when the 'feminist distinction between sex as a biological category and gender as a social one had not been established' (op. cit., p. 13). In its place, Barrett (super)imposes 'gender', said to be a 'social' distinction, but what is meant by 'social' is left implicit in Barrett's argument. This lack of attention to the social, we suggest, takes for granted the historical constitution of this category.

The taken-for-grantedness of the social (what might be termed a form of social essentialism) is evident in Barrett's use of the Marxist concept of 'reproduction', which is divided into 'human reproduction' and 'social reproduction'. In relation to these two different types of reproduction, Barrett operates two different understandings of gender. In her brief discussions of human reproduction, she implies that 'gender' is merely an extension of biological or natural understandings of 'sex'. That is, while 'sex' and 'gender' are explicitly set up in apparent opposition, they are, in effect, collapsed. So, for example, Barrett sees no need to fill out the categories of 'masculine' and 'feminine': they are simply located as the inevitable outcomes of 'sex'.

In contrast, in her discussions of social reproduction, an at least partially historically specified understanding of gender is developed. In this context, 'sex' is no longer one of Barrett's concerns, and is completely detached from 'gender' (in contrast to their collapse in the discussion of human reproduction just outlined). 'Gender' is now to do with social reproduction, and social reproduction 'is . . . closely tied to an account of class relations at the root of capitalist production' (op. cit., p. 29). Indeed, so closely is gender tied to capitalist production that it is defined more or less exclusively as the power relations involved in women's reproduction of men's labour power. This requirement is, for Barrett, the over-riding social determinant of 'gender' and, indeed, is held to constitute the whole of 'women's oppression'.

What was significant about this argument at the time it was made was that this was a way in which women could be written into history. But, paradoxically, what stands out in retrospect is the taken-for-grantedness of the understanding of the social through which women entered into history. What is visible now is that Barrett assumes that the social is made in, through and by the requirements of capitalism. But as she and others have since noted, the social has determinants other than those deriving from the requirements of capitalism.

The use of this limited understanding in the early work of Barrett and many other feminists not only took for granted a limited conception of gender, but actively reinforced it by making visible only those aspects of gender associated with the reproduction of class relations. Its take-up as a complete explanation of gender thus had the effect of universalizing limited aspects of women's oppression, and contributed to the marginalization of aspects of women's oppression, including those experienced most acutely by women of colour (as Barrett herself recognises in later work (Barrett and McIntosh, 1985)). However, despite the force of the critiques which responded to this argument and the development of new analyses on the bases of these critiques (Walby, 1986; Witz, 1990), we believe that 'the social' as an analytic category has, implicitly at least, continued to be so closely tied to the relations of capitalist production that its value for feminist analysis has been made to seem untenable. Indeed, we believe that it is for these reasons that it has largely been replaced by understandings of gender as a cultural or ideological phenomenon. This, we believe, has its own problems, and is especially worrying for feminism at a time when not only 'society' but also 'the social' as a site of political contestation is under attack.

THE REFORMULATION OF THE MATERIAL: A BROADENING OUT OF THE SOCIAL?

The continued use of a limited understanding of both the social and gender is, for example, evident in Cynthia Cockburn's influential analysis of the 'material of male power' (1981). At first sight this may not be apparent, especially since Cockburn questions the over-working of the ideological or the cultural as an explanation of gender in other Marxist feminist analyses of the labour market. Specifically, Cockburn takes issue with the degree of significance to be attached to the ideological, and asserts the importance of material relations in the formation of gender. In doing so, she argues for a revised understanding of the material to include not just the economic but also the 'socio-political' and 'the physical'.[1]

However, while in some ways this reformulation of what is meant by the material redressed some of the problems arising from Barrett's limited definition of the social, it produced further problems since the relationships between the material, the social and the economic were not addressed. For example, Cockburn argues that the economic formed part of the material, but does not address the issue of whether the economic itself is gendered or not. Instead, once again, as in Barrett's account, the economic is held to be gender-neutral. Indeed, the question of what the economic consists in is explicitly put to one side: she herself says she will 'allow the economic to retire into the background'. As a consequence, the relationships between the economic, the socio-political and the physical are not addressed, even though they are all held to be part of 'the material'.

We want to spend some time reflecting on what we see to be this rather premature retirement of the economic. Throughout her analysis, Cockurn maintains that her retirement of the economic is connected to what she sees as the problems associated with an economic reductionism. In particular, she sees economistic accounts as having ignored other important sources of women's oppression. But we think there is more to this retirement than a straightforward rejection of economism. We believe Cockburn's reluctance to confront the economic arises because of her assumption that the economic is solely related to the capitalist mode of production. For her, the sex–gender system appears to be exclusively defined in terms of the physical and socio-political and can be understood independently of the economic. As a consequence, men may have power over women in the sex–gender system, and this results in the social category 'women', but this power is only effected through men's sex and not through the economic.

We see here the continuation of a limited understanding of the social, as in Barrett, although in Cockburn's formulation the determinant process recognised in the sex–gender system is male sex-power rather than ideology. Thus, for Cockburn, the social constitution of gender is exclusively defined by male sex-power, and she fails to consider other potential sources of gender, including the economic or the sexual. Moreover, because the social category of gender is not understood to include the economic, while women may be dominated by men they can never be the subject of their appropriation.

The difficulties with such restricted understandings of gender have since been acknowledged by some feminist labour-market theorists. But this has led, not to reworkings of the categories of the social or indeed the economic, but rather to a complete bypassing of the social. Thus, in more recent feminist analyses of the labour market we find only two modes of social formation: the economic and the cultural. In these analyses, however, the economic is not merely retired, but is laid to rest, and it is the cultural which is located as the principal determinant of gender.

THE BYPASSING OF THE SOCIAL: GENDER AS A CULTURAL PROCESS

In Pringle's (1989a, b) analysis of the gendering of the labour market, for example, she concentrates:

> on discourses of power rather than analyses of the labour process. . . . I have wanted to avoid a framework which latches on to the 'tangibles' and instead bring into the centre issues which have less frequently informed studies of 'work' . . . [including] the connections between domination, sexuality and pleasure. (1989a, p. *x*)

Here Pringle outrightly rejects the idea that sexuality can be brought into analyses of the labour market via 'the economic' (i.e. the 'tangibles' such as the labour process) or 'the social' (which is almost entirely absent from her account). Instead, she seeks to give weight to the sexual via an analysis of the ways in which power relations between men and women in the workplace are discursively produced, the cultural meanings embodied in occupations and the formation of workplace subjectivities.

What is especially interesting about Pringle's analysis from our point of view is that within her analysis of the symbolic and cultural production of power relations, she stresses the significance of family and sexual relations in the workplace as key constituents of these processes. In doing so Pringle therefore tackles the significance of sets of social relations which, due to the use of restricted understandings of the social, earlier feminist labour market theory had tended to neglect. Pringle, however, argues that both sexual and family relations are key in terms of the formation of gendered subjectivity within the workplace and in terms of the production of power relations between men and women. In particular, she argues that gendered workplace power relations relate to the operation of a number of (often overlapping) discourses based on family and sexual imagery which locate men and women in a number of different subject positions.

In her study of the boss–secretary relation, for example, Pringle argues that the operation of these discourses is central to the formation of gendered workplace identities and power relations between men and women. In particular, she argues that these discourses construct secretaries exclusively in familial and sexual terms – as office wives/mistresses, mothers/nannies or daughters. As a consequence, the variety of gendered subject and object positions produced through these discourses allows bosses to establish a number of forms of sexual and familial control over secretaries (including controls over their appearance, and the organization of their private lives). While Pringle stresses the limits of women's authority in the workplace and the range of controls to which secretaries are subject, she also argues that bosses exert this control not simply by force, but also by 'definitions of pleasure and selfhood' (1989b, p. 165). She shows, for example, how by gaining intimate knowledge of secretaries' personal lives, bosses can exert control by claiming to know what is 'best' for their secretaries, for instance, what gives them pleasure and self-esteem (1989b, p. 172). Indeed, Pringle locates control through pleasure as one of the key strategies of male domination in the workplace. In turn, this leads Pringle to argue for a recognition of the significance of domination based on desire in terms of the construction of workplace power relations, and to the significance of unconscious processes, repressions and fantasies which may structure such desires (1989b, pp. 174–7). She thus makes use of psychoanalytically informed understandings of occupational positions to fill out previously missing dimensions of subjection in the labour market.

In stressing the cultural and symbolic construction of jobs and locating the formation of workplace identities as key for the construction of power relations between men and women in the sphere of employment, Pringle's analysis broke new ground in feminist analyses of the labour market. But despite Pringle's attempt to move on from old paradigms, we believe that her understanding of gender as a purely cultural phenomenon, and the continued retirement of the economic relies on a taken-for-granted understanding of gender, and, as a consequence, continues to produce a limited understanding of the structuring of gender in the labour market.

The common-sense understanding of gender is evident in the ways Pringle simply assumes that to be a symbolic father/master/naughty child automatically confers power and the ability to control women on men. Similarly, she assumes that to be a symbolic daughter/mistress/mother–nanny confers submissiveness and subordination on women. That is, she reads in a (common-sense) gendered hierarchy to the subject and object positions without explaining the sources and conditions of the hierarchy. Thus, while she says that the subject and object positions 'are not equally available to men and women' (1989a, p. 170) she cannot explain how these subject/object positions become gendered in the first place, nor how individual workers come to occupy these positions. Rather, these occupational positions are described in terms of a range of psychic positionings, or identifications, distributed via the operation of powerful, but apparently arbitrary, discourses. The processes by which individuals come to occupy these positions is not explained; instead, pre-gendered workers are simply slotted in. This slotting in is, we believe, a consequence of her evacuation of the social as an analytical category and means that gender as a collective category is marginalized while gender, understood more or less exclusively as an identity, is defined as a cultural phenomenon.

Pringle's evacuation of the social is made clear in her later discussions of the possibility of the non-gendered nature of subject/object positions:

While masculine and feminine identities are to some extent 'fixed' in early childhood they also have to be constantly reproduced. They are never fully or permanently constituted and are always, in some sense, in a state of flux. Most discourses are gender differentiated so that subject and object positions are not equally available to men and women. But since the meanings have to be reproduced in specific situations there is room for negotiation and change. There is space for games to be played and roles to be reversed. (1989a, p. 54)

It is also clear in her conclusion that sexual pleasure can be used to disrupt male rationality and that women can 'get what they want on their own terms'. In both cases, the conditions under which gender may be detached from relations of power cannot be specified because the terms of their existing association have not been made clear. This leads to a kind of sexual voluntarism, in which agency, pleasure and desire, understood as relations of individual identification, are dissociated from the collective category 'gender'.

Pringle's limited understandings of the social and of the formation of gender contribute to a fundamental ambiguity about the relationship between the symbolic or the cultural and the economic in her analysis. For instance, while Pringle shows that women's workplace identities may be structured in sexual or familial terms (as in, for example, the case of the 'attractive mistress', or the 'sexy secretary'), the issue of the relationship between these workplace identities and the formation of men's economic and other advantage in the labour market remains unclear. Indeed, this is the case despite the fact that throughout her account Pringle argues for the centrality of discursive power relations for the gendered organization of work. But it is not clear from Pringle's account how the symbolic and discursive processes she identifies relate to such organization. Indeed, because the economic and the social are absent in Pringle's account, the significance of such cultural and symbolic processes for the relations of production, and therefore the organization of work relations between men and women (including the specificity of service work) cannot be considered. It then becomes impossible to consider the ways, for instance, that sexual, emotional or bodily subject positions available to men and women in the workplace may relate to the gendered nature of the relations of appropriation (including job specifications, criteria of quality and productivity, occupational resources and occupational hierarchies). Instead, the effectivity of cultural and symbolic processes is reduced to the performance of (gender) identity.[2]

REBUILDING THE SOCIAL: BEYOND THE UNGENDERED ECONOMIC

In contrast, in Adkins' (1992, 1995) research, the economic is neither retired or killed off, but is recognized as central in terms of the social structuring of gender. Moreover, the economic is not assumed to be an ungendered category; on the contrary, it is seen to be fundamentally organized in terms of gender. This gendered structuring of the economic is uncovered through studies of the conditions of men and women's employment in tourist organizations.

In these studies Adkins shows that, regardless of occupations, women are employed on quite different terms to men. Within tourist employment, women workers are recruited not simply on the basis of the particular skills or resources needed for particular jobs, but also on the basis of fulfilling a set of conditions relating to appearance. Thus, in a number of organizations Adkins found that if women were to get a job at all they had to fulfil criteria of visual attractiveness. Not only were women required to have an attractive, pleasing appearance to be employed, but part of the women's jobs once inside the workplaces involved the maintenance of their looks. Thus, if the women looked tired, wore too little or too much make-up, or failed to wear their uniforms in the prescribed manner (for example, if they failed to wear their dresses off the shoulder) they were instantly warned to correct their appearance problems – and if they did not were subject to dismissal. For men in these organizations no such conditions were in operation. There were no additional criteria they needed to fulfil as a group in order to become employees, and their jobs did not require the maintenance of their personal appearance.

Adkins goes on to show that the conditions relating to women's appearance acted to constitute women workers as a sexually commodified workforce. Thus, the appearance of women workers was the object of routine sexual attention in the organizations. Men customers, co-workers and managers routinely made sexual innuendoes about women's appearance, for example on how they liked the way they looked and found them attractive in their uniforms. This sexual attention from men was so routinized that the women developed various strategies to deal with the sexualized interactions. Thus, they would, 'laugh it off', 'look flattered', 'smile' and 'play along with it'. By engaging in these interactions women were routinely engaging in forms of sexual work. Moreover, this work was compulsory – if the women complained or got angry with the men they risked losing their jobs. Knowing how to

deal with the sexualized interactions and doing sexual work was therefore 'part of the job'. The conditions attached to women's employment meant that part of 'women's work' was the work of sexually
commodified labour. Indeed, women could only be workers – they
could only 'exchange' their labour – if they fulfilled the conditions of
being a sex-worker. Men and women were therefore constituted as
different kinds of workers in these organizations – to be workers women
had to be sexually attractive and carry out forms of sexual work, while
men did not have to do this work. Men and women therefore participated in the labour market within qualitatively different relations of
production. The work of the women at the tourist organizations, for
instance, did not simply involve serving food and drinks, selling sou-
venirs and clearing tables, but also involved the provision of sexual
services (amusement and titillation) for men. The conditions attached
to women's employment ensured that this work was performed whenever it was required – it was compulsory if women were to have access to, and retain their jobs. Thus, men (co-workers, managers and
customers) had access to, and could appropriate sexual servicing from
women workers.

The gendered nature of the relations of production, appropriation
and exploitation shows how, in contradistinction to Barrett, not that
these terms do not have any purchase in terms of understanding gender, nor that the economic (cf. Cockburn) or the 'tangibles' of the
labour process (cf. Pringle) should be left to retire through fear of
economism, but rather that men's power over women is, in part, produced through the (gendered) structuring of economic relations. In
Adkins' research, it is made clear that the gendered structuring of the
relations of production actively produces 'sexuality' in the labour market.
Thus, the gendering of production placed women in a position where
they were consistently sexually objectified by men and their sexual
work was routinely appropriated and exploited. The relations of production therefore located women as sexual objects and men as sexual actors/
subjects – who were able to initiate sexual interactions and access forms
of sexual servicing. In other words, the relations of production produced a form of sexuality which was structured in terms of men's
dominance.

Indeed, Adkins goes further in looking at the constitution of men's
economic/material advantages over women in the labour market through
the gendered structuring of production. Thus, she shows how the definition of women as a group of undifferentiated (sexual) workers, allows
men co-workers, not only access to forms of sexual servicing from

women workers, but also power to participate in occupational structuring. Specifically, because men were not constituted as a homogeneous group of workers in the way that women were, men were able to make claims to occupational resources (for example specific occupational skills) in ways which women could not counter because of their primary location as sexual workers (Adkins and Lury, 1992). In short, women as women were denied the ability to possess particular skill-based occupational resources because the 'primary labour market resource women were recognized to possess was that of their value as sexual servicers' (Adkins, 1992, p. 230).

We believe Adkins' research provides the basis for a more fully social understanding of gender compared to those developd in earlier feminist studies of the labour market. Adkins has been able to move towards such an understanding by rejecting the central assumption in the earlier analyses that the economic is a gender neutral category defined only by the relations of capitalism which is held to be irrelevant to the direct constitution of gender. We believe it is the assumption of the neutrality of the economic (as part of a limited understanding of the social) that leads to restricted understandings of gender. It underpins, for example, the inability to grasp the significance of sexuality in terms of a structuring force of gender and, in some cases, the failure to consider gender as a social phenomenon at all.

In Adkins' analysis, a much broader understanding of the social structuring of gender is effected. The recognition that the economic is not simply capitalist, but also patriarchal, allows gender to be seen in terms of the social constitution of hierarchically organized groups in which women workers are the subject of men workers', men employers' and men customers' appropriation and exploitation. Thus, the constitution of gender can be seen not simply to be effected through pre-given differences, male sex dominance or through the requirements of capitalism, but through the structuring of work relations (or relations of production) between men and women. In terms of the production of a feminist analysis of the labour market, such an understanding of gender also allows an appreciation of its determinants – including sexuality – which the earlier analyses had failed to theorize. The sexual is not simply a cultural phenomenon which is separate and distinct from the (ungendered) economic, but rather sexual relations are intrinsic to the economic.

A number of other contemporary feminist commentators concerned with analyses of the labour market have also recognized the problems associated with an ungendered understanding of the economic. Joan

Acker (1990), for example, explores the gendered constitution of 'workers' by interrogating the use of the abstract category of 'a job' which, in social and economic theory, is commonly held to be filled only by a disembodied worker who 'exists only for the work' (Acker, 1990, p. 149). Acker reveals the gendered structuring of jobs by arguing:

> The closest the disembodied worker doing the abstract job comes to a real worker is the male worker whose life centers on full-time, life-long job, while his wife or another woman takes care of his personal needs and his children. While the realities of life in industrial capitalism never allowed all men to live out this ideal, it was the goal for the labour unions and the image of the worker in social and economic theory. The woman worker, assumed to have legitimate obligations other than those required by the job, did not fit with the abstract job. (op. cit., p. 149)

Thus, for Acker, jobs and workers are 'deeply gendered and bodied' (op. cit., p. 150).

This is similar to Carol Pateman's argument in *The Sexual Contract* (1988). Here, Pateman suggests that women are not free to exchange their labour with employers on the same terms as men because of prior claims on women's labour:

> Women cannot become 'workers' in the same sense as men . . . the employment contract presupposes the marriage contract . . . the construction of the 'worker' presupposes that he is a man who has a women (a housewife) to take care of his daily needs. (Pateman, 1988, p. 131)

Thus, for Pateman, only men are free 'workers' and the ability to be a worker is founded on men's control and appropriation of women's labour in marriage.[3]

THE SOCIAL AS AN HISTORICALLY SPECIFIC FIELD

From our point of view, what is particularly interesting about both Acker's and Pateman's analyses is not only their recognition of the gendered structuring of the economic, but that this recognition rests on a historically specific understanding of the constitution of the social.

Indeed, both Acker and Pateman see the gendering of the economic or the capitalist market as being tied up with the birth of the social. Thus, for Acker:

A 'job' already contains the gender based division of labour and the separation between the public and the private spheres. The concept of a job assumes a particular gendered organization of domestic life and social production. (Acker, 1990, p. 149)

Similarly for Pateman, the development of the social (in particular the development of the civil or public sphere and capitalist relations) is seen as underpinned by what she terms the sexual contract – the medium through which modern patriarchal right is created and upheld. Indeed, Pateman sees the emergence of the public civil sphere in terms of the development of what she terms 'fraternal' patriarchy – a brotherhood in which only men are constituted as actors and in which men exercise the law of male sex-right. For example, Pateman demonstrates that all social contracts through which participation in the public sphere are effected are gendered. In particular, they assume male sex-right over women and the continuance of the gender division of labour. Thus, not only can women never be workers on the same terms as men but neither can they be full civil individuals. Indeed, Pateman shows that the public sphere is founded upon the appropriation and exploitation of women's labour:

Without the sexual contract there is no indication that the 'worker' is a masculine figure, or that the 'working class' is a class of men. The civil, public sphere does not come into being on its own, and the 'worker', his 'work' and his 'working' class cannot be understood independently of the private sphere and his conjugal right as husband. (Pateman, 1988, p. 135)

What stands out from Acker's and Pateman's analyses is their appreciation of the historical emergence of the social, and of its intrinsically gendered nature. In other words, these are analyses which define the social and gender in terms of their mutual constitution. Thus, unlike early feminist analyses of the labour market, Acker and Pateman do not operate ahistorical understandings of the social. We saw earlier how such restricted understandings of the social (such as the assumption that it is synonymous with the requirements of capitalism), have led to limited understandings of gender (such as an understanding in terms of the reproduction of class relations or simply in terms of 'male sex-power') and more recently has led to the abandonment of the social in feminist labour market theory.[4] But because Acker and Pateman understand the social and modern social formations (such as class, capitalism, modernity, imperialism and the nation) to be instrinsically gendered (indeed, they see that the social exists through and by the constitution of patriarchal contracts) they are, in turn, able to produce a historically specific exploration of the social structuring of gender. In other words, rather than hollowing out or abandoning the social, Acker and Pateman show how specific forms of women's oppression are structured by the gendered organization of the social itself.

THE UNIVERSALIZATION OF THE CULTURAL: A FREE MARKET IN IDENTITIES?

However, Adkins, Acker and Pateman are at odds with most other feminist analyses of the labour market. As we discussed earlier, the cultural is now being foregrounded as the key determinant of gender. However, we feel that feminists should be wary of accepting the view that the value of the social as a category of analysis has been exhausted and is no longer of use in understanding the constitution of gender. The writers we have discussed faced problems in theorizing the operation of sexuality in the labour market because they unproblematically adopted a universalist understanding of the social. Our argument has been that feminists should revise their understandings of the social rather than abandon it as an analytic term. We fear that the recent turn to the cultural as it is being currently conceived in the analysis of gender may not offer a way out of the problems raised by the use of restricted understandings of gender, but, rather, will be complicit with the universalizing tendencies of certain uses of the cultural as a category of analysis.

In much recent social theory the contemporary economy is increasingly being seen to be 'culturalized'. In many of these arguments, a kind of cultural essentialism is at work. To put this rather too simplistically, culture is seen as a set of meaning resources universally available to the individual in the project of self-transformation; it is understood as the source of identity and the gender-neutral medium of difference. This implicit essentialism, we shall argue, is reproduced in many recent feminist analyses of the labour market. While it is rarely visible in the form of a grand theory, it surfaces in the use of 'identity' as if it was an ungendered (and unraced) term, and in the assumption that culture is an identity resource equally available to all; as if, indeed, there were a free market in identities. This use of identity arises, we believe, because of the failure to theorise the ways in which identity practices may be constituted in relations of appropriation.

In Pringle's analysis, for example, although she argues:

> In so far as all discourses are gender-differentiated, the subject and object positions are not equally available to men and women,

she continues,

> Since they have to be constantly reproduced by *specific* men and women there is room for change, play and experiment. (Pringle, 1989a, p. 29)

It seems as if while the discourses may be gendered, men and women, as specific individuals, are more or less equally able to 'change, play and experiment'. This assumption of mutability and dynamism appears to depend upon an unspecified principle of performativity that requires a self-transforming subject, a position from which, through relations of appropriation, as we go on to show, women are likely to be excluded.

While much recent feminist philosophy and political theory has been concerned with the issue of performativity, some of it has stressed the need to redefine it critically in such a way as to avoid a voluntaristic interpretation of the term. So, for example, Judith Butler stresses that performativity should be understood 'not as the act by which a subject brings into being what she/he names, but, rather, . . . that reiterative power of discourse to produce the phenomena that it regulates and constrains' (Butler, 1993, p. 2). She further argues that it is necessary to link the process of 'assuming' a sex with the question of identification', and with 'the discursive means by which the heterosexual imperative enables certain sexed identifications and forecloses and/or disavows other identifications' (op. cit., p. 3). She thus points to the importance of locating what she calls the 'conditions of intelligibility' within which individuals come to assume a sex and seeks to relate them to what she calls heterosexual hegemony.[5] In this way, she points to the importance of recognizing that culture, or what she calls the conditions of intelligibility, is not a gender-neutral resource for self-transformation.[6]

But, in many uses of the notion of performance or identity in analyses of the labour market, the question of gendered access to and ownership of identity is not even posed. So, for example, while Pringle's 'central concern is with the way in which power is associated with definitions of pleasure, and coercion itself is defined as pleasurable' (Pringle, 1989a, p. 29), she does not articulate a theory of 'institutionalised heterosexuality' or 'the family', the two terms she consistently uses to ground her analysis of power relations. We believe that if feminists fail to analyse how the ownership of identity itself, not just specific identities, is achieved in workplace practices, and is thus constituted as an occupational resource in gender-differentiated ways, they will continue to fail to see all the ways in which gender is a mechanism of appropriation in the labour-market.

The issue that needs to be explored from our point of view is how identities are related to organizational processes, such as the labour process. To fail to consider such relationships is to essentialize identity as a cultural property of the individual. It assumes the ability to freely exchange identity for a wage is universal. But, we might ask, how does an individual come to possess an identity? And can such an identity be freely disposed? Can women possess an identity in the same way as men? Or are their identities possessed differently through, for example, practices of appropriation? What are the sources of identity? If the source of workplace identities is said to be culture, how is this culture to be understood? Is the contemporary formation of the cultural gender-neutral?

Adkins' research suggests that it is not. It shows, for example, that identities are not universally available as resources and, in particular, that identities are not constituted as the cultural property of the individual which all workers are equally free to exchange. We discussed earlier how in service workplaces producing and maintaining a sexualized identity for women is 'part of the job'. Presenting a certain appearance and a sexualized way of being, or a sexual 'self', is both required, and subject to appropriation. Such identity practices for women cannot be detached from their person, contracted out, and freely exchanged; on the contrary, these identity practices are rendered intrinsic to women workers through relations of appropriation. That is to say, the gendered relations of production in these sites ensure that women's labour (including the production of workplace identities) is always embodied as part of their selves. Thus women cannot 'own' (and therefore contract out) their workplace identities because their 'selves' are produced through the relations of production and are the subject of appropriation. In this sense, they are not individuals at work, but rather they are gendered workers, that is, the social group 'women workers'.

Men, on the other hand, are more able to (although none actually ever reach, and some are more able than others) to come close to the ideal of the abstract individual at work. That (some) men are able to do so is because they are not required to produce and maintain a particular 'self' as part of their jobs. As a consequence, men as workers are better placed to detach their labour (including the performance of work identity) and make use of their identities as a resource. Put simply, because men are not required to have a particular 'self' (and their selves are not equally the subject of appropriation) they are more able to determine their own 'self-hood' (that is, be the source or the author of their own individual identity). Thus, unlike women workers, men may claim their 'selves' or their workplace identities as their own property which they may contract out and exchange, and make use of as a labour market resource, that is, they may act as culturally individualized workers, with performable identities.

Clearly, we think that rather than being universally available to all, and differentiated from labour market processes, the ability to own a workplace cultural identitity as a property which can be disposed of (that is, that can be performed as an occupational resource) is both gendered and achieved through workplace practices (gendered relations of production and appropriation). The emergence of the cultural as a determinant of sexual identity at work should not therefore be seen as ungendered. Adkins' work shows how the 'cultural' should not be unproblematically accepted as a universal (re)source by feminist labour market theorists, for to do so is to fail to see the cultural itself as gendered and to fail to recognize how cultural identity practices form part of gender oppression in specific historical circumstances. It suggests that it may be useful to look at what Sedgwick calls, 'the representational contract' between one's body and the world (Sedgwick, 1994, p. 230): to fail to do so is, as Sedgwick argues, to understand a constructivist analysis in terms of either compulsion or choice. As she has commented, there

> is a frightening ease with which anything that our capitalist/consumer culture does not figure as absolute compulsion (e.g. addiction), [is instead recast] as absolute choice through the irresistable metaphor of the marketplace. (op. cit., p. 226)

This is not an argument to suggest that understandings of the cultural have no place in explaining the significance of gender in the labour market. Rather, in this chapter we have attempted to show that there are problems with the acceptance of understandings of both the social and the cultural in the explanation of gender which do not first consider how those terms themselves, that is, the social or the cultural, and indeed the distinction between them, may be already gendered. Just as we did not agree with the hollowing out of the social in explanations of gender inequality in the labour market, so we do not advocate the abandonment of the cultural here. Rather, we believe in the importance of recognizing the historical specificity of both the cultural and the social, and suggest that we need to see how the emergence of both, and the distinction between them, is related to the appropriation and exploitation of women.

NOTES

1. Cockburn uses the term 'socio-political' to refer to male organization and solidarity, while the term 'the physical' is used to address questions of bodily physique and its extension in technology, in buildings and clothes, space and movement.
2. Pringle makes use of a very specific understanding of culture here. The definition of culture has been much debated, but Pringle's use might be characterized by its almost exclusive focus on personal gender identity at the expense of a concern with the collective and historical dimensions of the category of gender.
3. See also Delphy and Leonard (1992), who argue that the gendered and generational structuring of the family means that family subordinates' whole labour capacity is appropriated and, as a consequence, are not free to sell their labour power to an employer in the same way as heads of household.
4. Interestingly, in her recent work, Cockburn (1991) does make use of some of Carol Pateman's ideas. Thus for example, she argues that the exploitation of women's labour by employers is 'constructed within the terms of the sexual contract, her subordination to husband, her responsibility for child, other dependents at home' (Cockburn, 1991, p. 84). In addition, Cockburn discusses Pateman's ideas regarding the emergence of modern fraternal patriarchy (op. cit., pp. 19–21) and the patriarchal structuring of capitalism (op. cit., p. 85). Unfortunately however, this discussion of Pateman's ideas does not lead Cockburn to a reformulation of gender and/ or the social. Thus, she continues to separate out the 'mode of production' from the 'sex–gender system' (op. cit., p. 10) and, in her discussions of bodies, emotions and sexuality operating in the labour market,

continues to treat the 'economic' as an ungendered set of relations and indeed, entirely abandons the 'social'.
5. In doing so, Butler herself indicates some anxiety about the adoption of the cultural as a catch-all; she suggests, that, 'for the sake of argument [she] will let "social" and "cultural" stand in an uneasy interchangeability' (op. cit., p. 5).
6. While we recognize that there is much debate concerning whether or not Butler reduces gender to performance (an understanding we would not uphold), what is important here is her recognition that performance itself is gendered.

REFERENCES

Acker, J. (1990), 'Hierarchies, Jobs and Bodies: A Theory of Gendered Organizations', *Gender and Society*, **4**: 2, pp. 139–58.
Adkins, L. (1992), 'Sexual Work and the Employment of Women in the Service Industries', in M. Savage and A. Witz (eds), *Gender and Bureaucracy* (Oxford: Blackwell).
Adkins, L. (1995), *Gendered Work: Sexuality, Family and the Labour Market* (Buckingham: Open University Press).
Adkins, L. and Lury, C. (1992), 'Gender and the Labour Market: Old Theory for New?', in H. Hinds, A. Phoenix and J. Stacey (eds), *Working Out: New Directions for Women's Studies* (London: Falmer Press).
Barrett, M. (1980), *Women's Oppression Today: Problems in Marxist Feminist Analysis* (London: Verso).
Barrett, M. and McIntosh, M. (1985), 'Ethnocentrism and Socialist–Feminist Theory', *Feminist Review*, **20**, pp. 23–47.
Butler, J. (1993), *Bodies That Matter. On the Discursive Limits of 'Sex'* (London: Routledge).
Cockburn, C. (1981), 'The Material of Male Power', *Feminist Review*, 9, Autumn, pp. 41–58.
Cockburn, C. (1991), *In the Way of Women: Men's Resistance to Sex Equality in Organizations* (Basingstoke: Macmillan).
Delphy, C. and Leonard, D. (1986), 'Class Analysis, Gender Analysis, and the Family', in R. Crompton and M. Mann (eds), *Gender and Stratification* (Cambridge: Polity Press).
Delphy, C. and Leonard, D. (1992), *Familiar Exploitation: A New Analysis of Marriage in Contemporary Western Societies* (Cambridge: Polity Press).
Pateman, C. (1988), *The Sexual Contract* (Cambridge: Polity Press).
Pringle, R. (1989a), *Secretaries Talk: Sexuality, Power and Work* (London: Verso).
Pringle, R. (1989b), 'Bureaucracy, Rationality and Sexuality: The Case of Secretaries', in J. Hearn, D. L. Sheppard, P. Tancred-Sherrif and G. Burrell (eds), *The Sexuality of Organization* (London: Sage).
Sedgwick, E. K. (1994), *Tendencies* (London: Routledge).
Walby, S. (1986), *Patriarchy at Work: Patriarchal and Capitalist Relations in Employment* (Cambridge: Polity Press).
Witz, A. (1990), *Professions and Patriarchy* (London: Routledge).

Index

academic feminism, 79, 96
Acker, J., 173, 174, 175, 205, 216, 217, 218
activist feminism, 80–3, 96
Adkins, L., 8, 9, 10, 174, 175, 183, 188, 213, 215, 218, 220, 221
Adler, Z., 58, 59, 61
agency, and structure, 2
Albrow, M., 173
Allanbridge, Lord, 55
Altman, D., 2
Anthias, F., 122, 125, 136, 141
anti-sexist living arrangements, 41–50
Armstrong, L., 83, 91

Babuscio, Jack, 114
Backett, K., 69
Baldwin, J., 130
banking, and heterosexual office culture, 184–7
Barker, R., 69
Barrett, M., 204, 205–7, 208, 209
Barry, K., 81, 82
Barthes, R., 118
Bartky, S., 25, 26, 29
Beck, U., 1
Beck-Gernsheim, E., 1
Bem, S. L., 36, 105
Berk, S. F., 45, 47
Bernad, J., 200
Bonnett, A., 125
Bordo, S., 103, 109
Bowes, J., 69
Brannen, J., 69
Bremer, J., 105
Brodribb, S., 102
Brown, B., 57, 58, 59, 61, 62, 66
Bunch, C., 37
Burman, M., 57
Burrell, G., 174
Burton, S., 5
Butler, J., 20, 23, 26, 107, 111–12, 113, 219

Callas, M., 174
Cameron, D., 17, 22, 23, 77–8
Campbell, B., 29, 157
Chambers, G., 58
'Chantal', 200
child abuse, 84–7
Clark, D., 50
Clarke, A., 84
class
    and heterosexual relationships, 146
    and Irish men in England, 135–40
Clifford, J., 124
Cockburn, C., 79, 174, 175, 176, 183, 197, 204, 208, 209, 214
Cohen, P., 127, 129
Collard, J., 69
Collinson, D. and M., 177, 178, 179
commercialized feminism, 79–80, 96
confluent love, 5, 7, 146, 158, 160
Connell, R. W., 180, 187
Cowie, C., 164, 200
Cowie, Lord, 55
Crisp, Q., 106
Croghan, R., 40
cultural identity, and the labour market, 218–22
Curtis, L., 127

Davies, B., 129
Davis, A., 112
Delphy, C., 21–2, 24, 27, 28, 44, 46, 205
D'Emilio, J., 105
Dobash, R. and R., 68, 83
Dollimore, J., 113, 118, 131
Drewal, M. T., 113
Duberman, M. B., 105
Duncombe, J., 45, 69, 146, 160
Dworkin, A., 28
Dyer, R., 113, 114

Edgell, S., 69
Edwards, S., 58
Ehrenreich, B., 69, 70
Elson, D., 200
embodiment
  gender and sexuality, 7–9,
    102–18
  in organizations, 173–89
Emslie, Lord, 64–5
Enloe, C., 79, 138
Epstein, D., 128
Estrich, S., 87
Evans, J., 124
Evans, M., 23

Fanon, F., 130
feminism
  and heterosexuality, 35–50
  re-defining, 78–83
Firestone, S., 206
Ford, N., 145
Foucault, M., 17–19, 20, 36
Frank, A., 102, 108, 175
Frankenburg, R., 125
Fraser, N., 19
Frazer, E., 17, 22, 23
Freedman, E., 105
French, D., 200
Frye, M., 40, 41
Fuss, D., 26

Gaag, N. van der, 202
Gagnon, J., 1, 18, 20, 21, 158
Game, A., 102
Garber, M., 105, 106
gay identities, 2, 4, 110, 113–17
  Irish in England, 6, 122–41
gay politics, 1
gender
  as a cultural process, 209–13
  division of labour, 4, 25, 39,
    43–7
  and heterosexuality, 4, 27–30
  and the labour market, 204–22
  and sexuality, 2, 6, 7–9, 18,
    21–2, 102–18, 174
genital identities, and
  heterosexuality, 6, 102–18
Gergen, M., 26

Gershuny, J., 69
Gerson, K., 69
Giddens, A., 1, 56–7, 68, 69, 146,
  148, 156, 158, 159, 160, 163,
  164, 167
Gilbert, L., 69, 88, 89, 90
Gilbert, N., 87
Gilfoyle, J., 151
Goodnow, J., 69
Gordon, L., 84
Gramsci, A., 125
Grant, K., 79
Gray, B., 139
Greenslade, L., 125, 129
Gribben, P., 125
Griffin, C., 68
Griffin, G., 80

Haldane, D., 50
Halford, S., 7
Halson, J., 68
Hanmer, J., 68
Harvey, M., 88
have/hold romantic discourse, and
  male heterosexuals, 159–64
Haywood, S. C., 148
Hazelkorn, E., 125
Hearn, J., 24, 174
Heath, S., 21
Henriques, J., 129
Hertz, R., 45, 69
heterosexuality, 1, 2
  and anti-sexist living
    arrangements, 41–50
  and feminism, 35–50
  and feminist theory, 3–4, 15–30
  and gender, 4, 27–30
  and long-term monogamous
    relationships, 39–40
  male, 7, 145–68
  socio-economic characteristics of,
    4
Hickman, M. J., 125
Hochschild, A., 44, 46, 69, 175,
  197, 198
Holland, J., 1, 17, 30, 68, 146,
  154–5, 156, 157
Hollibaugh, A., 28
Hollway, W., 19, 27, 29, 30, 37–8,

69, 130, 151, 155, 156, 158, 159, 163, 167
Hope, Lord, 55

Irish gay men, 6, 122–41
Irish society, and feminism, 139

Jackson, M., 17
Jackson, P., 173
Jackson, S., 3–4, 6, 19, 21, 22, 27, 29, 125, 146, 159, 163, 164, 167
Jamieson, L., 4–5, 7
Jeffreys, S., 17, 22, 23, 28, 29, 39, 84, 106
Johnson, A. M., 145, 148
Johnson, M., 199
Jones, C., 112
Julien, I., 135

Kappeler, S., 17
Keane, F., 139
Kelly, L., 5, 22, 68, 77, 79, 82, 83, 84, 86, 87, 90, 92, 93
Kent, V., 163
Kimmel, M., 69
Kitzinger, C., 27, 29, 35, 36, 40, 41, 83
Kitzinger, J., 157, 164
Kleihans, Chuck, 114, 115
Koss, M., 87, 88

labour market, gendering of, 204–23
Lacan, J., 20
law, and sexuality, 5, 55–70
Leeds Revolutionary Feminist Group, 36
Lees, S., 21, 58, 68, 112, 164, 200
Leonard, D., 24, 44, 46, 205
lesbian identities, 2, 4
lesbian politics, 1
lesbian separatism, 35–6, 50
lesbianism
  and monogamy, 39
  and radical feminism, 17, 105–6
  and sexual identity, 25, 26–7
  as a social practice, 36–7
Lewis, C., 69

local government officers, 181–4
Luckman, 110
Lury, C., 8, 9, 10, 174, 215

Mac an Ghaill, M., 6, 10, 126, 129, 133
McCarthy, C., 122
McIntosh, M., 1, 8, 9, 107, 207
MacKinnon, C., 16, 55
McNay, L., 20
Mahony, P., 112
Mailer, N., 89
Mandziuk, R., 108
Mansfield, P., 69
Marcus, G., 124
marriage, and heterosexuality, 24–5, 49–50
Marsden, D., 45, 69, 146, 160
Marshall, J., 186
Martin, B., 153
Marxism, and feminism, 205–6
Mellor, P., 109, 110–11
Mercer, K., 135
Miles, R., 125, 127
Millar, A., 58
Millett, K., 192, 193, 206
Modleski, T., 97
Morgan, D., 146, 150, 175
Morley, B., 86
Morrill, C., 114
Moss Kanter, R., 177, 186
Moss, P., 69
Mullender, A., 86

Nava, M., 41, 129
nurses, 177–81

O'Brien, M., 69
O'Loughlin, E., 139
oppression, identifying against, 104–6
organizations, sexuality and gender relationships, 7–8, 173–89
Osborne, Lord, 55, 66, 67

Paglia, C., 78, 81, 89, 90, 92
Pahl, J., 69
Pajaczkowska, C., 129
Parker, A., 123